THE
CREATIVE
SPARK

THE
CREATIVE
SPARK

How Imagination Made
Humans Exceptional

AGUSTÍN FUENTES

DUTTON

DUTTON

An imprint of Penguin Random House LLC
375 Hudson Street
New York, New York 10014

Copyright © 2017 by Agustín Fuentes

Art Credits: Page 58, Oldowan Tools: José-Manuel Benito Álvarez. Page 62, Acheulean Tools: Public domain. Page 234, Ochre Engravings: Christopher S. Henshilwood. All other illustrations by Daniel Lagin.

LIBRARY OF CONGRESS CATALOGING-IN-PUBLICATION DATA
Names: Fuentes, Agustín, author.
Title: The creative spark : how imagination made humans exceptional / Agustín Fuentes.
Description: New York, New York : Dutton, Penguin Random House, an imprint of Penguin Random House, LLC, [2017] | Includes bibliographical references and index.
Identifiers: LCCN 2016030260 (print) | LCCN 2016049511 (ebook) | ISBN 9781101983942 (hc) | ISBN 9781101983966 (trade pbk.) | ISBN 9781101983959 (ebook)
Subjects: LCSH: Philosophical anthropology. | Imagination. | Creative ability. | Human behavior.
Classification: LCC BD450 .F79456 2017 (print) | LCC BD450 (ebook) | DDC 153.3—dc23
LC record available at https://lccn.loc.gov/2016030260

Printed in the United States of America
1 3 5 7 9 10 8 6 4 2

Set in Garamond Premier Pro

To everyone past, present, and future
who dares to imagine, create, and learn

CONTENTS

PART FOUR

THE GREAT WORKS: *How Humans Made the Universe*

THE
CREATIVE
SPARK

TRUMPETING CREATIVITY AND
A NEW SYNTHESIS

When we consider creativity, we might think of Shakespeare or Mozart, Albert Einstein or Marie Curie, Charles Dickens or Mary Shelley, Andy Warhol or Annie Leibovitz, Jamie Oliver or Julia Child, Beyoncé or Prince. We often see the capacity for creativity residing in a single person or a select group of people. But creativity is not limited to the United States and Europe or to rich people or to people born in the last 500 years. It is not, after all, a solitary endeavor limited to the work of a genius or some particularly original thinker. Creativity is built on interconnections of ideas, experiences, and imagination. Whether in the physics lab, the artist's studio, the mechanic's garage, or even in figuring out how to make a small paycheck last until the end of the month, creativity is everywhere in the human experience. We are creative every day. But we do not accomplish this miraculous feat on our own.

Writer Maria Popova tells us that creativity is our "ability to tap into our mental pool of resources—knowledge, insight, information, inspiration, and all the fragments populating our minds . . . and to combine them in extraordinary new ways." Archeologist Ian Hodder agrees, telling us that creativity is the space between the material reality and our imagination where intelligence, adaptability, agency, interpretation, and problem solving all come together, but he also emphasizes that it is a thoroughly social process. Anthropologist Ashley Montagu highlights the fundamental human ability to project our ideas onto the world and transform them into materially resounding reality. This book illustrates the clear connection between these views of creativity and the extraordinary story of human evolution.

Countless individuals' ability to think creatively is what led us to succeed as a species. At the same time, the initial condition of any creative act is collaboration.

Every poet has her muse, every engineer an architect, every knight a squire, every politician a constituency, but it's rarely just two or three or four people in the collaboration. More often it's hundreds or even thousands who collaborate over time and space to produce the most profound creative moments. Dancer-choreographer Twyla Tharp writes, "sometimes we collaborate to jump-start creativity; other times the focus [of collaboration] is simply on getting things done. In each case, people in a good collaboration accomplish more than the group's most talented members could achieve on their own."

By delving into our past and drawing on the best and most current scientific knowledge, we shall see that creativity is at the very root of how we evolved and why we are the way we are. It's our ability to move back and forth between the realms of "what is" and "what could be" that has enabled us to reach beyond being a successful species to become an exceptional one.

The nature of humans' creative collaboration is multilayered and varies widely. But our distinctively human capacity for shared intentionality coupled with our imagination is how we became who we are today.

This cocktail of creativity and collaboration distinguishes our species—no other species has ever been able to do it so well—and has propelled the development of our bodies, minds, and cultures, both for good and for bad. We are neither the nastiest species nor the nicest species. We are neither entirely untethered from our biological nature nor slavishly yoked to it. It's not the drive to reproduce, nor competition for mates, resources, or power, nor our propensity for caring for one another that has separated us from all other creatures. We are, first and foremost, the species singularly distinguished and shaped by creativity. This is the new story of human evolution, of our past and current nature.

The Four Big Misconceptions of
Human Evolution

But aren't we modern humans supposed to be the progeny of demonic males? Weren't we stamped with a deep evolutionary history in which natural selection favored more aggressive males, leading to a biological proclivity toward violence and sexual coercion? In other words, aren't we the species that is supremely good at being bad—naturally selfish, aggressive, and competitive?

No! says this professor.

We are the species that is naturally caring, altruistic, and cooperative, distinguished early in our evolution from other primates by privileging the sharing of our food and other resources, self-sacrifice, and service to the good of the group over self-interest—are we not? We are, in short, a species of supercooperators, supremely good at being good.

Nope, that's not it either.

Well, isn't our nature shaped primarily by the happenstances of the environments we lived in and the challenges and opportunities they presented? And aren't we therefore a species still better adapted to traditional lives as hunter-gatherers than to modern, mechanized, urbanized, and tech-connected life? Hasn't this modern disconnect with our evolutionary roots led to mental health issues and widespread dissatisfaction with our lives?

And didn't our intelligence allow us to transcend the boundaries of biological evolution, rising above the pressures and limits of the natural environment and molding the world to serve our purposes—increasingly to the planet's peril? Aren't we the Promethean breed, who, having made all the world our dominion, are now running it, and ultimately ourselves, into ruin?

Sorry, but no, again.

These are the four currently predominant arguments about human evolution and human nature. Compelling as they all are—with voluminous research literature behind them, as well as eloquent journalists and scientists making strong cases for each—they are also radically incomplete, each leaning too heavily on certain evidence and preconceptions while either actively casting aside, or simply overlooking, the wider body of important findings. These include a flood of revelations in anthropology, evolutionary biology, psychology, economics, and sociology over the past twenty years. While each of the four arguments has been instrumental in pushing our understanding of human nature forward, each has also led to gross simplification and some serious misunderstandings—such as the ideas that we're naturally disposed toward conflict and that we're divided into different biological races. Perhaps most important, these popular accounts have obscured the wonderful story at the heart of our evolution—the story of how, from the days of our earliest, protohuman ancestors, we have survived and increasingly thrived because of our exceptional capacity for creative collaboration.

It's the epic tale of all epic tales: the story of a group of highly vulnerable creatures—the favored prey of a terrifying array of ferocious predators—who learn better than any of their primate relatives to apply their ingenuity to devising ways of working together to survive; to invest their world with meaning and their lives with hope; and to reshape their world, thereby reshaping themselves.

A New Synthesis

Whether it was eluding predators, making and sharing stone tools, controlling fire, telling stories, or contending with shifts in climate, our ancestors creatively collaborated to deal with the challenges the world threw at them. At first they did so in ways that were just marginally more effective than those of their prehuman forebears and other humanlike species. Over time, that minor edge of advantage expanded, refined, and propelled them into a category all their own.

Recent discoveries and theoretical shifts in evolutionary theory and biology, such as the insights about how our environment and life experiences affect the functioning of our genes and bodies, along with new findings in the fossil record and ancient DNA, have changed the basic story of humanity. A new synthesis demonstrates that humans acquired a distinctive set of neurological, physiological, and social skills that enabled us, starting from the earliest days, to work together and think together in order to purposefully cooperate. Our genes tell only one aspect of how we became creative at increasing levels of complexity.

Using these abilities, our ancestors started to help one another care for the young, whether or not those young were their own. They began to share food for both nutritional and social reasons and to coordinate activities beyond what was needed for survival. Acting in ways that benefited the group, not just the individual or family, became increasingly common. This baseline of creative cooperation, the ability to get along, to help one another and have one another's backs, and to think and communicate with one another with increasing prowess, transformed us into the beings that invented the technologies that supported large-scale societies and ultimately nations. This collaborative creativity also drove the development of religious beliefs and ethical systems and our production of masterful artwork. Of course, it also tragically fueled and facilitated our ability to compete in more deadly ways. We applied essentially the same creativity in killing other members of our species as we did to manipulating planetary ecology to the brink of complete devastation. Nevertheless, while humans are obviously capable of intense damage and cruelty, our tendency toward compassion plays a larger role in our evolutionary history.

The goal of this book is a far more nuanced, complete, and judicious account of our evolution than has previously been possible. This new story is based on a synthesis of the full range of relevant research, old and new, across evolutionary biology, genetics, primate behavior, anthropology, archeology, psychology, neuroscience, ecology, and even philosophy.

The new synthesis that I present in this book is embedded in the cutting-edge contemporary understanding of evolution that has taken shape only over the last few decades. Evolutionary theory has changed considerably since Charles Darwin and Alfred Russel Wallace first proposed evolution via natural selection more than 150 years ago. Today our best understanding of evolutionary processes is called the extended evolutionary synthesis (EES), in which a range of different processes, beyond just natural selection, are central in explaining how, and why, animals, plants, and all living things evolve.

Evolution as we know it today can be summarized as follows: Mutation (changes in the DNA) introduces genetic variation, which in interaction with the growth and development of the body (from conception until death) produces a range of variations (differences in bodies and behavior) in organisms. This biological variation can move around within a species by individuals moving in and out of populations (called *gene flow*), and sometimes chance events alter the distribution of variation in a population (called *genetic drift*). Much of this variation can be passed from generation to generation through reproduction and other forms of transmission and inheritance. Then there's natural selection.

Natural selection does not mean what most people think it means. Rather than being a lethal competition for survival in which the biggest, baddest, and "fittest" battle it out on the playing field of life, natural selection is a filtering process that shapes variation in response to constraints and pressures in the environment. Imagine a giant strainer with openings of a certain size (that vary as environmental conditions vary), and then imagine that organisms come in different sizes and shapes (variation). These organisms have to pass through the strainer in order to get to the next generation (to reproduce and leave offspring). Those that fit through the strainer's openings successfully reproduce, and those that do not, don't. Some of the successful variants fit through better than others due to their particular size and shape, which results in their leaving more offspring (who inherit that specific size and shape). This process, the filtering of variation from generation to generation based on pressures in the environment, is what natural selection is. So in evolution the type and pattern of variation and the pressures of the environment matter a great deal.

We now recognize that four systems of inheritance can all provide patterns of variation that influence evolutionary processes.

1. *Genetic inheritance* is the passing of genes, encoded in DNA, from one generation to the next.
2. *Epigenetic inheritance* affects aspects of systems in the body associated with development that can transfer from one

generation to the next without having a specific root in the DNA. For example, certain stressors on a mother during pregnancy can affect the development of the fetus, who may in turn pass those altered characteristics on to her or his offspring.

3. *Behavioral inheritance* is the passing of behavioral actions and knowledge from one generation to the next and is common in many animals, such as when mother chimpanzees help their offspring learn how to crack nuts with rocks or fish for termites with sticks.

4. Finally, *symbolic inheritance* is unique to humans and is the passing down of ideas, symbols, and perceptions that influence the ways in which we live and use our bodies, which can potentially affect the transmission of biological information from one generation to the next.

So we have to recognize that evolutionarily relevant variation can come in the forms of genes, epigenetic systems, behavior, and even symbolic thought.

There are two other key contemporary theoretical findings that are especially important for this new synthesis. They are: (1) a distinctive brand of cooperation and (2) the process of *niche construction*.

Humans have evolved to be supercooperators. Cooperation occurs within communities of ants, between cells, and among hunting dogs, meerkats, and baboons—but never as intensively, or as frequently, as it does for humans. Cooperation has many definitions, all of which fit into the general idea of working together for a common goal. *Wikipedia* (a cooperative endeavor itself) defines cooperation as "the process of groups of organisms working or acting together for their common/mutual benefit, as opposed to working in competition for selfish benefit." *Merriam-Webster's Online Dictionary* tells us that cooperation is the "association of persons for common benefit." We all know what cooperation is because we cooperate every day. In some countries we agree to drive on the right-hand side of the road; in others, on the left. We line up at grocery store checkouts. We help others in need, whether it be by carrying a grocery bag, holding open a door, or passing along contact information. We have governments, hold birthday parties, go to school, and donate money to charities. Cooperating is central to everyday human life.

Most species do cooperate but to a lesser extent. African hunting dogs and female lions coordinate their hunts; meerkats take turns watching out for predators; and many monkeys join together to build social alliances to deal with life's daily challenges. Many animals simply group together to avoid predators or gather for the social interactions that do them all a bit of good. This type of cooperation is common among most living things, even bacteria. The communities of microorganisms living in your gut form complex cooperative and symbiotic relationships with one another and with you. Basic cooperative interactions among microorganisms early in the history of life are what set the stage for the appearance and development of more complex multicellular animal forms, including dogs, cats, eagles, tyrannosaurs, and humans. However, targeted, complex, and coordinated, not to mention potentially costly, long-term cooperation is less common, except in humans. No other animal exhibits the same intensity, constancy, and complexity that we see in our own cooperation.

Why is that?

A popular theory suggests that competition, and not cooperation, serves as the main stimulus in evolution. Darwin argued that it's the environmental conflicts and challenges that stimulate evolution. Many researchers have since gone on to argue that it's not just the general environmental challenges, but rather the competition between individuals (or even individual genes) in those conflicts that serves as the true driving force in the history of life. Their basic idea is that individuals—not species or groups—face the challenges of the environment and that the competition between these individuals is what drives evolution. So cooperation—doing good for a common benefit—would not be a good strategy. If most individual organisms cooperated and a few did not, the cheaters would reap all the benefits without having to pay the same costs and put in the same effort as the cooperators. Consequently, the cheaters would come out ahead. They would "win" the evolutionary game.

Many problems with this argument have been noted.

A population where most individuals always behave selfishly and cheat would not do very well if they needed to react to challenges as a group. They would go extinct. If being in a social group is critical to success, then members of that group can use the threat of punishment or expulsion to ensure that selfish cheating does not get out of hand. Recent modeling work in evolutionary theory and economics uses equations that include the costs and benefits of cooperating, defecting, or being neutral. These equations also factor in relatedness and familiarity, and we use them to play out various scenarios in order to understand why organisms might cooperate. This sophisticated mathematical modeling demonstrates that cheaters and defectors do not win out over the long term, and that cooperating, in many cases, is a good strategy (even if one doesn't do it all the time). The math supports what we see in the natural world. Cooperation is pretty common across the animal kingdom (and plants too), as much as is competition. Our ancestors didn't invent cooperation out of thin air; they just put a novel spin on it.

Many animals focus cooperative behavior on those that share similar genes with them: their relations, their kin. But humans extend the scope of cooperation well beyond. We cooperate with friends, collaborators, strangers, other species, and even enemies upon occasion. We also practice cooperation between generations, between sexes, and between groups. These are all occurrences that happen from time to time in other animals, but not nearly as consistently or widely as in humans.

We humans have the distinctive ability to think about times and places in the past and the future (our "off-line thinking") and to convey the information via language and symbol. Human cooperation, unlike, say, that of ants, involves groups of individuals who recognize their individuality, who reflect on it, and yet who still cooperate. Humans can calculate much more effectively the outcomes of possible cooperation or competition. This cognitive complexity has long been part of our tendency to cooperate. It has also enabled amazingly innovative ways of cheating, which we do more often than it is comfortable to admit. We don't always get along, but when we do, we achieve greatness. Our ability to be supercooperators, amazing collaborators, even while competing and sometimes cheating, is a large part of what sets us apart from the rest of the species on earth.

While all the processes in the extended evolutionary synthesis are relevant to the story of human evolution (and appear throughout this book), one process is particularly important: niche construction. New ideas can sound like jargon, but I ask you to bear with me. Originating in the 1980s, niche construction is a truly groundbreaking new idea in evolutionary science.

Niche construction is the process of responding to the challenges and conflicts of the environment by reshaping the very pressures that the world places on (each of) us. A *niche* is the sum total of an organism's ways of being in the world—its ecology, its behavior, and all the other aspects (and organisms) that make up its surroundings. In short, the niche is a combination of the ecology in which an organism lives and the way it makes a living.

Many organisms "do" niche construction. Beavers build dams, changing the compositions of fish and crayfish, water temperature, and water flow around their houses and thus altering the kinds of pressures they face in the world. Even earthworms niche construct. When arriving in a new place, they work their way through the soil, ingesting it, changing its chemical structure, and loosening it, making it a better environment for the subsequent generations of worms living in that same place. However, humans are in a class all our own when it comes to niche construction. Towns, cities, domestic animals, agriculture—the list goes on and on. The cooperative and creative responses to the conflicts the world throws at us, and to those we create ourselves, reshape the world around us, which in turn reshapes our bodies and minds. We are the species that has a hand in making itself—niche constructors extraordinaire.

We've coshaped our bodies, behavior, and minds by our actions and the evolutionary pressures we've faced. The history of this process is the heart of the new synthesis and not only tells us how we got to where we are today, but also offers significant insight into where, and who, we might be in the future.

Humans on the Tree of Life

To tell the story of human evolution, we must try to establish a starting point, but a single spot in space and time will elude us. Perhaps a better way to see humans' place in nature is to first ask what we were before we were human.

As the evolutionary biologist and author Stephen Jay Gould passionately argued, all too often we see human evolution as that classic image of a series of figures lined up, growing from a chimp-like creature on the left to a full-blown human on the right. This image is scientifically wrong and doesn't even tell an interesting story. The real evolutionary tree for humans is represented by a giant and dense diagram showing humans as one teeny twig on one small branch of the primates, who themselves are one small twig of the larger group of mammals, who are one small branch of the larger group of vertebrates (things with backbones), who are another small branch of a gigantic group called animals, who are just one of the many branches on the tree of life on this planet. We know that all of life shares a common ancestry and the forms of life that share the same core branches and side branches are even more closely related. While a human might share 24 percent of her DNA with a Chardonnay grape, 44 percent with a honeybee, and 84 percent with a dog, she shares more than 90 percent with all primates and more than 96 percent with our closest cousin, the chimpanzee.

Unlike the misguided linear diagram of human evolution suggests, chimpanzees (or even chimpanzee-like things) are not our ancestors. We are both part of a family (called "hominoids," or apes). However, each of our lineages has been evolving for at least 7 to 10 million years independently of each other (the lineage humans belong to is called the "hominins"; that of the chimpanzees is called the "panins" or the "Panina"). We do share amazing amounts of biology and history with chimpanzees, and with all the primates. But evolution creates continuities *and* discontinuities. In order to understand what makes humans distinctive, we need to know what we share with the other primates, but even more important, we need to know how and why we've diverged from them. So, while we share more with the other primates than many early detractors of evolution could countenance, the differences tell us more about who we are as a species than do the similarities.

We'll begin with what we know about humans as primates and what we know about the hominin lineage over its roughly 7-million-year history. After that we delve deeper into the revelations of the new synthesis and discover exactly how we became *the* creative species. The secret of our creative spark is something that can continue to serve us today.

PART ONE

STICKS AND STONES

The First Creativity

CREATIVE PRIMATES

I was under the immense banyan tree in the central plaza of the Padangtegal monkey forest in Bali, Indonesia. I'd been here for months watching a few groups of macaque monkeys, immersing myself in their society. A small group of macaque monkeys sprinted up into the trees and the terraced hillside above the main temple. The dominant troop meandered in to take their place. Teardrop, an adult female so named for a white birthmark in the shape of a tear just below her left eye, trailed by about thirty feet from any other monkey. She always traveled apart from the rest of the group. I didn't give her much thought. My attention switched to Arnold, the dominant male, and Short-tail, the alpha female, who teamed up to take a cluster of papaya leaves and a prized half coconut from two low-ranking males. I looked down and again noticed Teardrop, who now sat only ten feet away from me, staring at a leaf on the ground and nonchalantly scratching her side. I turned to scan the plaza to get an idea of the groups' spread; the males, females, and young formed small clusters like little families. I felt a gentle pressure on my right leg. Teardrop was now right next to me, her left hand on my thigh. Over the next few minutes she calmly leaned into me. We did not look at each other, nor did we move, for about ten minutes. Then she got up, looked around, cast a sideways glance at me, and walked away.

I discovered in time that Teardrop was unable to have offspring, and as such she was never able to work herself into any of the clusters of females and young that made up the social core of the macaque group. But she did, on occasion, sidle up next to humans and lean into them. Teardrop, like all monkeys, needed physical and social contact to live, and like all monkeys she occasionally got socially creative to satisfy those needs. After all, there were plenty of these other large-bodied, relatively hairless, seemingly willing primates with whom to score a bit of contact time. She had a problem, and she figured out a novel way to solve it.

Teardrop is a primate and so are we. As such we share the trait of social creativity—a prime component of our evolutionary success. In order to understand the human story, the grand narrative of our creative journey, we need to recognize that we (humans, that is) are mammals and members of a specific mammalian order (Primates). We are also members of a specific subset of primates called "anthropoids" (monkeys, apes, and humans), as well as a specific subset of anthropoids called "hominoids" (apes and humans). Humans are members of a specific subset of the hominoids called the "hominins," which are humans, our ancestors, and a set of extinct humanlike beings.

Envision the history of life on this planet as a gigantic branching bush with millions of branches, twigs, and leaves. Those leaves and twigs closest to one another are close evolutionary relatives. As such, we do share a branch with Teardrop, but our respective twigs split off in different directions 25 to 30 million years ago. So, whatever commonalities we have with all monkeys are shared traits that were present in the original branch from which both of our lines (the twigs) arose. If we look to our closest primate relatives, the African apes (gorillas and chimpanzees), our lineages split off from a common ancestor about 7 to 10 million years ago, so we might expect even more similarities between us and the apes than between us and the monkeys. In any case, before getting to what is distinctive about humans, we need to know what it is about us that's not distinctively *human,* but rather distinctively *primate.*

As Teardrop, in her way, demonstrated for me, social relationships are at the heart of monkey and ape societies. Getting along, touching, and spending time with their relatives, friends, and potential mates are the main things these primates do. Sound familiar? The social landscape is the key factor in any primate society. It is made up more or less of hierarchical relationships, friendships, aggressive behavior, and sex.

Imagine yourself in the midst of one of the groups of macaque monkeys in the Padangtegal monkey forest in Bali, but this time we are watching the female named Short-tail, so named because she had only the nub of a tail. For a species called *long-tailed macaques,* one might think not having a tail would be a problem, even a disability. It wasn't. Short-tail was the highest-ranked female in a troop of nearly eighty monkeys—the opposite of Teardrop. She would swagger through the forest and temple grounds surrounded by her daughters, granddaughters, and even great-granddaughters. Other females would move out of her way or grimace in submission when she came near. Her favorite daughters and their friends would hand her their infants to hold and groom, she had access to the best foods, and she always took center stage when fights between her group and other groups in the area broke out. She often even led the charge, outpacing the big males in her tenacity for defending the group's space.

Male long-tailed macaques are 50 percent larger than females, with huge fangs (canine teeth, to be exact) that can shred flesh very effectively, so in most cases these males easily dominate females in any one-on-one conflict. But the females that make it to high rank are never in one-on-one contexts—they are savvier than that. Short-tail had a whole cohort of relatives nearby and ready to defend her. This meant that the high-ranking males, instead of trying to dominate her, would seek her out and groom her and hang out with her, especially when they needed a favor.

Social Hierarchies Aren't Hierarchies

Throw a banana on the ground between two monkeys, and nine times out of ten they won't both charge for it. Rather, one will look quickly at the other and back away, ceding the banana without a fight.

Understanding where you fit in the hierarchy, who is more or less dominant than you, helps primates navigate their daily lives. In a group with a set of well-defined dominant relationships, there's little doubt

about who gets access to the better food, sleeping sites, grooming partners, potential mates, and so on. When relations are less well defined,
there might be one or two "top dogs" (or top monkeys), and most in the
group are on more or less equal footing. In any case, primate hierarchies
are neither strict nor static—dominance relationships are negotiated
with friends and foes. Mostly it takes only a quick look at the other to
determine who is in the more powerful position. This flexibility reflects
a primate knack for creative social solutions.

Primates change dominance ranks and roles throughout their lives,
and each primate species has a different pattern through which individuals gain dominance or compete for resources. Young individuals
have to learn these patterns as they mature. These patterns develop via
direct fights, accumulating supporters, and manipulating one's opponents. Once dominance relationships are developed in this way, they gain
some stability but nevertheless remain mutable.

The local Balinese called one particularly vicious and aggressive male
macaque Saddam, a reference to the Iraqi dictator (this was back in the
late 1990s). My colleagues and I called him M1. He was the sole fully
adult male in the smallest of the three groups at Padangtegal, made up
of him, a few nearly adult males, six females, and about ten youngsters.
One could easily recognize a female from M1's group, as she always had
patches of hair missing and/or scars on her back from M1's sharp canines.
He dominated every individual in the group with an iron fist. In fact, he
even dominated many humans in the vicinity, often chasing them and/
or biting them when he wanted to displace them or steal their food. He
was a merciless dictator—until everything changed.

M1 had a fall and broke his leg. He could still get around, but he was
slower and less capable of chasing or attacking other monkeys and people. Two of the young males in his group, who previously cowered anytime he got within ten feet, took advantage and got creative. They began
pushing him, tentatively at first, then more frequently. At the same time,
they stuck next to, groomed, and curried the favor of Ma, the largest female macaque around and the oldest in M1's group. That did the trick,
the social tide shifted, and they made their move. M1 lost his rank and
eventually left the group.

Dominance is not a biological characteristic of an individual; it's a social position. Individuals can move through different dominance ranks across their lives. You may identify some of these aspects of primate dominance in your own life, but it's a lot more complicated for humans. We are multifaceted in how we build relationships and how we alter or destroy them. Still, the ways in which monkeys and other primates creatively navigate their social worlds serve as a guide to how the spark of primate creativity became the five-alarm inferno of human creativity.

When we think about other animals, especially primates, we often think about aggression and violence, but social creativity is about much more than that. As with many primates, long-tailed macaque males have those fangs. One good bite could open an eight-inch gash two inches deep in a person's thigh. If they made a habit of aggressively using their teeth, we'd see massive injuries on a regular basis, but we don't. Most aggression in primates is limited to low-key threats and chases, with real physical fighting being far less frequent. And when aggression does occur, the resulting wounds are less grievous than one might expect. Primates check their violence, usually devising creative solutions to meet the challenges of social life.

After being evicted from his group, M1 hung out in the general area, sticking by himself for almost four months. Then, gradually, he began hanging around the central group (Short-tail's group), but only on the outskirts. Next, he approached a few low-ranking females and their offspring and did something that really surprised all of us watching him: He made nice. He would offer to groom these females and even play with their young. At first the females were wary; they'd seen him from afar in his previous group and knew he was not the warm-and-cuddly type. But as he persisted they gradually changed their tune. After a few more months, M1 was in the middle of the group, playing with five or six young, lounging with a cluster of females, and looking downright mellow. When the resident males came around, he showed signs of submission and they left him more or less alone. Shortly thereafter he started having sex—lots of it—with the females: His calm demeanor and frequent grooming and playing with the young had placed him in good favor. Even after a few years this pattern remained the same, M1 seemed like a totally different primate. But he wasn't; he was just doing what primates do so well—living a complex and dynamic social life and coming up with a creative solution when new circumstances demanded it. The hierarchy didn't govern his life; it was simply something to work with.

This ability is easy to overlook and to undervalue, but, again, it is what sets the stage for the emergence of a particular kind of creativity, the spark that sets our lineage on fire.

What Can Happen in a Soap Opera

Living organisms change and adapt, or they fail to and suffer the consequences. Animals have to respond to the pressures of the world to survive. But unlike a hermit crab that employs a dead snail's shell to make itself a home, or an earthworm that through digestion changes the chemical makeup of soil to make it livable, primates respond to the pressure from the world around them not just by physically reacting to the environment, but also by constructing a network of peaceful and aggressive relationships with the other monkeys around them—a social niche. So while all the socializing, fighting, making up, and jockeying for social position that goes on in primates' lives might resemble a soap opera, these behaviors reflect a suite of successful responses to life's pressures. This gives primates a buffer most other species don't have. If primates successfully use this buffer against life's pressures, they can carve out more space in their lives to innovate—just like the macaques at Padangtegal.

These Balinese macaques have it pretty good. They get food from the surrounding forest as well as from the temple staff and tourists. They are healthy, they don't have to go far to find food, and the food that they do get is very high in nutrition and easy to consume. This scenario results in something that scientists call an "ecological release." It's not that the macaques don't have to respond to pressures in their environment; it's just that the pressures they face are not particularly harsh. These macaques have a good deal of free time.

Time enough for, say, new hobbies.

At Padangtegal, young and old, male and female, monkeys spend time playing with rocks. They rub them on the ground, in circles, and in puddles of water. They stack them carefully, knock them down, and restack them. They wrap the small rocks in leaves or bits of paper and roll them back and forth across the ground. Every now and then they even use a rock as a tool, to pound a piece of food or to scratch an itch. Aside from being entertaining to watch (for humans) and fun to do (for the macaques), there is no apparent purpose to this behavior, and that is the point. In their leisure time these macaques combine their penchant for manipulating objects and their curiosity (both usually associated with getting food) into a behavior that is quite new. It is not sufficient that they have free time for this kind of play. They must be creative.

The Padangtegal monkeys are not alone in this interesting behavior. This same species of macaque, in Thailand and Burma, also uses stones and shells as tools. The researcher Michael Gumert and his colleagues describe the use of stones to break open shellfish by the macaques. He also reports that the monkeys grab one type of sharp, spiral snail shell off rocks on the beach and use it to pry open one of their favorite foods: mussels. Researchers across Africa have studied chimpanzees using rocks to crack open nuts, twigs to fish for termites, and leaves to drink water at numerous locations for more than fifty years. Investigators in Costa Rica report the use of stones and sticks by capuchin monkeys as well. Humans are not the only tool-using primates, nor are primates the only tool-using animals. It's not only the use of rocks, sticks, and shells that reflects the primate spark of creativity; it's the variety of ways distinct groups use them.

As you move across Central Africa from west to east and stopping at various chimpanzee communities along the way, one of the most striking discoveries is the variation in what stones and sticks are used, how they are used, and how sometimes they are not used at all. In some regions female chimpanzees use sharp sticks as minispears to skewer small sleeping primates called galagos. At other sites, chimpanzees gather in groups at nut trees and use the stones to crack the nuts—and there is evidence that in some locations this tradition has gone on for more than 200 years. In still others, chimps carry light twigs on long walks to reach their favorite termite mounds, where they've left large, heavy sticks, and then use a combination of the two types of wood to crack open the mounds and fish for the tasty termites inside.

In all of these cases, the role of creativity is to manipulate physical items to assist in the procurement of food—a way to cope with scarcity when it arises. Many other animals do this, albeit with less ingenuity; the primate order has a way of going to extremes. While environmental pressures such as scarcity in the food supply explain much in many animals' evolutionary history, they are by no means a complete explanation of how innovation in the natural world happens, the source of the spark of creativity that humans have made a bonfire of. Note the *variation* in the solutions to food procurement—not just in tool use across different primate communities, but also in their social traditions. You can't have that kind of variation if there isn't a spark that is specifically creative, that is, more than just a response to environmental pressures.

A social tradition is a shared bit of creativity. It is a component of the group's social lives and is transmitted via some kind of social learning. In primates some social traditions are related to stones or sticks used as tools, but many are not.

Many human groups create special ways to greet one another, from spoken salutations to secret handshakes, and so do other primates. For example, when two chimpanzees greet each other after being apart for some time, they often approach each other and raise their arms into the air, touching each other as if doing a high five. However, in some groups they clasp hands when they do this, in others they cross wrists, and in still others they bend at the elbow and press their arms into each other. And even more interesting, when a female moves from one chimpanzee community to another, she will take the version of the hand clasp from her group into the new one; sometimes it spreads into the new group and other times it does not.

The primate spark of creativity emerges from the way that primates have made social lives and social innovation central in how they deal with the pressures of the environment. As we look to those species with whom humans share the most in biology and ecology, we see more and more complexity in social traditions, both in the use of objects as tools and, more important, in the creation of novel social behaviors. While never reaching anything near the extent that humans do it, other primates do create novel ways to meet life's challenges and do invent new ways to relate to one another.

We know that the primate group that includes monkeys, apes, and humans, the anthropoids, exhibits complex social lives. The hominoids from which both our and the ape lineages derived probably had even more social complexity. In turn the hominins, arising from the hominoids and eventually giving rise to our lineage, followed the trend toward social complexity and began making social niches, tools, and social traditions.

PRIMATE TAXONOMY

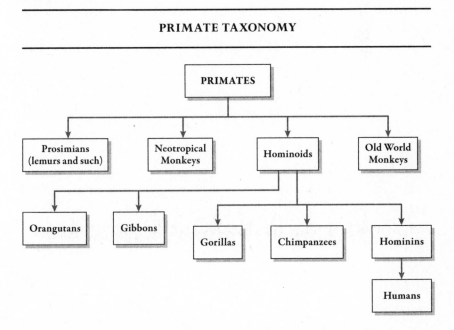

In the 7 million years of hominin evolution, we see the growing sophistication of social niche construction, dynamic social groups, social traditions, and simple tool manufacture and use. We see the primate creative spark taken to a new level, making tools rather than just using them, ratcheting up social learning and cooperation, and in sum constructing an entirely new way of making a living on this planet—a way that would eventually beat everything else, ever.

THE LAST HOMININ STANDING

I f we traveled in a time machine back to the African forests between 11 and 8 million years ago, we might catch a glimpse of the most sought-after target in human evolution: the last common ancestor between humans and chimpanzees. Dubbed "LCA" by scientists, these creatures are not the "missing link" we know from so many sci-fi tales. In fact, there's no such thing as a single missing link—no sole ancestor that gave rise to us all. That's not how evolution works. LCA was really a population, or a few populations, of apelike creatures living in clusters spread across much of Africa and possibly the Mediterranean region. In all likelihood the LCAs lived both in the trees and on the ground but spent more of their time in the trees. They were probably somewhere around four feet tall, and while they were certainly members of the ape family, they bore no close resemblance to chimpanzees, humans, or any other living apelike form. But in their DNA, their bodies, and their behavior lay the kernels of potential that gave rise to both the chimpanzee and hominin lineages.

The LCAs probably lived in small groups of around ten to thirty individuals, spending time in smaller clusters during much of the day, searching for fruits, young leaves, and the occasional fungus growing on tree bark. It's likely they'd come back together at night to sleep in the trees, wary of the large cats and other predators that ruled the nighttime. The LCAs groomed one another and actively engaged in the standard primate soap opera of relationships, fights, makeups, and sex. They had one offspring at a time, which probably took as many as five years to mature into a youngster able to fend for itself. But the basal influences on chimps and humans didn't stop there. LCAs also likely used twigs to poke at insects and small lizards and had figured out how to use a rock or a heavy piece of wood to crack open nuts. This skill is what set them apart from the other primates and animals around them—a small creative edge. They lived alongside a range of other apelike animals, monkeys, big cats, small-hooved mammals, and a few early piglike creatures.

Between about 7 and 9 million years ago, different populations of these LCAs separated. They moved into new areas, encountering novel evolutionary pressures. These separate groups gave rise to many other populations and types of apelike beings, which eventually stretched across Central, Eastern, and Southern Africa in two distinct lineages: the hominins and the protochimpanzees (the panins). The chimpanzees' lineage is not our story, but the hominins' is.

Since we don't have a time machine, none of this process can be captured in real time by observers, but we do have the next best thing: fossils and other signs of activity that these earliest ancestors left behind. Using this record we can track the steady increase in creativity.

Early Glimpses of Human Creativity

In trying to understand the emergence of human creativity from the fossil record, we face two core questions:

1. When is an early apelike thing no longer an ape, but rather a hominin?
2. What is it about the early hominin fossil remains that illustrates a new creativity?

Hominins habitually walk on two legs, and because of this, the skull sits on top of the spinal column at something close to a ninety-degree angle and the shape of the pelvis and lower limbs reflects this distinctive pattern of moving (called bipedality). So when we want to know if a fossil is a hominin as opposed to some other apelike primate, we know what to look for: signs of bipedality.

Apes sit upright and stand on two legs occasionally, but when they move they often walk on all four limbs, so the skull connects at an angle that lets them hold their head comfortably in both positions. For hominins, this kind of movement is difficult. When humans try to move around on all fours, it's quite uncomfortable to hold our heads up to see in front of us for any period of time. This anatomical challenge, standing upright and looking straight ahead, is met with the foramen magnum—science-speak for *big hole*—through which the brain is connected to the spinal cord. It is directly under the skull in hominins, but more toward the back of the skull for other apes (who walk on all fours when on the ground). This means that an "apelike" skull that has the foramen magnum underneath as opposed to in the back is likely to be bipedal and, thus, a hominin. Additionally, hominins have canine teeth that are smaller and more in line with the rest of the teeth, whereas apes, especially the males, have larger, more protruding canines.

Among the earliest hominins, there are three contenders for the distinction of being our first ancestors. They are all relatively apelike, but their fossils reflect evidence of bipedalism, and they have reduced canine teeth. They all come from Africa.

- The first is called *Sahelanthropus tchadensis*. This fossil, found in what is today the country of Chad, is somewhere between 6 and 7 million years old and has aspects of the skull that suggest bipedalism, but the specimens we have comprise only pieces of a skull and some teeth—not much to go on.
- The second, from around the same time, is called *Orrorin tugenensis*. The researchers who found it in the Tugen Hills region of central Kenya argue that the few bits of bone discovered suggest that it, too, was bipedal. Neither of these two earliest possible hominins provides much insight or excitement in regard to new avenues for creativity. A far better starting point is the third fossil.

- *Ardipithecus ramidus* roamed the forests and mixed woodlands of Eastern Africa between 4.4 and about 5.8 million
  years ago. One member of this species, nicknamed "Ardi," is
  one of the most complete fossils ever found (most of her skeleton is preserved). On the ground, Ardi moved on two legs
  with head held high, but her long arms, long, grasping fingers,
  and big, grasping toes enabled seamless movement between
  the forest canopy and the ground beneath. Her bipedalism
  was different from ours today—imagine having your big toe
  stick out to the side like your thumb. Unlike most apes or
  apelike creatures, the male *Ardipithecus* were only slightly
  larger than Ardi, and both sexes' canine teeth were about the
  same size. *Ardipithecus* teeth and jaws tell us they had a general omnivorous diet and they collected their food from trees
  and the ground. The capacity to be at home in the trees and
  to be bipedal on the ground freed their hands from the
  process of walking. Those hands didn't stay idle.

Imagine Ardi and five or six others in her group visiting a giant fruiting fig tree early in the morning, collecting armfuls of fruit, and walking
across a shallow stream to their favorite sleeping tree and the rest of the
group. There they sat, gorging themselves on the ripe fruits, while across
the stream monkeys, birds, squirrels, and a bunch of arboreal rats fought
it out in the fig tree for the rest of the fruits.

It's possible that *Ardipithecus* were the first in our lineage to regularly
carry things in their hands and arms. We have no direct evidence that
they used sticks or rocks as tools, but given that all other descendants of
the LCAs do, it's likely that they were at least as creative. *Ardipithecus*
could carry more, and larger, sticks and rocks—and food they'd
gathered—with them over longer distances. Walking on two legs introduced a host of new transport options.

Ardi and her species created new social spaces, which became options
for later hominins. In many primates, including the apes, males with
large canine teeth and much larger bodies than females exhibit a high
degree of conflict and competition between the sexes. So in *Ardipithecus,*

the relatively small canine teeth and the small amount of dimorphism between males and females suggest that Ardi, and other female *Ardipithecus,* had stronger social and bonding relationships with males—a hint of things to come. While we don't know for sure, it's a good bet that the ability to carry and manipulate things with their hands—and the possibility that they had more collaboration between the sexes and among individuals—represents early versions of the patterns we know became central to the success of later hominins.

The only problem with the story so far is that there's no current agreement in the scientific community that *Ardipithecus* was a direct ancestor to the human lineage. It was a hominin but may have been just a cousin to our line. Regardless of the direct link, it does show us that the hominin lineage, which we are undeniably a part of, had acquired abilities enabling novel creative behavior by 4.4 million years ago. Over the next million and a half years, a whole range of hominins—some in our direct lineage and some not—evolved from the earlier hominin groups and took these abilities further than any species had before.

Once, in the Afar region of Ethiopia, seventeen hominins (nine adults, three teenagers, and five young children) traveled across the mostly open grassland dotted with clusters of trees. They never made it to their destination. Just over 3 million years later, in 1975, scientists discovered their collective remains covered by a fine silt that held them together as they fossilized. This cluster of hominins, sometimes referred to as the "first family," belonged to a hominin species called *Australopithecus afarensis,* which existed in Eastern Africa from about 4 million until about 3 million years ago, was bipedal, but had long arms and hands with long fingers (like *Ardipithecus* but more humanlike), which suggested they found climbing trees useful.

The way the fossils are spaced together makes us reasonably sure that all seventeen died at about the same time and that this was not caused by a flash flood or some localized disaster. While some have suggested that the whole group consumed poison, a better hypothesis is that they were attacked, probably by one or more very large cats or some other large predators.

We don't know how big the actual group of these hominins was—there may have been more than seventeen—but it is unlikely that it was very much larger. We also know that predators, even when there are three or four or five of them hunting together, make one or even a few kills in a group of prey, then stop to consume the prey or take the carcasses away to another spot to eat them. So this means that most, or maybe even all, of the group of hominins may have stayed to try to assist the others, and in the end they all perished. If this is what happened, it represents a kind of extreme group cooperation, in the face of such intense danger, that is not at all common for most animals, not even most primates. Such a tragic event might be early evidence of hominin groups collaborating and bonded with one another in ways that are stronger and more cohesive than seen in other animals—even at the expense of their own lives.

About 3.2 million years ago the famous fossil now known as Lucy was a living adult female, nearly four and a half feet tall. This *Australopithecus afarensis* fossil, like Ardi, changed our view of human history. Discovered by Don Johanson and colleagues back in the 1970s, and so named because they happened to be listening to the Beatles the evening of the discovery, Lucy was the oldest and most complete hominin fossil ever found (at the time), and she finally put to rest an old debate about whether our lineage became bipedal before our brains got big or after: We were bipedal first. A series of fossilized footprints dating to about the same time as Lucy's demise shows us that her bipedality was closer to ours than to Ardi's. So while she did not have a brain any bigger than that of *Ardipithecus* or the LCA, she did walk in a more humanlike way, with her head on top of her body and her eyes front and even sometimes turned up to the nighttime sky. Johanson and his colleagues named what they thought to be our oldest ancestor, the root of our creativity, after Lennon and McCartney's "Lucy in the Sky with Diamonds." Creative indeed.

Lucy's and her kin's creativity becomes particularly evident at the site of Dikika in Ethiopia, with the oldest evidence of animal butchery. In 2010 researchers discovered marks on animal bones that are about 3.4 to 3.6 million years old, the oldest evidence of animal butchery ever found. It is almost certain that these marks do not reflect hunting, but rather a kind of opportunistic scavenging: getting to the meat of someone else's kill. These earliest marks on the ribs and femurs of good-size antelope-like animals were made by stone tools, but no tools were found at the site.

Some of the marks on the bones are clear lines and scrapes, showing that flesh was cut and scraped off. Other marks show that stones were used to hammer at the bones to either break them or loosen the meat. In this case, a group of organisms had the bones with meat on them, used stone flakes and pieces of stone to remove the meat, and then carried it, and the stone tools, away with them. The most likely candidates for having done this are *Australopithecus afarensis* or one of the other two closely related hominin species around at the time (called *Kenyanthropus platyops* and *Australopithecus deyiremeda*).

The butchered bones at Dikika represent one of the first times in the history of the planet that an organism came up with the idea to take a sharp piece of flaked stone and use it to more efficiently cut meat off the bone. The sharp flakes allowed the hominins to separate meat from the bones and carry that meat away to safety—thus increasing the value of getting meat and reducing the processing costs of doing so.

In 2015 researchers working at a site called Lomekwi 3, near Lake Turkana in Kenya, made a breakthrough discovery: the earliest evidence of definite stone tools. The tools are mostly cores of stone with flakes that were deliberately knocked off them to produce specific shapes and edges on the stones. The toolmaking site includes larger "anvil" stones that the toolmakers used as platforms on which to work the smaller stones into their final forms. At 3.3 million years old, these are the oldest examples of stone tools ever found, a clear signal that our ancestors had crossed a critical boundary in creativity.

By 3 million years ago, hominins were working together in groups and in the manipulation of stones to create new ways to deal with the world. They went from taking what the world gave them and making the best of it to taking something as hard as stone, seeing within it a new suite of possibilities, and then reshaping the rock to meet their needs. Hominins began to shape their world. And, if you think about it, the creative process of envisioning, experimenting, and creating stone tools and the ways in which they are used and carried about requires some pretty elaborate collaboration and communication.

If you or I saw someone making stone tools and wanted to try to replicate them, we'd be asking, "What are you doing?" "Where are you getting the best rocks?" Once we'd learned the skill and taught it to others, we'd tell them, "Do it this way and it works better," and so on. But these hominins had no language—their brains weren't even half the size of ours. So how did this happen? It is a bit of a mystery, but we know that some primates are capable of learning to use rocks and stones as tools by watching others and getting the gist of the process, and then using lots of trial and error to figure the process out. But hominins took that to the next level: They started to show each other how to select and shape rocks—not with words, but with gestures and a keen ability to watch one another, learn, and imitate. The hominins were getting better at focusing on a specific task and trying to work together to get it done.

Humans Emerge from the Evolutionary Bush

Stepping back and looking at all the fossil evidence we have between 2 and 4 million years ago, we see not a clean line of human ancestors one after the other, but a bushy cluster of possible human ancestors from which our lineage arose.

In both Eastern and Southern Africa we find hominin fossils in wooded and savannah-like environments, and they fall into a few different types or species. From 4 to 3 million years ago or so, the main hominin finds we have are from Eastern Africa:

- *Australopithecus anamensis* (a few finds),
- *Australopithecus afarensis* (the most common),
- *Australopithecus deyiremeda* (one find), and
- *Kenyanthropus platyops* (a few finds).

Most researchers agree the *Australopithecus afarensis* arises from *Australopithecus anamensis,* but not many agree on what to do with *Kenyanthropus* or *Australopithecus deyiremeda. Kenyanthropus* has a really flat face, unlike *afarensis*, and *deyiremeda* has teeth that are pretty different from most *afarensis* finds. It is possible that these last two are just variations on the *Australopithecus afarensis* theme, but it is also possible that

THE FIRST HOMININ LINEAGES
(FOSSIL LOCATIONS AND ATTRIBUTES)

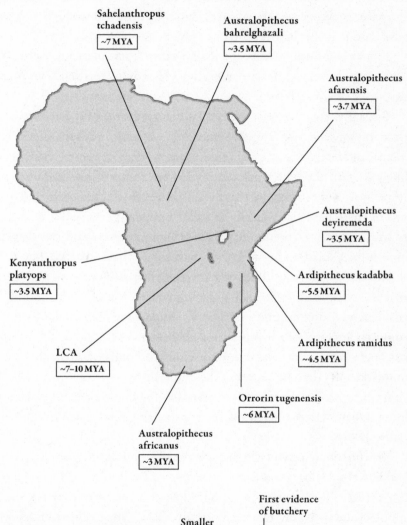

Sahelanthropus
tchadensis
~7 MYA

Australopithecus
bahrelghazali
~3.5 MYA

Australopithecus
afarensis
~3.7 MYA

Australopithecus
deyiremeda
~3.5 MYA

Kenyanthropus
platyops
~3.5 MYA

Ardipithecus kadabba
~5.5 MYA

Ardipithecus ramidus
~4.5 MYA

LCA
~7–10 MYA

Orrorin tugenensis
~6 MYA

Australopithecus
africanus
~3 MYA

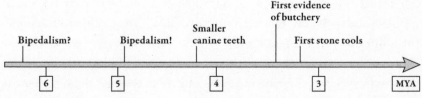

Bipedalism?   Bipedalism!   Smaller
canine teeth

First evidence
of butchery

First stone tools

6   5   4   3   MYA

they are separate species of hominins. We know that there was increasing instability in climate toward the end of this period and lots of variation in habitat and ecologies, so the opportunity for isolation and speciation was there. Also, all of these hominins lived in very small populations, there were never very many of them, and the pressure from predators was always on their heels. They did not have it easy.

From 3 to 2 million years ago the hominin story gets a new twist: We get clearly different lineages emerging and moving in their own directions, one of which is ours.

Basically, two types of hominins emerge: ones that have massive chewing muscles and jaws and ones that are a bit more slender in the mouth and face. We came from one of the slender-face groups. It is highly likely that all these hominin lineages used, and possibly made, simple stone tools, but only one of them started to grow a larger brain and only one of them gave rise to descendants who would eventually spread to colonize the whole planet. Both the massive chewers and the slender-mouth forms had bodies from the neck down that look like they were slightly modified from those of Lucy and the first family, so it is likely that *Australopithecus afarensis* is the shared ancestor of all the hominins that emerged after around 3 million years ago, much like the LCA is the common ancestor of the human and chimpanzee lineages. Most hominins between 3 and 2 million years ago had hands and feet that were more like ours than like Lucy's. These hominins were starting to wholly commit to life on the ground, forever leaving behind the long primate love affair with trees (setting aside the undying joy we still find in tree houses).

The big-chewing-muscle lineage, which show up in both Southern and Eastern Africa, are called *Paranthropus*. They are not directly on the human line. Rather, they were our close cousins, were bipedal, made simple stone tools, and ran from predators a lot. Their claim to fame was the ability to process really tough foods with their massive teeth and chewing muscles. So when times got tough, when food was hard to find, their massive jaws, chewing muscles, and teeth enabled them to live on grasses and seeds without needing to find more creative ways to eke out a living. *Paranthropus*'s mouths were their main tools. Combining the use of rudimentary stone tools, some level of collaboration between group members (inherited from Lucy and her kind), and the ability to rely on tough, harsh foodstuffs in times of stress was their way of navigating the changes in the world. They actually did pretty well with this strategy, lasting from about 2.7 million years ago until about 1.2 million years ago. But over this time they did not change very much, their brains did not increase much in size, and their tools and behavior likely stayed largely the same.

The slender groups have a different story. The earliest and best known of them are called *Australopithecus africanus* and are quite similar to Lucy and her kin, with some slight differences in the hands and feet. They existed in Southern Africa for about half a million years (from about 3 to 2.4 million years ago). There is also another similar form in Eastern Africa called *Australopithecus garhi,* which might be associated with stone tools (at around 2.6 million years ago) that look a little more advanced than the Lomekwi tools from 3.3 million years ago. But we have very little fossil material for this hominin, so not much is known.

In Southern Africa *Australopithecus africanus* either overlapped or gave rise to the most recently discovered member of this group (in 2008), *Australopithecus sediba,* which lived in Southern Africa around 1.8 million years ago and which looked a lot like one might imagine a mash-up between *afarensis* and the earliest members of our line would look, with some other strange quirks thrown in. One of the most striking is that it was bipedal in a way different from those slightly before it (*afarensis* and *africanus*) and slightly different from the other hominin lineages living at the same time. This shows that there was a lot of diversity in the hominins at this time, lots of natural experiments in evolution, as fluctuating environments, predators, and other evolutionary pressures challenged small populations spread across Africa.

The challenge for the slender hominins was to construct a niche that gave them a slight leg up relative to all the other similar forms out there.

Our lineage (*Homo*) emerged as part of what researchers call an "adaptive radiation" in the hominins, a grand evolutionary experiment in form and function. Across the landscape at about 2.5 to 2 million years ago there were three groups of hominins: *Paranthropus* in Eastern and

Southern Africa, the slender forms *Australopithecus africanus* and *sediba* in Southern Africa, and a slender form that we call *Homo* (which turns out to be our lineage), in Eastern and Southern Africa. We are not quite sure what to do with *Australopithecus garhi* because we have such a small sample, so we'll leave that one out for the time being.

Adaptive radiations are a key way in which diversity in life forms develops. It's been observed in many groups of species. Lakes in Africa today contain hundreds of different kinds of cichlid fishes (like tilapia, more or less), which all stem from one common cluster of ancestral lineages. In the past the original populations flourished so well that they began to crowd one another out. That didn't work for any of them—too much competition. In response, many groups branched out, trying new ways of making a living: The cichlids expanded into a surprisingly wide range of different ecological niches. When a new range of environments open up or when pressures force a cluster of similar lineages to compete for different ways to make a living, the processes of evolution facilitate a bunch of experiments in form and behavior; some work and some don't. In this case many groups of cichlids began to experience slightly different feeding pressures, leading to modified mouthparts; others changed the way they mated or the depths they swam in. The cichlids diversified into a suite of new forms and functions in an adaptive radiation.

We living humans are part of the hominin adaptive radiation. Today we are members of the genus *Homo,* species *sapiens,* and subspecies *sapiens:* We are the last hominin standing, the only one of the entire 7-million-year hominin experiment that made it. Our genus has a few physical characteristics that separate us from the pack of other hominins; our brains and bodies got bigger and our teeth got smaller, but the key difference, the one that truly matters, is that our lives got a heck of a lot more adventurous, collaborative, and creative.

The earliest fossil that is possibly of the genus *Homo* is a 2.8-million-year-old mandible found in Ethiopia at the site of Ledi-Geraru. This jawbone and some teeth look a lot like both the earlier forms (such as *Australopithecus afarensis*) and the later members of the genus *Homo.* It looks like a transitional jaw. Not everyone accepts this jawbone as a member of *Homo,* but it is at least very close. There is also a fascinating

cluster of fossils found in a South African cave that researchers are calling *Homo naledi*. These fossils are not yet dated, but they have humanlike hands and a really distinct skull shape. *Homo naledi* are similar in
some ways to other early members of the genus *Homo* but different in
others. It's not yet clear where this fossil fits in our story, but it is likely
part of the cluster at the root of the human lineage. Between 2.4 and
about 2 million years ago we see fossil skulls, teeth, and some limb bones
that most agree are members of the genus *Homo,* and there is good
evidence that brains are getting somewhat bigger.

Pretty much all my fellow researchers agree that by 2 million years
ago, hominins from our specific lineage are found in both Southern and
Eastern Africa, and that is when things really start to change. Within a
few hundred thousand years of emerging alongside other lineages in the
hominin radiation, our ancestors did something no hominin ever did
before: They moved fast and far. Some groups of *Homo* left Africa. We
find fossils and tools of *Homo* in Central Asia (at a site in the country of
Georgia called Dmanisi) and in Southeast Asia (on the island of Java in
Indonesia) by about 1.8 million years ago.

Between about 1.8 million and about 400,000 years ago, our genus
diversified as they moved back and forth, in and out of Africa, around
Central, Southern, and Southeast Asia, and into East Asia. In this time
period there are many different populations of the genus *Homo* that vary
in their bodies, the tools they make and use, and aspects of their behavior. Among researchers who focus on the fossil record of this time period,
there is a vociferous debate as to how many species come and go—a debate that is not going to be resolved anytime soon.

New tool types, new behaviors, new ways of making a living and
adventuring over most of Africa, Asia, and southern parts of Europe
became commonplace. These *Homo* populations remained small, often
on the move, and not always connected to other related populations, and
thus were very susceptible to extinctions. The fossil record shows a lot of
starts and stops, dead ends, narrow misses, and total failures. It is very
hard to tell which of these populations between 1.8 million and 400,000
years ago contributed their genetic and behavioral legacy to those of us
here today. Many did, but many more did not.

HOMININS AND THEIR INNOVATIONS SPREAD AROUND THE WORLD

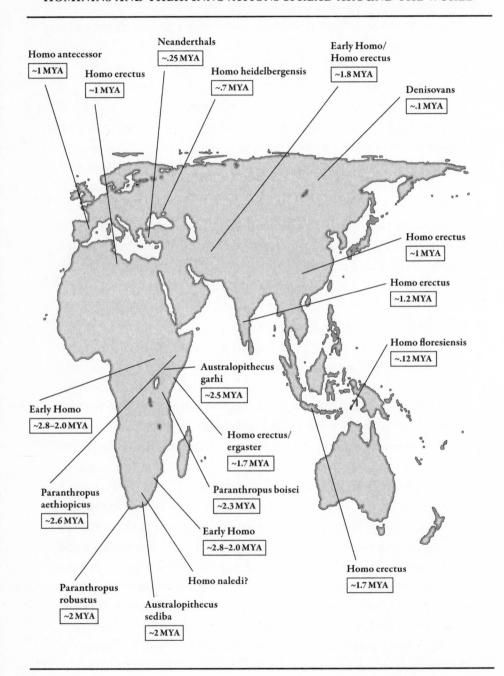

Homo antecessor
~1 MYA

Homo erectus
~1 MYA

Neanderthals
~.25 MYA

Homo heidelbergensis
~.7 MYA

Early Homo/
Homo erectus
~1.8 MYA

Denisovans
~.1 MYA

Homo erectus
~1 MYA

Homo erectus
~1.2 MYA

Homo floresiensis
~.12 MYA

Australopithecus
garhi
~2.5 MYA

Early Homo
~2.8–2.0 MYA

Homo erectus/
ergaster
~1.7 MYA

Paranthropus
aethiopicus
~2.6 MYA

Paranthropus boisei
~2.3 MYA

Early Homo
~2.8–2.0 MYA

Paranthropus
robustus
~2 MYA

Australopithecus
sediba
~2 MYA

Homo naledi?

Homo erectus
~1.7 MYA

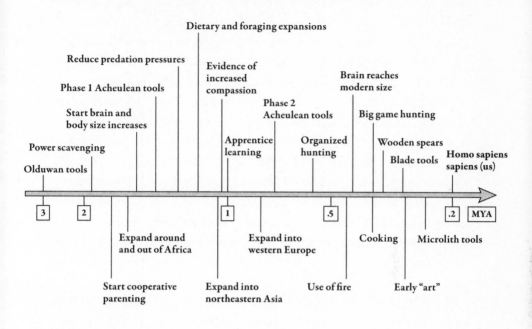

Little Winners

If we were to step out into the Eastern African woodlands around 1.8 million years ago, we'd be amazed at how small the early members of our own genus were and how large, and dense, the predators were. Most members of the genus *Homo* at the time hovered around five feet tall, lived in groups of about fifteen to twenty-five, were foragers who moved across the landscape searching for food and shelter, and had a few simple stone tools and sturdy sticks as their only weapons. Across the African landscape roamed giant hyenas, saber-toothed cats, giant lions, leopards, and even huge eagles, all of which were particularly keen on eating the easy-to-digest, two-legged packets of protein running around. So how did these small-bodied, upright, naked primates with no horns, fangs, or claws survive? They began to meet these threats creatively.

Early *Homo* had other hominin company in the members of the genus *Paranthropus*. As we know, while these other hominins had bodies similar to early *Homo* and probably even made, or at least used, the basic stone tools that *Homo* used, their niche required them to be able to chew tough foods in times of food scarcity or stress. Early *Homo* took a different path: Their brains were growing larger, and they began to rely more on tools and other things outside of their own bodies to deal with the challenges the world threw at them. We don't know how *Homo* and *Paranthropus* got along, or if they even interacted, but they did share the landscape, and evidence suggests that large predators hunted both of them. The threat of being eaten and the pursuit of protein were the two key challenges that our ancestors responded to creatively and that possibly doomed *Paranthropus*.

Obviously, both *Homo* and *Paranthropus* wanted to avoid getting eaten and did their best to get away from the predators. And both hominins' lack of natural weaponry and speed put them at a disadvantage. The solution that our ancestors hit upon was to make themselves less likely prey than, say, *Paranthropus*. But how?

Larger brains differentiated *Homo* from the other hominins and the other animals around them. Brains are the most expensive organ to run, and to grow a larger one you need two things: a longer childhood (growing time) and more calories (energy to build and run the more expensive brain). This leads to a dilemma: The easiest way to get more calories and protein is to eat meat, and the best meat is large and fast, not susceptible to capture via a few sticks and stone tools. However, hunting is not the only way to get meat. Predators sometimes leave remains. So, scavenging is an option, but then one needs to compete with other scavenging animals for the leftovers. What if one develops a method to take kills away from predators and/or to ensure access to the remaining meat once predators move on?

Homo of 1.8 million years ago was limited to sticks and stones and simple ways of communicating (no language yet). They could not defeat the main predators in direct combat, nor could they convince *Paranthropus* (or any of the other prey animals also sharing the landscape, such as baboons, impala, or pigs) to offer themselves up as the main menu item. With no language, no bargaining chips, no substantive weapons, what could *Homo* turn to?

One another.

Working together, communicating through gesture and by example, our ancestors learned to cooperate in ways no one else could. *Homo* likely began, slowly but surely, to watch the big cats and hyenas, to see when the predators used certain areas, what they did when not hunting, and how they interacted with one another (or didn't). Our ancestors learned how to ascertain which predators were hungry and on the prowl versus those that were satiated and posed no threat at all. They discovered that when predators have young they are especially dangerous, yet simultaneously vulnerable. They recognized that the predators fought among themselves and that many would steal one another's kills, scavenging more than hunting. It's possible that *Homo* began to use gestures and vocalizations as signals at this point, not just to indicate the presence or absence of a predator, but as ways of getting the group to act together and react to the behavior of the predators, and even to imagine what the predator might do next and respond to it before the predator knew what was happening. That would be a more complex, and creative, mode of communication than most other primates employed. It would be the basis of language.

Using these experiences and sharing them via collaborative interactions among group members, eventually *Homo* learned to stay one step ahead of the predators (most of the time), and every now and then they might rush to a carcass after the predator left and use their sharp-edged stone tools to rapidly and effectively remove chunks of meat and bone to take back, safely, to their sleeping places. By doing this as a collaborative group, some could strip the carcass while others stood guard, shooing away the vultures and smaller predators competing to scavenge the kill. Still others could watch the horizon and make sure no large predators were approaching. All the while this would have required communicating to one another with grunts and gestures; reassuring and bonding; creating new levels of teamwork.

We can bet that some groups of early *Homo* took chances from time to time. Building on the cooperative coordination they had used to protect scavenged kills and what they had learned about predator behavior, they might take a chance and pick out a weaker or older predator and follow it. Then, when it made a kill, the *Homo* group would, in unison, rise, stand erect, shake their sticks and wave their arms, make hooting and grunting noises, throw stones at it—in short, freak out the predator, which would flee from the cluster of coordinated, stick-holding, stone-throwing, screaming, upright hominins.

If this worked, the kill was theirs; if not, the *Homo* group ended up a little smaller. With each new lesson learned, they would improve, and as most groups of *Homo* within a region became adept at this, a new niche was constructed.

Predators undoubtedly noticed that one of their previously easy prey no longer was so easy. It was getting harder to find them, riskier to hunt them, and at times even dangerous to be around them. As is often the case in food chains across different kinds of ecosystems, when one prey item gets difficult to obtain, it drops lower in the "preferred prey" category and predators shift the focus to another, more reliable source to make up the difference. This is where *Paranthropus* might have come back into the story. While it was likely not intentional, our ancestors' creative ways of dealing with predators and feeding protein to their growing brains probably made life all the more difficult for the other lineage of hominins sharing the African forests and savannahs with them. Given the many other hardships of being a short, upright, weapon-less, apelike thing living in the Pleistocene, *Paranthropus*'s demise became inescapable. Our ability to deal with challenges via cooperation and creativity probably hastened the demise of at least one other close hominin lineage.

Once our lineage spread around and out of Africa (from about 1.8 million years ago, as land connections became set between Africa and Eurasia), different populations encountered a wide array of new ecologies and new challenges. This spurred a diversity of creativity across the continents. Sometimes the resulting innovations spread when populations or groups came into contact; often they didn't because groups were frequently isolated, separated by deep seas and ice-capped mountains. Imagine much of Europe and North Asia covered in glacial sheets, slowly retreating and advancing, creating valleys and mountains; the

Mediterranean region and South Asia covered by plains shifting to forests and then to swamps and even deserts over the course of hundreds of thousands of years; and Southeast Asia, as sea levels rose and fell, going from hundreds of isolated islands to one large land mass and then back again. As early humans spread, the landscapes they discovered were dynamic and challenging. Progress happened sporadically.

E Pluribus Unum?

Up until the last 10,000 years or so, there were never many members of the genus *Homo* alive on the planet at any given time—probably less than a million or two for much of the more than a million years of our history and less than about 8 million up until the last 20,000 to 30,000 years. That means that for the vast majority of our history, all the humans on the planet at any given time would not even fill New York City (they'd fill Manhattan and maybe a bit of Brooklyn). Today there are more than 7 billion humans—enough to fill 1,800 Manhattans. And today we are all the same species, even the same subspecies, which was not always the case.

There are a lot of different populations, shapes, sizes, and behaviors over the about 2-million-year history of our genus, *Homo*. Strong disagreements as to how to best categorize them rage on, but most researchers agree that there are four general clusters, which might be divided into as many as eleven different species or subspecies: the early forms (*Homo habilis* and *rudolfensis,* and maybe *Homo naledi*), the middle-range forms (*Homo erectus, ergaster,* and *antecessor*), the later forms (*Homo heidelbergensis, floresiensis,* and *neanderthalensis,* and the Denisovans), and us (*Homo sapiens sapiens*). We've already met the early forms, but the most interesting story unfolds from the middle group through to us.

Homo erectus is used to describe pretty much all populations of *Homo* from about 1.8 million years ago until around 400,000 years ago. *Homo erectus* moved around and out of Africa, encountering all of those new environments and being pushed to expand the creative and collaborative journey. It is in *Homo erectus* where fully modern-looking bipedalism appears, brain size reaches from 750 to nearly 1,000 cubic centimeters (average modern size is about 1,250 cubic centimeters), the childhood period gets longer, and new types of stone and wood tools, foraging, hunting, and even the use of fire emerge. Different populations of *Homo erectus,* as a result of these new pressures and changes, underwent evolutionary transitions to give rise to later forms and are the ancestors of *Homo heidelbergensis,* the Neanderthals and Denisovans, the Flores people, and us. But others seem to have diverged from the main lines and continued to change in isolation, not connected to the larger human gene pools, and eventually went extinct. The last isolated pockets of these late *Homo erectus* populations are found as recently as 30,000 to 40,000 years ago in Southeast Asia on what is now the Indonesian island of Java.

The later forms are generally divided into three clusters: The *heidelbergensis* line, which gave rise to the Neanderthals and Denisovans, the Flores line, and us.

The Flores peoples (*Homo floresiensis*) are a group of very small-bodied hominins that have their origins in *Homo erectus* populations of Southeast Asia. They likely became isolated on the island of Flores (today part of Indonesia) about 1 million years ago and underwent some extraordinary changes, including a kind of extreme dwarfism, before they went extinct around 60,000 to 100,000 years ago. We've found nothing else like them in the genus *Homo.* It's likely that there were many little isolated pockets of populations like this in the story of the genus *Homo.* Once our planet seemed really big—until very recently, when there were not many hominins to spread across it, and most of them went extinct.

The *heidelbergensis*-Neanderthal line consisted of populations of larger-bodied, big-brained (sometimes larger than ours) hunting and foraging peoples who lived from about 400,000 years ago until about 30,000 years ago in Northern Africa, much of Europe, the Middle East, and parts of Central Eurasia. They looked similar to us but were not quite the same. The Denisovans are known only from a few bones found in Siberia (dated to between 30,000 and 48,000 years ago) and some DNA researchers were able to extract from those bones, so we know pretty much nothing about their lives. Some argue that representatives of the *heidelbergensis*-Neanderthal-Denisovan line are also found in East Asia, but we don't yet have a good enough fossil record in that region to know for sure.

The populations in this lineage had increasingly complex stone and then wood tools, used fire, and were able to live in pretty cold and harsh environments (they were the first into Northern Europe and Russia). They also made small bits of art and body-adornment jewelry and, at least on occasion, buried their dead. They were innovative, creative, and very collaborative, and we even carry small bits of their DNA with us today, but they were not our direct ancestors.

It's not wholly clear exactly why or how it came to be that we have some Neanderthal and Denisovan DNA in us, but one thing is obvious: We all mated. Our lineages intermingled in more ways than one. We mixed genes, behaviors, and maybe even ideas. How and when that occurred is less than clear, but the DNA doesn't lie. So Neanderthals and Denisovans were probably not different species than our immediate ancestors. They were more like sister groups from a common ancestor (*Homo erectus*) whose populations got a bit separated from those of our direct line. They were certainly human and did many, but not all, of the things our direct ancestors did.

Populations of *Homo erectus* moved into, out of, and around Africa, undergoing changes in body and behavior effected by those movements. The changes the different landscapes presented to them, their responses, and the shifting gene pools and mixtures caused by the movements began to produce a particular pattern in body and behavior on some of these small populations. By just under 200,000 years ago, some populations in Africa developed skulls, brains, bodies, and minds, like ours.

By about 100,000 years ago (probably earlier) some of our direct ancestors moved across Europe, Central Asia, and East Asia. By about 60,000 years ago they developed seafaring skills and made it to the islands of Southeast Asia and Australia. By 15,000 to 20,000 years ago they mastered the hard-frozen Arctic and moved across it down into the Americas. In this hundred-millennia process they encountered, here and there, other groups of humans, the Neanderthals and Denisovans, maybe even the Flores peoples. We know that sometimes they mated (at least with the Neanderthals and Denisovans), sharing practices, ideas, and affection. But it's also likely that at other times they did not mate, they may have fought, or more likely they avoided one another, wary of the very similar but unnervingly different other peoples. Regardless, by about 25,000 years ago, there were no more "others."

There is certainly something distinctive about us.

HOMO SAPIENS SAPIENS SPREAD AROUND THE WORLD

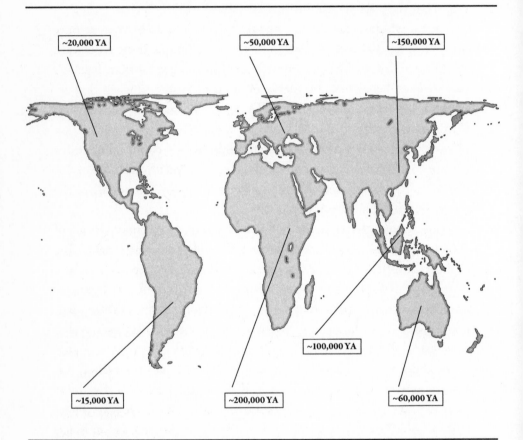

Our Shared Trajectory

All this talk of subspecies of hominins in some sense competing for survival can get confusing. They sound like different races. In the biological sense, a *race* is a population or group of populations in a species that are on a different evolutionary trajectory from the other populations in that species. Biologists call this a "subspecies." Subspecies are still in the same species, they can interbreed and share more in common with each other than they do with members of other species, but they are under different evolutionary pressures, producing significantly different versions of the same species. There are many ways to measure whether a cluster within a species is different enough to be labeled a subspecies, and they include both genetic and morphological (body) measurements. This sounds like the same kind of categorization as black, white, Asian, and so on that we see on census forms (and in popular notions of race) today. But it is not.

Apply any measurements of biological race (subspecies) to humans today and you always get only one race. We are all the same subspecies. Neither genetics, nor behavior, nor height, nor body, face, or head shape, nor skin color, nor nose or type of hair, nor any other biological measure divides modern humans into subspecies. If you compare the genetic differences between any two humans from anywhere on the planet, they are much, much smaller than those between any two chimpanzees from Eastern and Western Africa. It is a stunning fact. Humans are spread across the whole world and chimpanzees are found in only a relatively tiny swath across the center of Africa, but humans are far more genetically similar to one another. This pattern is the same for almost all comparisons between humans and any other mammal—we are among the most genetically cohesive and most widespread of any animal on the planet, a combination that is amazingly rare in the animal kingdom. In this measure, as in so many others, we are truly distinctive.

Thirty thousand years ago, and earlier, there were subspecies of humans, such as the Neanderthals. It's highly likely that there used to be more than one human biological race sharing the planet. Nonetheless, *Homo sapiens sapiens* is not what people usually mean when they say "race." We still use *white, black,* and *Asian* as labels for groups of humans as if they referred to biological races, and they don't.

Race as we use the term today is a socially, historically, and politically created and maintained category, not a specific and identifiable cluster of genetic or morphological variation, and it does not reflect our evolutionary history. As a social reality it has repercussions that will need thoughtful attention for a long time yet, but they are not the focus of this book.

The human evolutionary story demonstrates why racism is fundamentally misguided and just how amazingly biologically close to one another all humans are, despite the wide range of differences among societies across the world today. But the differences across societies and groups of humans, in dress, languages, food, religion, sports, living arrangements, and political beliefs, all come from the key characteristic that enabled us, the race of *Homo sapiens sapiens,* to be the last hominin lineage standing.

Understanding the details of how the human creative process worked in relation to the way our ancestors got food, dealt with the planet and one another, and channeled creative energies and capacities into ever-expanding innovations can give us a better grasp of our place in the world and help us shape our future. Ours is the story of how we got from a small group in the hominin lineage that could make simple stone tools and creatively cooperated to avoid being eaten, to the controllers of fire and the hunters of large game, to the creators of art, farming, science, religion, cities, and nations, and even to piloting spaceships to other planets and beyond while we investigate the beginning of the entire universe. Our next steps had best be creative too.

PART TWO

WHAT'S FOR DINNER?

How Humans Got Creative

LET'S MAKE A KNIFE

For decades in the late twentieth century academics assumed that it was our ancestors' ability to hunt that separated us from the other hominins and explained our evolutionary success. A famous conference (and subsequent book) in 1966 entitled "Man the Hunter" laid out the basic concept: Early man (and they meant only males, not females) made a place for himself and his group in the world by banding together and using sharp sticks and edged stones to hunt down animals, kill them, and consume them. This was a first in the primate world and it had a cascade effect: Men who were better hunters became leaders, and hunting and the aggression associated with it became a central aspect of the human evolutionary story. Men hunted, fought, and provided; women gathered, raised the kids, and tended the hearths; and the story of how we got our food gave us insight into gender, aggression, and human nature.

Except it was wrong.

Active and organized hunting shows up pretty late in our evolutionary trajectory—scavenging, gathering, and innovating with diverse foods all precede it. Being the hunted rather than the hunters is the reality at the start of our lineage, and gender differences associated with food that we see today are not evident in our deep past. The "man the hunter" scenario as it used to be told is a myth slain by the fossil, archeological, and genetic evidence.

It is true that hunting, and the creativity associated with it, plays a special role in human evolution. But what happened in our lineage before we became successful hunters, what preceded the development of our capacity to be the top predator, is more fascinating than any myth—or TV show.

Top Chef

On the TV show *Top Chef* the most important test is the Elimination Challenge. In it the top chefs are given specific ingredients and a limited set of tools and preparation options and are challenged to create the best meal possible. In one episode the chefs were sent, with no forewarning, into a swamp and challenged to use some of the local denizens (alligator, turtle, or frog) and outdoor cooking gear to create a dish with an innovative twist. The teams tackled the task with gusto—the winning dish was curried turtle meatball, chayote slaw, and chutney with raisins. Top chefs usually do pretty well when creatively challenged. A well-trained chef's talent for such culinary art has a history millions of years in the making.

Nearly 2 million years ago, on the borders of what used to be a lake in the Turkana region of eastern Kenya, our ancestors previewed a top chef challenge of their own—and it involved catfish and turtles. Living around the edge of a lake where it butted up against swamps and woodlands provided many opportunities for a wide range of animals, but almost all of them specialized in what kind of food they sought. The grazers ate grasses, the predators ate the grazers, and the small mammals and birds ate the berries and nuts and seeds and tried to avoid being eaten themselves. Creatures that lived in the water ate other creatures that lived in the water, and the ecosystem went along, everyone in their niche. But members of the genus *Homo* in this East African ecosystem didn't stick to the recipe book.

Food stress is a killer. Even in rich environments like that of the Turkana region 2 million years ago, changes in temperatures, a few drought years, or even a volcanic eruption or earthquake can shift the scene from feast to famine. Thus, the better an organism's ability to establish options—the more choices of food sources it has, the more creative it can get with finding and getting food—the better its chances are.

Our ancestors were already great at gathering salads of fruits and leaves and getting better at occasionally scavenging from a carcass left by predators by 2 million years ago. But unlike other species, when challenged with food stress, our ancestors did not double down on their go-to favorites; they branched out.

Early *Homo* were not tied exclusively to the tools or weapons that their bodies provided. They had the ability to make and use sharp stone flakes and hammer stones and to hold and carry sticks and stones and food for distances, and they increasingly relied on one another, working together to get things done. This capacity to create tools out of items in the world around them and their tendency to work through problems together enabled them to take a more thoughtful look at their surroundings.

Homo would sometimes forage near the lake's edge and in the swamps for grasses and plant foods, occasionally catching any small animals that wandered within arm's length. Around them they saw baboons wading into the shallows, pulling up water snails and the roots of water plants. On the edge of the lake they'd sometimes see a leopard grabbing a turtle and flipping it over but often unable to crack the shell. They saw the medium-size fishing cats swiping their broad claws at fish in the shallows, and sometimes even the hyenas would charge into the water in usually futile attempts to grab a large catfish from the mud. Like the top chefs in the bayous of Louisiana, our ancestors got creative.

Totaling all these images and experiences up, our ancestors began adding to their menu. We find specific evidence of this expansion at the FwJj20 site at Koobi Fora in Kenya, dating to about 1.95 million years ago. There are turtle shells with clear evidence of cut marks from stone tools, indicating that the shells were cracked open and the meat cut from the interior. There are large catfish that have been filleted and have marks indicating that tools were used to scrape even the meat from their skulls.

We don't know exactly how early *Homo* actually captured these high-quality freshwater resources, but we do know they cut the meat from the bony catfish bodies and sliced through the turtle shells to the goodies inside. Aquatic food items like these offer a valuable nutritional alternative to a more landlocked diet. The researchers who reported on this find saw these advantages:

- a reduction in the energy it takes to capture and process nutritionally rich food,
- a reduction in competition with other species (most can't do this kind of foraging), and
- a decrease in the risks associated with the scavenging of large terrestrial carcasses (and running into, or competing with, predators).

Homo had come a long way from the novelty of carrying fruit, nuts, and seeds to safe places to process them; they'd created a new menu.

Our ancestors created novel ways to access the energy needed to expand their brains, bodies, and behavior over the course of the next million and a half years. They did it by modifying stones and wood, working together to expand their food options, and eventually mastering fire. Increasingly creative ways of getting food facilitated our lineage's move from being the main course to being the top chef. What they ate led to changes that eventually enabled us to win the evolutionary elimination challenge.

Getting an Edge

Food is shorthand for the energy that our bodies need to function, to grow, to live. If an organism can meet the challenges of food head-on, and win, it is doing well in the evolutionary game. However, these are rarely easy challenges.

Calories are the way we measure energy that bodies use. So when one consumes part of a plant or an animal, the first goal is to convert the calories stored in that chunk of fruit or flesh into calories that the body can store and burn as needed. This is what we call the "macronutrient

challenge." Macronutrients are carbohydrates, proteins, and fats (technically called *lipids*), and they are what bodies use for energy. A second goal
is to get enough of the micronutrients that the body needs to run well.
These micronutrients are vitamins, minerals, and the ever-critical water,
the key items for fine-tuning and lubrication to keep the body going. Different kinds of plants and animals produce and store different
combinations of macro- and micronutrients. The goal is to have a diet
with the best possible mix of the two.

Of course, plants and animals actively avoid being eaten—they make
you work for it. The more work one has to put into getting the food, the
more calories and water one burns and the more macro- and micronutrients one needs to make up for it. Getting enough of the right kind of
food is an active process. So animals forage or hunt, or both.

Carnivores like lions and cheetahs hunt by chasing down big game.
Leopards use stealth and ambush their prey, and meerkats spend much
of the day searching for lizards, grubs, and beetles, eating the occasional
fruits and roots as supplements. All do this with specialized bodies for
tearing, gnashing, clawing, and sprinting. Primates, in general, are not
much in the way of hunters, but humans are the extreme exception.

Most monkeys don't hunt animals and are primarily fruit and leaf
eating, needing a third or more of their day to forage for and ingest the
right plants and plant parts. Most of the apes spend their days eating
fruit, with chimpanzees, and occasionally orangutans, sometimes hunting animal prey. No monkey or ape has much in the way of honed hunting skills or bodily weaponry for it. And no other primate has as diverse
a diet as humans. You may have seen a seagull drop a shell on a paved
road or rock to break it open, but no other animals process their foods to
the extent that humans do, and no other animal cooks. Human foraging,
hunting, and eating are quite distinctive.

Our lineage created new ways to get food, increased the diversity of
what was consumed as food, created new ways to process food, and eventually even developed techniques to alter the chemical and biological
properties of food to make it better, easier to use, and tastier. The evidence
of this exceptional capacity starts with our lineage's ability to reshape
rocks into tools.

In 2015 a space probe NASA launched in 2007 made it to Pluto and sent back amazing images from 3 billion miles away. That probe was a human-constructed tool, and the creative innovation behind it is a direct descendant of modifying rocks to have sharp edges a couple of million years ago. Looking at the early stone tools from today's vantage point of steel knives and food processors, let alone spacecraft, they don't look like much, at least at first glance. But these shaped rocks were the starting point of a distinctive history of changes to our brains and bodies. The simple sharp flakes and edged stones of the earliest tool industry are the first hard evidence of our lineage's ability to see more than what is simply in front of us, to create new form and function in the world.

Crows use rocks to break open snails, tits (small songbirds) use sticks to puncture milk caps in bottles on the porches of British homes, dolphins use sponges to help them catch fish, and some primates regularly use rocks, sticks, and other items to crack nuts, fish for termites, drink water, and even, on occasion, hunt other animals. Using stones or sticks as tools, especially in the search for food, is not uncommon in the animal kingdom, but significantly altering stones or sticks to make better tools is.

The most creative tool use, outside of the human lineage, is found in our cousins the chimpanzees. For more than fifty years we've known that chimpanzees select specific rocks in order to crack nuts, fold leaves into cups in order to drink from streams, and take the leaves off small twigs and break the twigs to the right lengths for termite fishing. The anthropologist Crickette Sanz and her colleagues demonstrated that chimpanzees think through using multiple tools for a single task. In the Central African site of Goualougo they've observed chimpanzees carrying small "fishing" sticks over long distances to their favorite termite mounds. At the mounds are large sticks left there during previous visits. Once a chimpanzee gets to the mound, she puts the small stick in her mouth and grabs one of the larger sticks. Using one foot and two hands to grasp the large stick, she uses it like a shovel to break open the ground at the base of the giant termite mound. Once she's opened up a crack in the mound, she sets the large stick aside, crouches down, and takes the small stick from her mouth. Artfully inserting the small stick into the mound, she wiggles it just a bit to annoy the termites, which attack it. In a quick motion she extracts the small stick with tens or even hundreds of termites locked onto it and whips them into her mouth, crunching down on a "forkful" of juicy, protein-rich food. All the while her young son has been hanging on to her back or standing at her side and watching, occasionally reaching to grab a few termites from the corners of her mouth. Research shows that young chimpanzees hang out with their moms for years and during that time pay very close attention to Mom's tool use (and a whole range of other behaviors) and slowly, with lots of trial and error, acquire the tool-using skills.

This example, and related research, tells us three things. First, chimpanzees are quite skilled in using lightly modified sticks and unmodified stones as tools. Second, because this skill set shows up (to some extent) in all the apes and in humans, it is likely quite old and may even be as old as the LCA (last common ancestor between great apes and humans), making this kind of tool use a basal part of hominin capacities—a jumping-off point for the evolution of our lineage. And third, using tools in this manner is not something that an individual just invents each generation; it is learned through exposure to others of the group, a kind of social facilitation and maybe even a bit of teaching.

The fact that chimpanzees will strip the leaves of a good termite-fishing twig and even break it to a specific length, or that they will leave a large stick at a site for future use, demonstrates that they have the capacity to understand that there are differences in the shapes and sizes of the sticks that translate to better or worse tools. This capacity is not confined to primates; we also see it in crows and other birds in the size and shape of the rocks and sticks they use. Animals that use tools tend to select rocks or sticks of sizes and shapes that work well for the intended task. For young chimpanzees it can take years to learn, through observation, how to effectively fish for termites or crack nuts with rocks. But no other animal in the wild, not even chimpanzees, can look at a rock, understand that inside that rock is another more useful shape, and use other rocks or wood or bone to modify that rock—and then share that information with the members of her group. This is exactly what began to happen 2 to 3 million years ago, at the very start of our lineage.

Making and using stone tools involves much more information, collaboration, and creativity than selecting a rock or stick, as it is, to use. The simplest and earliest stone tools associated directly with our lineage are the work of the Oldowan industry, which takes its name from the Olduvai Gorge in Tanzania, where these tools were discovered by the archeologist Louis Leakey in the 1930s.

OLDOWAN TOOLS

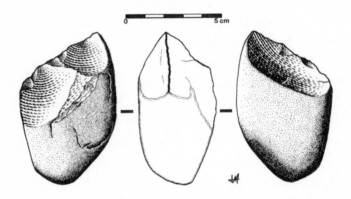

The making of the Oldowan tools required a set of manipulations made possible by hands like ours and a capacity for predicting the outcomes of hitting the rocks in certain ways (physics!). Most important, each group seems to have had many toolmakers (and possibly everyone in the group was a toolmaker). This suggests a process of sharing information, passing around the knowledge to make and use these tools within groups and across generations—the first tangible sign of our collaborative creativity.

But just how "creative" does one need to get in order to make sharp flakes from rocks? Actually, it is a lot harder than it appears, especially if it has, so far as you know, never been done before.

The most common Oldowan tool is a sharp stone flake created by striking a stone core (often called a *cobble*) with another stone, called a *hammer stone*. In order to make these efficiently you need to be able to do a number of things in sequence. First you have to find a core and hammer stone of a good size, shape, and composition. Not all stones are equally good for making flakes, as density, grain, and crystal structure vary across types of rock. That means you need to search for, locate, and repeatedly go back to the same sources, or at least be able to access the same rock types and sizes, in order to get the best raw materials. Once you collect the basic stones, you need to find a safe place to make the tools (a loud and intensive process—try smacking rocks together quietly). Remember, there were a lot of large predators living in the same time and place as early *Homo.*

Making the flakes presents a series of challenges. First one must examine the core for shapes and patterns in the rock, selecting the specific site to strike the core to create the best flake. You have to support the core in a certain way to get a clean strike. You have to grip and swing your hammer just so. It is an art.

Once one flake has been detached, one has to repeat the whole process again, but now with a modified core and a new set of possibilities: New shape of the core, new options for where to hit it, and the whole set of steps in the flake-production process starts again. Today it usually takes university students many, many hours or even weeks to learn to reliably make good Oldowan tools, and this is with instruction from a skilled teacher, using language, video guides, and books and already having the best materials delivered to the lab or classroom—things that none of our early ancestors had. University students don't have anything trying to eat them either.

This simple stone toolmaking process opened up a space for our ancestors to grow their brains and increase social and cognitive complexity: two core features of our evolutionary history.

We know the brain is exceedingly expensive to grow, using 20 to 30 percent of the body's energy during peak growth, between two and seven years of age! There had to be a pretty extreme increase in nutrition between 500,000 and 2 million years ago to power the massive increase in brain size we see in the fossils. The earliest members of the genus *Homo* (from around 2.3 to 1.8 million years ago) have brains in the 600- to 650-cubic-centimeter range (about 30 percent larger than apes of approximately the same body size); by 1.5 million years ago we see *Homo erectus* fossils with brains hitting the 750- to 900-cubic-centimeter area; and nearly modern-size brains (more than 1,000 cubic centimeters) appeared by 400,000 to 500,000 years ago. Cleverly invented and utilized tools made the necessary increase in consumed calories possible.

These tools also had an interesting by-product. The behavior and collaboration involved in making tools actually changed the way our ancestors used their brains and resulted in changes in the way their (and our) brains work.

We have fossil evidence of the fact that brain size increased over the evolution of our lineage, but we also have laboratory-based research to help us understand how this might have happened. Recently teams at the University of St. Andrews in Scotland and Emory University in the United States began programs training people how to make stones into tools (including Oldowan-style tools). The researchers paired the toolmaking process with a series of brain scans in order to see what specific areas of the brain might be affected by the process of learning how to create these tools and then becoming skilled at making them. Both sets of researchers reported seeing changes in the connections and organization in the brain associated with training hours and actual performance of making the tools.

The Emory group demonstrated that learning how to make Oldowan tools creates different patterns of activity in the visual cortex at the back of the brain before and after practice, indicating that the act of toolmaking shapes the way the brain responds to stimuli and that learning (when making stone tools) can shift brain activity. The areas where more complex toolmaking activity had the clearest effects were the supramarginal gyrus in the parietal lobe and right inferior frontal gyrus of the prefrontal cortex. These brain areas are associated with planning complex actions, advanced cognition, and possibly the development of skills in language. The Emory group also showed that experienced contemporary stone toolmakers had marked increases in activity in the supramarginal gyrus in their parietal lobe. But they also found that other individuals *just watching* the toolmakers could experience some increases in activity in that same brain area as well. This suggests that the action of toolmaking, and the watching, imitating, and communicating about toolmaking, can set up and expand the activity and dynamics of particular areas in the brain—areas that we know began to grow between 2 and 1 million years ago, and areas that are eventually associated with language and other high-level cognitive behavior.

The complexity of toolmaking and the diversity in types of tools increase as does brain size and diversity of food types: It looks like there is a feedback process in action. As I've mentioned, this is what we call niche construction—the tools, brains, and behavior all interact to facilitate a specific pattern of relations between *Homo* and their environments. This produces a series of feedback loops that affect one another, creating outcomes of increased efficiency and effectiveness. But the remodeling of the way the brain works is not done in one fell swoop.

By about 1.5 million years ago we start to see a new type of stone tool in the archeological record in Africa and then in other parts of the Old World as our lineage spread. These tools are more varied than the Oldowan tools and have new features, and forms, that make them both better to use and harder to make. This tool industry is called the "Acheulean" and can be divided into an early phase, about 1.5 million years ago to about 700,000 to 900,000 years ago, and a later phase, around 700,000 to 250,000 years ago.

The early Acheulean industry produced more than just choppers and cutters, and it adopted the increasingly common method of refining tools by removing smaller flakes on both sides of the edge, thus making sharper and more resilient edges. It is in this phase of toolmaking that hand axes start to show up, and they last as part of the human tool kit almost into contemporary times.

A key pattern underlying these innovations is greater premodification of the core (the rock from which a flake is knocked off) to create specific patterns in the surface of the core such that the likelihood of getting a really good flake is improved—more preplanning and a more multilayered visualization of what the end result could be. This is different from the earlier Oldowan method; there are even more steps of preparation, of envisioning multiple stages to the process, before it is even begun. This requires more involvement of different areas of the brain and increasing flexibility of cognitive function.

ACHEULEAN TOOLS

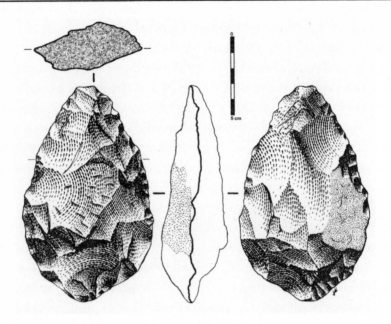

What this actually means for the production of such a tool is that a group of our ancestors would have to go to the rock outcrop near some low cliffs, or the litter of stones near a dried streambed, likely one that their group had been visiting for years, and collect armloads of cores to take back to a safe place. Or if the area where the stones were found was reasonably safe, they could sit, taking turns standing watch, and start to hammer out the stone tools (again, not a quiet activity). But even after this process, they still had to carry armloads of the tools themselves back to their sleeping sites or wherever they preferred to stash them (remember, these are rocks, and heavy). The paleoanthropologist Rick Potts of the Smithsonian estimates that to cut the hide of, and deflesh, a good-size ungulate (like a small wildebeest) would take about ten to twenty-five pounds of stone and about 50 to 100 flake tools. Imagine a few individuals carrying around five or ten pounds of rocks across rough terrain in eighty- or ninety-degree heat searching for some food to chop up. Inevitably the load would get shared among the group's individuals, and along with that a culture of collaboration would develop.

We find evidence for some creative storage systems for these tools. We know that from pretty early on our ancestors left piles of tools across the areas over which they roamed, planning for kills or scavenges or plant-gathering events, or just storing them in many places to keep them safe from others. Maybe they were just too heavy to carry around all the time. More than a million years ago our ancestors were using parts of their landscape like a toolshed (or kitchen cabinets), making sure that some tools were always close at hand or in a reliable spot when they needed them. Again, such a system takes a lot of collaboration and innovative problem solving. Such materials—possessions—also introduced the risk of theft—and gave our ancestors more to think about, plan for, and create with.

To make the Acheulean tools, our ancestors had to modify cores via specific small strikes to prep a place for them to directly hit with the hammer stone to create the first useful flake. Once they had the core modified and a specific target spot in sight, they would grasp the core (or maybe a few would secure it together), and one individual would raise the hammer stone high and aim to deliver the key blow. Anyone who has tried to make stone tools knows that this is the stage when the blood starts spurting. Because of the high quality of the rocks, the debitage (the small chips and flakes that fly off when you strike such rocks) are really sharp and can easily slice through flesh. That is, after all, the whole point. Even the best modern stone toolmakers get bloodied on a regular basis.

Once the first flake is knocked off, it would be set aside or handed to another individual, whose job was to start modifying that flake. Then the toolmaker would examine the core, rotating it in her hands and possibly knocking off bits here and there to prep the next strike. This brings in multiple areas of the brain involved in spatial and rotational analyses, in information processing, in hand-eye coordination, and likely in communication of these concepts.

This whole process gets even more complicated in the more advanced Acheulean, with the introduction of both hard and soft hammers (including bone hammers) and the use of multiple core-prep sequences to whittle a stone down to the ideal flake type, which is knocked off after four or five or six premodifications and other flake removals. The bottom line is that by 500,000 years ago, our ancestors were making new tools that required foresight, nuanced communication, some teaching, and a lot of manual dexterity.

The Oldowan tools were used to cut and mash parts of plants as well as meat. The new Acheulean tools provided more reliable ways to use stone, tools with sharper edges, larger tools that could be used with more flexibility and efficiency, and more types of tools, such that a wider range of uses became available. Sharpening wood became extremely important by at least 500,000 years ago. Scrapers, two-sided choppers, and smaller and more refined edges on tools appeared, and eventually new techniques for prepping cores, predicting and shaping flakes, and even reusing tools by sharpening them became commonplace. By about 100,000 to 200,000 years ago we start to see blades (flakes that are more than twice as long as they are wide) and a range of small tools called microliths, bone and wood tools, and dozens of different tool types in these new industries. And in the last 10,000 years we see the move from stone, bone, and wood to the metals of bronze, iron, and steel (and all the way to the dawn of plastics).

While ours is not the only lineage in the world to use things that are not part of our bodies to modify the world around us, we are certainly the masters of tool creation, innovation, complexity, and use. Take a look around your kitchen and revel in the products of our deep-seated, and distinctive, creativity (even if you never did quite get around to remodeling it). But before we get too excited about the advances of nearly 2 million years of toolmaking up to around 250,000 years ago, there is not what we'd call a rapid pace of technological advance compared to what we have seen over the last few thousand years. The Oldowan and Acheulean tools dominated the human landscape for well over 2 million years. It is not that our ancestors were simply resting on their laurels and unwilling to or incapable of change.

First of all, both the Oldowan and the Acheulean did their jobs very well—better than anything else out there at the time. Second, remember that it takes a lot of brainpower and complex communication to develop progressively more complex tools: It was through the early tools that our ancestors began to set in motion the processes that provided the possibilities of change (the new niche of increased nutrition, brain growth, creative collaboration, manipulation of the environment, and so on). So it took a great deal of time before the connections that linked bodies, brains, behavior, communication, and ideas could all line up effectively to facilitate moving to the next step in complexity.

We see that innovations did show up, in stops and starts, with some eventually catching on and spreading across populations of our ancestors—a process that took a very long time during the first 1.5 million years of our history. Why the relatively slow pace? Again, up until very recently there were simply not many members of the genus *Homo* on the planet. While some groups came into contact with a few other groups and others moved across large areas into new locations, on average most members of our genus did not interact with too many other individuals, or groups, across their lifetimes. This means that most groups died out, became isolated, or just lived many, many generations interacting with only the small populations right around them. So when new innovations in tools showed up in a group or set of groups, the most common outcome was for these innovations to eventually go extinct with the groups that had them, before being spread to other areas. Most of our history, and the individuals in it, is lost forever to the archeological record and to the mainstream of human evolution.

Over the course of the about 2-million-year history of our lineage, our ancestors went from being the first creatures to make stone tools to being the technological masters of the planet—and it all started with figuring out a better way to get food. But while getting better at getting food remained a key to staying alive, what about the other primary challenge related to food: how to avoid being someone else's?

Avoiding Being Dinner

Human bodies are very digestible (no spines, scales, fur, stinging barbs) and thus are quite desirable as food for many, many other animals. Our ancestors had a particularly risky trade-off to make between getting better and more diverse food and putting themselves more and more in the sights of predators. Increasing the quality of the nutrition they consumed meant getting, making, and using tools, getting more meat, accessing a more diverse diet, spending more time searching for the best kinds of foods, collecting them, and bringing it all back to some sort of base camp. All of these activities involve a lot of moving around in the open during the day. The risk of predation never totally disappeared; even today there are still instances of lions, tigers, alligators, crocodiles, and even very large snakes attacking and consuming humans.

To make simple stone-flake tools one must smack rocks together repeatedly, which is akin to yelling out, "Hey, over here: fleshy mammals with no horns, claws, or spines!" That's something one wants to minimize when large saber-toothed cats and giant hyenas are around. And because carrying armloads of rocks is not always possible or advisable, having to leave tools and raw materials at different locations across the landscape meant more travel, movement, and exposure.

The same is true for building a more mixed diet. Many monkeys mix fruit, leaves, and insects into their diet, but they do so by exploiting all three of those things in trees. Other monkeys, like baboons, mix it up, eating from both the ground and the trees. But they spend a lot of their time watching for predators and live in pretty large groups, and the big males have very large canine teeth. But leopards and other carnivores can still take a heavy toll. The easier thing for our ancestors would have been to just hang out in a few trees to get fruit, or simply make it a priority to always be in areas where the predators are not and eat what is available there. But instead they added more meat, more types of plants, and even some aquatic animals to the menu and started moving across more types of landscapes, spending more time processing foods, and often having their arms full as they moved across the landscape. In getting more creative with their menus, our ancestors started to do just the opposite of what most animals, even our close relatives, do. Eating well meant accepting a higher risk of getting eaten.

This increase in dietary diversity and complexity occurred as our brains grew larger. Larger brains enabled us to do more cognitively, to get creative with stones, wood, foods, and one another. Getting those large brains was all made more complicated by the fact that having brains growing for longer (which is how you get bigger ones) slowed down the pace at which kids developed, so by about 1.5 million years ago, the young of the genus *Homo* became more and more reliant on other members of the group to care for them for longer periods of time.

There is no chicken-or-egg conundrum—which came first: bigger brains or complex behavior? This interactive process represents a critical part of the early human niche, our ancestors' way of making a living in the world. Neither came first. There was a mutual feedback loop between the bodies and minds of our ancestors, mediated and made possible by changing behavior and the increases in nutrition that accompanied it. Creativity is a process, and as our ancestors began to construct their new niche around new ways to get food, more and more options began to open up—and not just for eating.

Carrying armloads of rocks, kids, and food, and moving around in high-predator environments with no fangs, claws, horns, or real weapons, does not sound like a sound strategy for evolutionary success. But it was.

KILLING AND EATING, ETC.

Our ancestors needed meat. They'd become adept at scavenging, using stone tools to cut meat from the remains of kills left by predators, more than 2 million years ago. But passive scavenging, taking the leftover scraps, was not enough. They wanted the best, and the most, meat so they began to "power scavenge," getting to kills early and attempting to take them away from the predators. Building on their cooperative coordination and what they learned about predator behavior while avoiding being eaten, our ancestors got creative. When they came across recent kills, or fresh carcasses with the predators still around, some in their group could charge in, shaking sticks, waving their arms, and making hooting and grunting noises. Others might have stood back, throwing stones at the predator. The predator would run off. When this worked, our ancestors got a fresh kill and lots of meat. When it did not work, the predators got one or more of our ancestors. But practice is everything, and over time, groups of *Homo* were growing smarter and becoming better able to imagine outcomes.

Getting to the carcass quickly, before the predator had stripped away the prime meat, was crucial. After chasing away the predator, the group could coordinate the removal of the flesh: cutting the ligaments and tendons with the sharp-edged small flakes; then switching to the larger-edged choppers to hack through the muscle; finally removing the meat from the heavy bones in strips and chunks and passing those into the arms of the group members not processing the carcass, standing watch for predators, or fending off other scavengers (large vultures, jackals, and even stray hyenas). The predators, or larger groups of the more dangerous scavengers, could be back on the scene quickly, so time was of the essence. Having different individuals armed with stone tools at each of the limbs and on the haunches, the group could strip the big carcasses of the loins, stomach fat, and rib and limb meat relatively quickly. Having removed what they could carry, the group would then leave the carcass to the smaller scavengers.

If most groups of *Homo* within a region were able to do this with reasonable success, then their combined actions would force small changes in the entire ecosystem. Predators would have to alter their behavior, causing other animals to respond, and if the groups of *Homo* kept up their creative activities, a new niche could be constructed. And it was. Power scavenging emerges as part of the *Homo* tool kit prior to hunting and is part of the suite of innovations including toolmaking and the expansion in both the types of foods gathered and how foods were processed that our ancestors began to develop over the first million years or so of their history.

The evidence for this behavior, and its emergence from a more passive mode of scavenging, is in the fossilized bones of larger grazing animals and the tools our ancestors left behind. In some of the earliest tool-use sites, those that predate even our lineage (*Homo*), evidence suggests passive scavenging: waiting until the predators who made the kill have had their fill and then stripping what meat remained. The bones of animals that have been eaten by Pleistocene carnivores and then processed by stone tools have telltale marks that enable us to reconstruct what happened. When a big cat or hyena strips the meat from a bone, it does so by grabbing the meat in its mouth and tearing. As it gets closer to the bones, the strong teeth dent, nick, and otherwise mark the bones in very distinctive ways. Once much of the easily stripped meat is removed, carnivores often gnaw on the bones (the meat at the bone surface has a lot of connective tissue—what we'd call gristle—that is really tasty). Think about the images of lions eating wildebeest in nature documentaries or a dog chewing, gleefully, on a bone with scraps of meat on it to get a good idea of what this looks like. Experts can examine a fossilized bone (or a nonfossilized one) and tell not only that a predator was eating it, but even what kind of predator it was and how big it was. There is also a whole other set of marks left by the last participants at the table: the scavengers and the rodents. Birds and small mammals usually do the final noticeable cleanup, leaving marks of their own, and while beetles and ants might pick the bones truly clean, those marks are the hardest to see.

These same techniques enable us to tell when stone tools were used on a bone because they, too, leave predictable and recognizable marks. When you cut into the meat attached to a bone, the edge of the tool can come into contact with the bone and leave a cut mark, but one that is very different from that left by the bite of a predator or the gnawing of a rodent. If the cut marks from stone tools are overlaid on the predator teeth marks—that is, if they cut into the teeth marks—then we know the stone tools were used on the bones after the predator had used its teeth. Most of the early examples of stone tool use on fossil bones (from 3.3 to about 2 million years ago) look like this and so are evidence of passive scavenging. However, starting about 2 million years or so ago we start to find the reverse: the predator tooth marks and other scavenger marks sit on top of the stone tool marks. This tells us that the stone tools cut the meat from the bones first; then the other animals got access to the kill. Now, we don't find any evidence early on that the stone tools were used to kill the prey animal, so we have no real evidence of actual hunting at this time. But the fact that the predators who likely took the kill down did not get much of a chance to eat from that kill leads us to a specific conclusion: Our ancestors were taking the kills away—they were power scavenging.

Whereas passive scavenging requires some creativity, power scavenging takes the creative process to a new level. Choosing when to try to take a kill from a predator, coordinating the behavior of the group to get it done, having the right tools handy, getting the meat from the carcass in a quick and organized fashion, and getting out of there before more predators show up is no easy task.

Research at the Gran Dolina site, at Atapuerca in Spain, clearly demonstrates this kind of collaboration by about 800,000 years ago. The site has evidence of a wide range of animal bones, many of which were modified by *Homo,* often before any evidence of other animal markings. Many of the medium-size and larger animals show evidence of being taken apart with stone tools, having the meat stripped from the bone and specific bones (with meat on them) cut from the larger body. The limbs and ribs and other specific bones with good meat attached to them are in abundance, whereas other bones (heads and backbones, for example) that are heavier and have less meat on them are not present, indicating that the members of the *Homo* groups at Gran Dolina coordinated butchering the carcasses and carried the pieces to different locations to share and maybe even store for later. The researchers on this project even state that from the evidence they've found, "we can deduce that several individuals participated in hunting parties and/or carcass transport. The potential variation in the number of participants is a complex issue, but it is nevertheless a clear sign of social cooperation within a group, food sharing and possible division of subsistence tasks, conceivably to ensure the group's survival."

Between around 2 and 1 million years ago, when our ancestors were exploring the savannahs and woodlands of Eastern and Southern Africa and expanding out into Eurasia, the climate was anything but stable. Large fluctuations in temperatures, rainfall, and weather patterns challenged animals, our ancestors included, and one successful way to deal with these challenges was to be flexible with food and get creative. Looking at the fossilized teeth of our ancestors from this time period shows that they developed a very mixed diet, not reliant on one type of food over another.

Meat was not the only item on the menu. Having stone tools enabled *Homo* to eat a wider range of fruits and nuts than most other primates or animals sharing the same environments. Chopping, cutting, and crushing nuts, large fruits, and even unripe fruits provided access to more types of nutrition from plant foods, and our ancestors' gift for sharing food got that nutrition spread across the group. They could have divvied up jobs, with some members making the stone tools, while others collected nuts and fruits and brought them back to a base camp; an egalitarian division of labor seems to be characteristic of successful human foragers. This is how the first granola was invented.

Some days they could have organized together to power scavenge, but others they might have used those same collaboration skills to extract another superrich source of food called underground storage organs (USOs)—basically big roots packed with water, carbohydrates, and calories. They were the yams, beets, and potatoes of their day. Many researchers have argued that these could have been a critical part of the diet for *Homo* early on. But getting USOs requires serious digging and often some kind of processing (mashing or pulping) to make them edible (if you don't yet know how to cook, that is). We don't have any concrete evidence of digging sticks, as wood rarely fossilizes, but we are pretty sure that early *Homo* had the capacity to use sticks in that manner. After all, it is simpler than making stone tools.

If the group worked together, young and old included, they could set off with their digging sticks to the best spots for tasty USOs and spend a chunk of the day digging (keeping an eye out for predators). Once they'd unearthed the rich roots, they could chop them into smaller chunks with a few stone tools they'd brought and then all carry the chunks back to a safe base (maybe leaving the stone tools at the site for a return visit). They'd then spend the afternoon taking turns back at their base camp mashing the roots with stone tools and end up with a few days' worth of carbs and calories for the whole group.

Scavenged meat and plants were not the only things on the dinner table. It is quite likely that early on our ancestors learned to exploit the work of others beyond simply taking kills from predators: They also challenged bees for their honey. Most animals consume honey when they can get it (some chimps even use tools to do it), so bees try to defend their hives by placing them inside the trunks of dead trees or in high, out-of-reach places. But that was not such a big challenge to our ancestors.

Work by the anthropologist Alyssa Crittenden and colleagues suggests that honey could have been an important source of protein and sugars for early *Homo*. Two or three individuals would have climbed into the tree and used their digging sticks to pry open the bark of the trunk to reveal the densely packed honeycomb, dripping with honey. The bees would be flying about, confused by this approach at first, so more of an annoyance than a danger. One could swing the stick around to keep the bees away while the other two used sticks and some stone tool flakes to cut the honeycomb out and drop it down to the rest of the group waiting at the base of the trunk. Carrying gobs of sticky honeycomb might have been made easier by sticking them on large leaves and maybe even rolling the leaves up to make less sticky and more transportable bundles. We have no direct evidence that they did this, but it is not much of a stretch to imagine that the same beings who could travel miles to find the right kind of rock and then create tools out of it and use the tools to deflesh a kill they've stolen from a large predator could figure out that transporting a sticky mess of honeycomb might be easier if it were wrapped in a large leaf.

And here is where it might have gotten even more interesting. The collection of the honey would have resulted in some spilling on the ground and even small chunks of honeycomb littered around the base of the tree. This would attract some smaller animals drawn by the strong smell of the super-nutrient-rich resource (honey). Members of the *Homo* group likely noticed this pattern (after all, they were already adept at noting, tracking, and even predicting the movements of the large predators) and realized that as soon as they moved away from the tree, these other small animals showed up to eat the remains. They also had sticks and stone tools handy . . . and some groups likely put two and two together.

If a few members of the group hung around, maybe crouching in the high grass near the tree with the hive, they might be able to use their sticks, and rocks, to add some meat to the menu. It is only a small step from chasing away predators from a kill to making the kill oneself—especially if there is a pretty low cost to the kill attempt (thus the focus on small animals). Creativity in getting food inevitably set the stage for experiments in early hunting.

Hunting Parties

Two of the three great apes (chimpanzees and orangutans) do hunt in certain conditions today, suggesting that occasional small-animal hunting might have showed up as early as the LCA. Both of these great apes (and some monkeys, such as baboons, as well) will opportunistically take small animals. For example, when a small deer or baby bushpig runs across their path, they might grab, kill, and consume it. However, both apes sometimes engage in premeditated hunting.

Chimpanzees, our closest cousins, hunt in two ways: socially and solitarily. In social hunts, large groups of chimps (mostly male but sometimes with females too) that come across monkeys high in the trees start to get a bit crazy. They become really excited, panting and hooting, and charge up into the trees after the monkeys (chimpanzees' favorite prey is a kind of monkey called red colobus). The chimps don't actually coordinate the hunt particularly well, but some of the better hunters play off the movements of the group and watch the directions and actions of the monkeys, heading them off for a capture if they can. And when they do, it is a sight to see. The successful hunter delivers a crushing bite to the head of the colobus or slams it against a tree to render it unconscious. Then it moves to a solid spot in the trees or on the ground and is surrounded by the rest of the chimps, arms outstretched, whooping, hooting, and begging for meat. Most of those on the hunt get no meat; the captor usually shares a bit only with his closest allies (and maybe his mom). Sometimes, if the successful hunter was a low-ranking male, a more dominant male will swoop in and steal the kill, sharing with his allies and leaving the actual captor with nothing. These hunts, especially if they are successful, are frenzied times for the group. Massive excitement and often small side fights break out; meat is a much-prized item, but they get very little of it. Hunted meat makes up less than 5 percent of the chimpanzee diet, and most communities of chimpanzees spend very little time in any efforts related to hunting.

Solitary hunting in chimpanzees is a bit different, done mostly by females, and with tools—spear-like sticks, to be exact. Work by primatologist Jill Pruetz in Senegal reveals that females will take sturdy sticks, strip them of their leaves and small branches, and break them so they have a sharp point. The female (often with her infant riding on her back) then takes to the trees searching for large trunks with telltale holes in them—these are the sleeping sites of a little nocturnal primate called the galago. Once she locates the galago nest, the female rams the spear into it, poking and stabbing until she hits pay dirt, and withdraws the impaled galago to consume. Interestingly, at the site where Pruetz has seen most of the hunting, dominant males rarely steal these kills from the females.

The chimps studied by Jill Pruetz are the only nonhuman primates who've been observed to hunt prey with weapons regularly, and it is in a savannah site, which is an uncommon type of area for chimpanzees to live in. Other chimpanzee communities hunt off and on, especially in times of fruit abundance, and hunts seem to happen when a large group of chimpanzees is traveling together and then comes into contact with a group of colobus or other monkeys. Chimpanzees hunt due to neither nutritional stress nor dire need for meat. Indeed, chimps seem to hunt more when they have lots of fruit available and lots of individuals around: Hunting is a social event rather than just a drive to get food. It's a sort of party.

In orangutans hunting is rare and done mainly by females. The few times it has been observed, it has entailed an adult female grabbing a small nocturnal primate called a loris (found only in Asia, but related to the African galago) and either slamming it against a tree or delivering a crushing bite to its head. Unlike among chimpanzees, hunting in orangutans appears to be done only when fruits and young leaves are scarce and thus is a rare, but creative, response to nutritional stress by a few populations of orangutans.

Because humans and some of the apes hunt, it is likely that the LCA was at least capable of opportunistic hunting. But at some point, probably around a million years or so ago, our ancestors made the shift from their path of power scavenging and some opportunistic hunting to regular hunting and changed not only their worlds but those of the animals they preyed upon. Groups of *Homo* collecting honey or digging and chopping up USOs or slicing the meat off a large ungulate had already sometimes grabbed and killed small animals. By around a million years ago, they lay in wait for the small animals, premeditating their kill.

Once *Homo* had some success grabbing (and eating) the small animals that came to clean up after them, it was only a few mental steps to noticing that such small animals ranged across many different habitats. Through a lot of trial and error, some groups of *Homo* got quite good at surprising and capturing small mammals, and the better they got at it, the more they realized that not only was this a great source of food, but there were many, many types of these small animals and that different ones probably had different challenges for capture and different benefits for nutrition (and maybe even taste?). The social and creative ways in which early *Homo* got food generated a feedback loop that shaped their evolution—and hunting ratcheted that process up.

This feedback loop connecting the nutritional stresses of growing brains and bodies, the shaping of stones and wood into tools, the collaboration and communication required for power scavenging, and USO and honey gathering and processing expedited the changing brains and behavior of *Homo,* increasing capacities for creativity. Human-style organized hunting soon followed.

What Drove Communication Skills?

Human coordinated hunting is much more than a bunch of primates running around trying to capture animals to consume: It is a group of individuals using communication, collaboration, and tools to capture elusive and sometimes dangerous prey. Consider a large, and meaty, animal like a deer or a good-size gazelle. At around 120 or more pounds, there is enough meat to feed a group of twenty for four or five days (supplemented of course with plants and fruits). Power scavenging such a kill is good, but if a group could get the deer by themselves—cutting out the middleman—it would be even better. Being the actual hunters meant they would not be reliant on finding a predator to shadow, hoping that the predator is successful, and effectively taking the kill away from the predator without much of a fight. Hunting would mean that the whole process of getting food could shift much more in their favor. The main problem is that deer are very fast and quite wary of predators and will (not surprisingly) do most anything they can to avoid being eaten. Our ancestors must have noted the way predators catch their prey, the long chase and eventual capture by lions, the ambush attacks of leopards, and the group mobbing by hyenas, and probably started to figure out how to mimic some of those approaches. But in each of these predators' hunting styles, the weapon of choice was a feature of its body: running speed, massive teeth and jaw muscles, sharp fangs, deadly claws, and so forth. Our ancestors had none of those things. But, as they had already done for more than a million years, *Homo* went with what they did have: creative collaboration.

It is not that other animals don't communicate when they hunt. Lions watch one another and take cues predicting where the fleeing prey might head. Hyenas, African hunting dogs, and some communities of chimpanzees follow the lead attacker's moves, either joining in the initial attack or circling around to head off the prey. But all of these hunters rely on their bodies as weapons and their experience from previous hunts to figure out what to do. The young hyena learns through socially guided trial and error, often making mistakes and sometimes being cut out of the shared kill because of it. The difference with human social hunting is twofold: We rely on tools or other forms of extending our bodies' capabilities, and we share information via language. We communicate about the past, the present, and the future in great detail—one need not have ever hunted to participate, successfully, in an organized hunt.

While probably not using language (yet), *Homo* at a million years ago likely had a system of communication that was distinctive and more intensive than that of any other primate. What would it take to effectively do all that they were doing by this time? Just try to make Acheulean stone tools, collect honey, and forage for roots—and do all of it while dealing with a group of twenty or thirty individuals of all ages and sizes: helpless infants and toddlers with fast-growing, expensive brains, a few older folks, and the whole group with no body weaponry or even real speed, and a serious need to avoid the large predators whose daily mission was to eat them. This requires reliable, nuanced communication.

Many other animals live in groups, and some even have very complex social lives (hyenas, monkeys, apes, and whales, for example), but none of them require the level of coordination and communication that a human group requires, and that our ancestors developed. Being able not just to communicate with one another about the immediate moment, but also to imply where one should be both during and after a hunt, a honey collection, or a predator attack, would have created a whole new series of options for *Homo*. And this is before they had any really good weapons.

Moving to being hunters was an important next step and a very attractive one, but the obvious approaches, like chasing a deer in the open, would rarely work. *Homo* had no choice but to innovate. Chasing a deer into a thick stand of bushes where others of your group are waiting for it armed with rocks and sharp sticks is another matter. Cornering a small herd of gazelle at a watering hole and having some members of the group charge from three different directions could trap the gazelles, keeping them from running away (at least away from the water's edge). Others in the group could circle around the sides to strike, with rocks and sticks, at the gazelles that made a mad dash sideways along the water's edge. Some groups might even have noticed how slow animals get when bogged down in mud or the immediate results one gets when an animal falls down a ravine or off a cliff. The goal of chasing a group of hooved mammals doesn't always have to be capturing them; if the end result is their deaths, then driving them off a cliff or getting them stuck in the mud works. Whichever of these strategies was chosen, to make it happen a group of *Homo* had to have the ability to communicate and coordinate sufficient information.

Once these processes were under way, the feedback among food, tools, behavior, and hunting enabled *Homo* to produce novel options for tools, ones actually geared toward hunting. By at least 500,000 years ago we have evidence that members of the genus *Homo* used sturdy spears and maybe even threw them by about 300,000 years ago. Between 500,000 and 100,000 years ago we see the development of a whole range of better tool types, much more use of bone and wood for finer and sharper points, and the appearance of blades. Blades—flakes twice as long as they are wide—are the first step to making really good knives and eventually things like stone-tipped spears and swords. In this same time period there is evidence of the hafting of stone and bone to wood with glue and rope, the first composite tools and a radical expansion in how good the tools (and weapons) were.

Along with the increasing complexity of tools and hunting weapons there is evidence of even more diversity in diets and of larger game being hunted and killed by *Homo*. By this point small groups were living all around Africa, the Mediterranean, the Middle East, the Indian subcontinent, and East and Southeast Asia, and even in the northern latitudes of Eurasia. From the seashore to the mountaintops, from temperate forests to open savannahs to dense tropical jungles, our ancestors spread, changing and adapting their diets to new animals and plants.

Remains, especially teeth, from 400,000 years ago at the site of Qesem Cave, in what is today Israel, show how far *Homo* and their food had come by this time period. The fossil teeth from this site are covered with deposits and marked and grooved with pits and striations. Signs of polyunsaturated fatty acids coating the tartar of the teeth show that they were eating a good deal of seeds, with those from plants like *Pistachia* (ancestral form of pistachios) and *Pinus* (pine nuts) the most likely sources. But their diet was a lot more diverse than that. There is evidence of fungal spores (mushrooms?), some pollen and strands of leafy plant material (chewy greens and maybe some flowers?), and even insect exoskeletons, including a butterfly! (Did it just fly into someone's mouth?) There are starches that suggest roots and some evidence of meat eating as well—a very diverse and innovative diet. But the most telling remains are those that illustrate the last major component of the creative eating of early *Homo*, one that makes hunting (and all other food gathering) even more effective. Embedded in the tartar on the teeth of the individuals at Qesem are microcharcoal fragments—they were inhaling a lot of smoke and eating charred food items. Clearly, they were using fire, regularly.

The Power of Cooking

Humans are the top (actually, the only) chefs on the planet.

People who argue that raw foods are the best for you are wrong. There are certainly benefits one can derive from raw vegetables, raw leafy plants and fruits, and even raw meat (especially fish). But contemporary humans who rely exclusively on raw foods are seldom sufficiently nourished to meet challenges of the kind our ancestors faced. Cooking softens plant food, breaks down the cell walls containing cellulose (which humans cannot digest), reduces the chemical bonds of fats and other key aspects of meats and fibers, and generally makes the process of chewing, swallowing, and extracting the benefits of food (all called digestion) easier. Cooking increases digestibility of starchy plants by 12 to 35 percent and of protein by 45 to 78 percent. Cooking can also nullify toxins found in plants (especially in USOs) and acts to kill dangerous bacteria that can grow rapidly on exposed meat (like that scavenged from a predator kill). It makes a big difference. But one needs to control fire to cook with it.

There are some good indications (burned bone and heated rocks) that at least a few groups of *Homo* used fire as much as 1.6 million years ago, but we don't see regular evidence of fire use at hominin sites (like hearths or evidence of smoke on bones and teeth) until about 350,000 to 450,000 years ago. The early examples of fire use are likely the products of lightning strikes or small patches of fire left after larger forest fires. Small groups of *Homo* would emerge from hiding places where they rode out large grass fires, hungry and a little bit freaked-out by the sounds, heat, and mayhem. Wandering over the once lush grasslands, they would come across charred carcasses, and being master scavengers they'd have immediately checked them for meat. Most were burned to charcoal, but some would have only been singed or cooked a bit; the warm meat would have peeled right off the bones, would have been so easy to chew, and would go down so smoothly. It even tasted different, smoother and sweeter. Being pretty smart at putting cause and effect together and imagining more possibilities than directly meet the eye by this point (remember stone tools and power scavenging), some early *Homo* would eventually realize that exposure to the heat and chaos of the flames caused changes in the meat that made it better. This might have led some groups to actively seek out areas after a fire for such goodies; maybe a few even realized that you could grab and transport burning branches and feed them with grasses and wood to keep them going. The group that had this fire for any amount of time would quickly also learn that it had two other very important side effects. Predators who were drawn by the light and activity were then also easily driven away by the flames, and the flames themselves offered light that enabled extra time for toolmaking and socializing.

The ability to be free from the constraints of daylight to work and to play was to become a crucial turning point in what made our ancestors human—fire and light became catalysts for colossal increases in our creativity and productivity.

From sites like Gesher Benot Ya'aqov in Israel, at about 790,000 years ago, to Beeches Pit in England, Schöningen in Germany, and Zhoukoudian in China, all about 400,000 years ago, and at many sites more recent than 300,000 years ago, we find evidence of the creation and maintenance of fire. This evidence includes fire pits and fossilized charcoal, flame-seared bones, stone tools heated to facilitate better flaking, and even wood that has been made into a sharp point and heated to harden it for use as a spear.

This evidence of fireplaces more or less matches the timing of the evidence for regular hunting. This time period (about 400,000 years ago) is also about the time that the populations of *Homo* who are most likely our ancestors had developed brains that are in the range of modern size. This is also the point when we start to see a great increase in the types and complexities of tools and the first appearance of materials we might call art. Fire is probably a critical component in the human niche at this point, a core aspect of the feedback system that helped speed technological and social change in our evolutionary story. Fire helped give us more than just food; it gave us cuisine.

One can sit down in Tokyo, Jakarta, New Delhi, Cape Town, Marrakesh, Madrid, Helsinki, New York, Mexico City, Lima, and Apia (Samoa) and have a plate of a white-meat, flaky fish. But it will not taste the same in every city. One of the most powerful and creative aspects of modern human eating is the variety, the diversity, and the ingenuity in how we prepare food. There is no reason that we need to do anything more fancy than heat it up and consume it. But we almost always do. Each culture, each ethnic group, each local community, has its own ways. Food becomes a signal of who we are and where we come from. The ancestral quest for food and the creativity exercised in getting it set the stage for fish and chips, paella, tamales, sweetbreads, sushi, curries, satays, and porridges. Top chef competitions, upscale restaurants, chili cook-offs, Sunday meals, and takeout shops across the world owe their existence to our evolutionary trajectory begun nearly 2 million years ago.

The story of human eating is a story of innovation, collaboration, and experimentation. Over the history of our genus, the making and carrying of food and tools and the ability to expand their range put them in contact with new kinds of foods and new challenges. Being able to deal with that effectively involved an emerging package of capabilities: power scavenging and eventually hunting, increasing the diversity of what they ate and how they got that food, moving from simple to complex tool types, and becoming experts at outsmarting predators. These capabilities lowered the chances of dying from outside sources, which effectively lengthened childhoods and allowed for the increase in body and brain size. Every single aspect of these changes requires innovation and collaboration at both the individual and the group levels—human creativity.

To understand the development and expansion of these features beyond those of a few hundred thousand years ago we have to shift our focus to another distinctive human pattern: the ways in which we create and live in communities. The focus on tools, food, and hunting has gotten us to what was going on by about 100,000 to 200,000 years ago, but we have not yet even mentioned how our ancestors created and lived in communities, which led to the villages, towns, cities, and countries we see today. Nor have we touched on the most important reality of food today: It comes primarily from domesticated plants and animals. Of course, these two realities are intertwined. Understanding the creation of communities as a force in our evolutionary trajectory, not merely an outcome, is the point of our next chapter.

THE BEAUTY OF STANDING IN LINE

I f you placed a group of related and unrelated chimps, monkeys, wolves, or hyenas at a table piled with turkey, sweet potatoes, cranberries, gravy, a fancy salad, and a pumpkin pie, you'd get a pretty violent holiday event. Not so with humans (at least not usually). Sitting down with family and friends to a holiday meal represents a lot more than stuffing oneself with turkey and quarreling over politics. No other species works together to collect, prepare, and share food the way we do, and certainly none do so as broadly and enthusiastically.

Humans deal with all the problems the world throws at them—food, shelter, safety, innovation, childcare, illness, even death—as a community. But our communities are not like schools of fish, or herds of wildebeest, where members just follow the movements of the group. We are even different from groups of other primates who have complex social lives and are bound together by social ties. Humans have a distinctive capacity for getting together. It is part of our niche, the way we "make it" in the world.

Next time you walk up to a movie theater, supermarket checkout counter, or bus stop and see a line, set aside your annoyance at least for a moment. It is a marvel of human nature. A group of unrelated people, who have likely never seen one another before, all wanting the same commodity, mutually agree to arrange themselves in an orderly sequence, delaying immediate gratification. Of course, things don't always go perfectly smoothly, and in some contexts there is a lot of pushing and jostling for position (think of the entrance to a rock concert or boarding a crowded commuter train), but in most scenarios, everyone knows what to do without so much as a word between them. There are almost no other species on the planet that could regularly replicate this same feat, and humans do it morning, noon, and night.

Barn raisings are mostly a thing of the past, but for Amish communities across the midwestern and eastern United States they remain a central part of community life. People from all over a larger community converge to help put together a barn for one of the community members. Tens, or hundreds, of individuals coordinate their activities, ranging from assembling the beams to erecting the sidewalls, to raising and sealing the roof, while others set tables and prepare food, watch over the children, or coordinate the cleanup after the day's work. All of this for a barn that will directly benefit only one family. Each individual knows that if he or she needs such community assistance, it will come to them as well.

In 2005, after the devastation of Hurricane Katrina, tens of thousands of people went to New Orleans as volunteers. They gutted and rebuilt houses; they offered skills of community development, food preparation, nursing, and teaching. They left their lives, not damaged or destroyed by the hurricane, to stand in solidarity with the people who suffered the worst of its effects. Using websites and social media, more than 200,000 people volunteered to shelter evacuees, many opening their homes to strangers. These people crossed economic, political, racial, and ethnic lines to help those in need, and they did this often with great risks and strains to their daily lives. Nothing else on this planet shows this kind of massive compassion and coordination in the face of adversity—but humans do, again and again and again.

Humans are by no means alone in working together to get things done. Many other animals live in groups and cooperate to defend their young or their territory. Large herds of wildebeest cover hundreds of miles as a cohesive unit during migrations, and gaggles of geese can fly thousands of miles together in tight formation on their journeys south or north. Thousands of ants and termites coordinate their activities via chemical and behavioral cues to build giant nests and earthen mounds. However, not many birds build nests for other breeding pairs, few lions or hyenas kill an antelope and bring it to share with another pride or clan, few if any ants coordinate their activities with another colony to build mutual mounds, and it is almost unheard of to see a group of animals traveling, suffering, and risking themselves for other members of their species that they do not know.

It is the capacity to develop this level of community, and the coordination and cooperation involved, that was a necessary precursor for our ancestors to make the leap from being excellent hunters and gatherers to the mastering of the manipulation of plants and animals we call "domestication." How did that happen?

Creating Human Communities

Whether you are a macaque monkey, a lion, a meerkat, or a hyena, the group is the place where you are born, where you grow up, and where you either stay or leave to join another similar group. The group is the cornerstone of life experience for social animals. This is true for humans as well, but with a twist. Humans live in communities, and from early in our evolutionary past, they have been more than just groups.

The human community is a collection of individuals who share a sense of belonging, what anthropologists call "kinship." For humans this kinship can be biological, historical, social, or all three simultaneously—they are the people who matter most to us. The community is the primary source of shared knowledge, security, and development, typically across an individual's life span. Communities share meaningful emotional bonds and experiences even when all members are not in the same place at the same time. But to build a community you first need to live together, and it turns out that there are many challenges to any animals trying to live together in a social group. The two most basic ones are coordination and size.

Coordination simply means being together, most of the time, and still being able to

- get along,
- get enough food, and
- not get eaten.

The getting along does not mean that all members of a group are always particularly nice to one another. Think about a household full of siblings or the group of macaque monkeys; their day-to-day experience involves a lot of little tiffs, but grooming and peacefully hanging out together take up most of their time. Some sort of coordination among them has to occur so that they can all get enough food (avoiding serious fighting over it) and not get attacked (or eaten) by other animals. In the macaques this coordination takes the form of dominance hierarchies for access to goodies like food, a high level of tolerance for young individuals around food, and joint defense by the group against predators or other outside-the-group threats. However, this kind of coordination gets very difficult the larger your group gets, especially if you have no language.

The psychologist and anthropologist Robin Dunbar many years ago proposed that there is a maximum size to have a successful coordinated social group and that this size limit is imposed by the number of close connections ("friends") you can manage. It turns out that this limit has to do with brain size and complexity—you can see where this is going. Humans, with bigger and more complex brains than most, can have larger social groups, and we do, but we didn't always.

Over the course of our evolution, our brains got bigger and more complex, and the same is true of our social groups; we see it in the fossil and archeological data. However, based on our current brains, the maximum size of a group (or community) for humans is somewhere around 250 individuals (at least according to Dunbar). Any look around you today shows that we have massively overtaken that and that we started to do so at least 10,000 years ago (and likely earlier). The capacity for larger and larger communal coherence is the result of our creativity. We already saw how our ancestors figured out how to expand their capacities for getting food from the world around them, a first step in building communities. Now we are going to see how they expanded their capacities to get along, to live in larger groups, and to eventually move from groups to communities—and then to towns, cities, and beyond.

It Takes a Village to Grow a Human Brain

The capacity for living in a group starts to grow at birth. The infant is born very dependent on its mom. This is different from most other animals, which are ready to go right out of the egg: Snakes are ready to slither off and feed, fish to swim and eat, and frogs to tadpole it for a while (also swimming and eating) until they transition to, well, frogging. Mammals, however, come out from Mom in varying states of readiness, but all need to hang out close to her for milk and protection for the first weeks, months, and, in some cases, years of their lives. That means that the very first thing mammals know is a tight social bond to another mammal, their kin. If we focus on the more social mammals (primates, whales, wolves, etc.), then we see that multiple members of a group interact closely with the young mammal and thus the infant's social world is complex from the get-go.

These realities have deep physiological impacts. For mammals it is critical to survival to have a strong bond and commitment from both mom and offspring to get along, a drive to be together. Over many millions of years, evolutionary processes have fine-tuned mammalian bodies to set them up for a strong physical sense of attachment and caring. Technically this is called a psychoneuroendocrine system, a complex of hormones, emotions, and affections. Humans took a basic mammalian trait and made it very complicated.

The primate version of the mammalian parenting style is to have infants be reliant on Mom for a very long time. This is also true with elephants, dolphins, and whales. Most monkeys are glued to Mom for the first few years of life, and some apes stick around Mom until they are seven or eight years old. This pattern is due to two related things: Primates have large brains that take a good while to develop, and primates have complex social lives, and it takes a long time to learn how to navigate them well. This means that the mother-infant bond lasts longer and is more intense in primates than in most other mammals. A second, less common but still important, primate twist is having multiple allomothers—that is, more individuals than just the mom take care of the infants from very early on. And these extra caretakers aren't always other females.

Think about humans. Today we have massively dependent babies. A baby horse can run hours after birth and a few-days-old macaque monkey can hold tight to her mother's body as she leaps through the trees and can tentatively climb on its own after a few weeks. But it takes months after birth before humans can even hold themselves up, let alone move on their own. It takes years for them to learn how to walk well and even longer to run effectively, and even longer for them to master language. In other words, human infants are pretty useless to the group. They are a drain on the group's resources, as they cannot produce or carry their own food, fend off predators, or assist in daily activities for at least the first three to five years of life (and in modern times some folks would argue that this period is stretched out into the late teens and early twenties). And herein lies the key to human success. By constructing a system in which we could have babies born well before their brains and bodies are developed, we have enabled a kind of learning, a complexity in brain development, and a potential for innovation, imagination, and creativity. And we did this by finding creative ways of increasing cooperation and constructing community.

We already know that it costs a lot to grow a big brain. But we did not go from a 600-cubic-centimeter brain in early *Homo* to the 1,300-cubic-centimeter brain of today overnight. It was across about 1.8 million years that these changes took place (from about 2 million to about 200,000 to 300,000 years ago). The critical creative act was to develop a social system, a way of living, that gave our ancestors the flexibility to have offspring that were helpless for longer amounts of time. That is, if early *Homo* infants began developing more slowly, inside of the womb and out, it enabled a greater amount of postbirth brain growth. Two things are required to make this happen: increased quality of food and increased abilities to care for the young.

The increased quality of food is indirectly for the infant—it is Mom who needs the extra nutrition. The anthropologist Leslie Aiello and colleagues demonstrated that *Homo erectus* females were under substantially greater nutritional demands than earlier *Homo* females. Gestation (when the baby is inside of Mom) is not the really costly part of reproduction; lactation (nursing) is. Mom has to consume enough nutrition to feed her body's needs *and* create enough milk to provide all the nutrition the infant needs for at least a year or two before being able to supplement the infant's diet with outside food sources. We know that in the time period when *Homo erectus* shows up and spreads around and out of Africa (1 to 1.8 million years ago) our ancestors began to expand and diversify their food supply.

However, in most other species of mammals, the mother is on her own for getting food and taking care of the infant(s) at the same time. It is also up to her to avoid being eaten by predators (and keep her young from being eaten). If you add on top of the additional food costs an infant who is not good at moving or doing much of anything for those first few years, you get a problem, especially in *Homo erectus*. We've already established that group members needed to work together to get all these foods, to get and make the stone tools, and to avoid the predators. Mom, just like everyone else, needed to be helping with the food gathering and predator avoidance, and if she was the only one in charge of caring for this costly kid, things would not go well.

But if others in the group also chipped in, then we have a different story. We know that in some other mammals, even a few primates, there is allo-care, where individuals other than the mother contribute significant effort in taking care of the infants. *Homo erectus* started to do this with a novel twist: It was not just the holding or "babysitting" of infants by some females other than Mom, or one specific group mate taking on much of the infant care burden, as in a few species of primates where the dad does most of the carrying of the infants. It was both of these things and more. *Homo erectus* developed the system that we refer to when we say "it takes a village to raise a child," even though they didn't have any physical village architecture.

The anthropologist Sarah Hrdy and other groups of researchers have demonstrated, very robustly, that humans have a distinctive system in which infants are nurtured not just by the mother but by a system of caretakers from day one. In this system (Hrdy calls it "mothers and others"), the members of a community take on substantial aspects of the care and development of children. Older females (grandmothers) can act as caretakers, enabling the younger mothers to participate in many of the group activities. Some researchers argue that this caretaking role is one of the reasons that human females, unlike all other primates, undergo menopause, where females live long after their reproductive cycling shuts down. Older siblings and other children could also hold, watch, and even carry infants, as the other members, including Mom, made stone tools, butchered scavenged kills, gathered USOs or fruit, or patrolled the water's edge for turtles and large catfish. When the group was moving, males and females without infants could take turns carrying infants over long distances, freeing Mom from the extra energetic costs of carrying all the time. The members of early groups of *Homo erectus* were moving from a group to a community.

It is important to note that *Homo erectus* did not have a modern growth pattern right off the bat (today humans have a few years of helpless infancy followed by at least a decade of childhood). Those patterns emerged slowly, over a million years or so, through the kinds of feedback loops that characterize the process of niche construction. Actions by *Homo* influenced the evolutionary pressures on them, which in turn helped shape their bodies, brains, and behavior over many, many generations. Each innovative change by *Homo* tweaked the system slightly, with resultant benefits. Going from only Mom as caretaker to having older females hold and care for this infant was one step; including older siblings and other kids was another; and then having males help with the carrying was a third. Each step increases the flexibility and resilience of the group but also increases the level of coordination and communication needed. The feedback loops were in place, and for *Homo erectus* the solution to the baby problem pushed the human evolutionary story toward a whole new chapter.

Initially, *Homo erectus* infants grew at a faster pace than ours do now, and their childhood period was about two-thirds of what ours is—they likely matured by their early teens. Over time, as *Homo erectus* tweaked the system via behavioral innovations like getting better at allocare, improving nutrition, and achieving more collaboration and coordination among members of the nascent communities, infant survival rates improved and childhood inched longer and longer. There are two processes to focus on that will help us understand how key parts of the human community developed over this time:

- the new ways of thinking involved in the transition from early stone tools of the Oldowan to the Acheulean and more complex tool kits, and
- the caretaking not just of infants but of one another with the emergence of compassion as a central part of the human community.

The Emergence of Compassion

Years ago when I was living in central Bali, Indonesia, I took a class from a master mask carver. I was the only foreigner in the class and the oldest person at twenty-four; the rest were boys in their early teens. The course began with us all sitting around the carver watching him as he took a block of wood and began to carve. We did that for a week. Four hours a day sitting and watching. I was starting to wonder what was going on. Then at the start of the second week we were all given a set of carving tools and a block of wood. The master carver told us to make the mask he'd been carving the week before. Okay. I did my best to remember his patterns, grooves, and strikes and got started. He walked around the room grabbing the hands holding the tools and showing, not telling, how to make the cut, carve the groove, or shape the pattern. When he got to me he just shook his head and sat down. He grabbed the block of wood, positioned it in his lap, grabbed my chin and positioned my gaze on the wood at a certain place, and began carving. He carved for fifteen minutes and an eye appeared. He pointed to the space just to the right of the eye he'd carved and gave the wood back to me. I started in again. In the month that I worked with the master carver we probably had a total of five or six conversations about the work itself, but never when I was actually working the wood. Eventually the second eye (and more) appeared. It was not by any stretch a good mask, but it was recognizable as one. Such apprentice learning has deep roots in our lineage.

We know that between 1.6 and a half million years ago, small communities of *Homo* across Africa and much of Eurasia made the transition from reliably making and using the Oldowan technology of flakes and chopping tools to innovating, experimenting, and developing a broader array of shapes, sizes, and functions of the Acheulean and subsequent stone tool kits. The skills were transmitted from individual to individual, from community to community, and across generations. It is this transmission involving learning and sharing, even more than the initial innovation, that is arguably the most creative act.

Remember that to make stone tools our ancestors had to be able to "read" the rock extremely well, imagine an end product, and modify the cobble via multiple strikes to develop the right platform for knocking off the first usable flake. Then they had to examine the core, rotate it, and possibly knock off bits here and there to prep the next strike. Over time, as they got more proficient, the whole process got even more complicated, and there were four or five or six premodifications and other flake removals just to get to the right shape to get the best possible flake—which, once it was knocked off, was refined and developed into a working tool. Learning how to do this process is a bit like when I learned to carve the mask. It is not easy and it requires some form of teaching.

We can see hard evidence of this process in the archeological record through recent work enabling reverse reconstruction of the flaking trajectories and the shape and pattern of the creation of stone tools. At some sites dating as far back as a million years (and older) we have all, or nearly all, of the flakes from a cobble (the debitage) as well as the final tools produced. This means that through a very painstaking procedure, researchers can actually reassemble the entire toolmaking process, flake by flake. They can reconstruct the patterns, the decisions, and the actual strikes that went into making a specific Acheulean tool. The bottom line is that making these kinds of tools is not possible without teaching.

Initially, some particularly skilled and insightful individuals took Oldowan flake-tool creating one or two steps further. As new and better variations happened by chance or intent, others noticed and tried to emulate them—and they would do so by working with the innovator, watching her, following her strikes and core preparation and experimenting with what they'd learned. But for such innovations to remain in a community and be passed down across time requires both the initial act of creativity (by an individual) and then the broader collaborations that enhance that initial act (by the group or community members). This kind of toolmaking process is not a skill one develops in each generation via trial and error or by oneself; it is a skill that, once developed, is maintained within the community.

The philosopher of biology Kim Sterelny took up this issue and asked: How did our ancestors without language as we know it or brains the size or capacity of ours develop and pass along such a complex and intensive skill set as complex stone toolmaking? Sterelny's answer is "the apprentice model," essentially the way I learned to carve my mask. Young members of *Homo* communities were exposed to older individuals who made the tools, traveled with members of the community to gather the right stones, and handled the tools themselves, using the tools and even playing with them. But all of this is without schools or guilds or anything we might recognize as formal instruction.

Today we think of society as split up into clusters of roles with special skills; in the deep past it was likely not so delineated. It is unlikely that, a million years ago, there were hard-and-fixed roles for "tool specialists," "hunting specialists," "entertainers," or "childcare specialists." But this flies in the face of almost any depiction most of us have seen in museums or in books of what our early ancestors were like. In these images and dioramas we pretty much always see the same stage set: a male standing with a medium-size dead animal slung over his back (the hunter), a female sitting or kneeling holding an infant (the caretaker), maybe another female tending a fire with a toddler at her side (the meal preparer), and then another male, usually a bit older, sitting making the stone tools (the toolmaker). It is important to realize that nothing, not a thing, in the fossil or archeological record suggests this specific sex or age makeup of who did what or that there were "jobs" like this in the past. We do know that in all apes, females use and make tools slightly more than males and the young learn to use tools primarily by watching their mothers. We also know that while male chimpanzees hunt most, females are the ones who primarily use tools to hunt.

Of course, in many contemporary human societies males do hunt large game more than females and females are often the main individuals charged with childcare. We also know that *none* of the apes or any other animal does anything like making complex stone tools and that modern society is technologically a million miles ahead of that, so looking to modern-day patterns in humans or in other animals is not the best way to reconstruct what the past of our lineage was like. Assumptions about gender and role specialization likely reflect some of the patterns in our ancestors, but they have restricted our perspective too much. Strict specialization shows up much more recently in the archeological record— and is an extremely important shift, changing the way communities work. But we need to keep that historic turning point in its place, which is not with early humans.

Of course, some individuals were likely better at stone toolmaking than others, just as some were better at leading the power scavenging, finding the best fruit trees, knowing where to find turtles, or more speedily digging up roots and tubers. The point is that rather than the others of the group ceding all responsibility to those individuals who seemed to have a better knack at the specific skill, they would learn from them. The knowledge spread within the community, taking hold such that most members became capable of at least passable performance of the critical behaviors: If such behaviors hadn't been shared, they would not have survived the passage of hundreds and thousands and millions of years.

In the apprentice model one learned via stages, incrementally, by emulating the actions one observed. This can be done via passive teaching— by having individuals simply sit around and watch the stone tool production process. Imagine a group of youngsters sitting around three adults as they work, across hours, shaping the stones, whittling down from large cobbles the sharp and finely honed double-sided cutters, cleavers, scrapers, and choppers. The young would pick up the flakes, the halfway-done tools, the initial cobble, and the final forms and touch them, follow and repeat the actions of adults, and even try to replicate the process from start to finish. Sometimes a bit more active instruction could have come into play. One adult, seeing a youngster who has been repeatedly alongside whenever the older one began the toolmaking process start working the side of a cobble, might grab the stone and reposition it in the hands of the youngster. The new position is closer to the right way to hold it. The youngster strikes the core and sees the result.

Adding this slight change to his repertoire, the youngster starts the process again, using a slightly better starting position he has learned. Much as I saw in Bali, apprentice learning still works. It was key for our ancestors and is still key for us today.

This transmission of skill via learning, doing, and sharing information is reflective of a specific and very human capacity that the anthropologist Tim Ingold calls "enskillment"—and it always involves watching, interacting, and acquiring the patterns of how to be a member of the community. The quality of compassion springs from the same set of circumstances.

Many animals exhibit concern for their group mates, sometimes even helping the sick or injured. It is common to see clusters of baboon or macaque monkeys mobbing a snake or a dog in defense of the group, but it is pretty rare to see any individual monkeys explicitly care for and share food with an injured member of their group (it does happen sometimes). Popular YouTube videos show a few older female elephants rescuing a young elephant in distress or two adult elephants assisting another injured adult to walk by holding her up on either side. There are examples of similar behaviors from a range of highly social mammals (dolphins, dogs, wolves), even across species, but they are all seen only sometimes, never regularly. In contrast, humans regularly exhibit a high level of compassion and assistance to others, even those not related to them. Of course, we also have an aptitude for cruelty unrivaled in the animal kingdom, which turns out to be part of the same package as compassion, but let's set that aside for now.

In forming and maintaining the kinds of communities our ancestors did over the last million years, there would have been many, many times when individuals would have fallen ill, been injured, or even just gotten old and lost some of their physical capacity. When this happens in other animals, that member of the group usually gets isolated, sometimes even attacked, and slowly moves off and disappears (usually dying). One of the amazing transitions in our lineage was the advent of behaviors that kept the injured, sick, and aged as part of the community. Individuals actively assisted others, even when it was taking energy from themselves that the others could not directly give them back. That same hormone-behavior system that drives the mother-infant bond spread beyond its initial use.

Work by the archeologist Penny Spikins and colleagues walks us through the fossil record to demonstrate this. She divides the last 2 million years into three stages in the emergence of compassion. From about 1.8 million to about 300,000 years ago we see evidence of the acquisition and sharing of meat from scavenged prey and other foods. We see the advent of allocare by males and females, young and old, and the subsequent lengthening of the childhood period. The sharing of food and the widespread caretaking across the group assisted our ancestors in being successful, and the feedback loops of their shaping and being shaped by the environment started to include these compassionate behaviors. We even have direct evidence of caretaking. At the 1.8-million-year-old site of Dmanisi in Georgia, we see that one of the adult individuals there had lost all but one tooth many years before he died (we know this, as all of the sockets except for the canine teeth were reabsorbed in the jawbone). This means others in the group had to have provided digestible food for him. Maybe they even prechewed it.

Another example comes from a site 1.5 million years old in Kenya where the remains of a female *Homo* show evidence that she was likely suffering from hypervitaminosis A, a disease caused by too much vitamin A in the diet (which you can get by eating too much bee larvae, so maybe this female was in an especially successful honey-gathering group). This disorder can cause problems with bone density and damaging bone growths. It takes quite a long time for this disease to manifest in the bones, and her fossil shows that she had a full-blown case. If she had the disease it would have taken weeks, even months to develop, causing her to experience nausea, headaches, stomachaches, dizziness, blurred vision, reduced muscle capacity, and fainting. These would have seriously limited her ability to contribute to the group or even fend for herself, but she survived. She was cared for.

At the famous site of Sima de los Huesos in Spain, about 530,000 years old, there is evidence of a child (maybe eight years old) with a birth defect called lambdoid single suture craniosynostosis, where the bones of the skull fuse very early and cause serious problems with brain growth, leading to developmental disabilities, locomotor challenges, and disfigurement of the face and head. This child lived at least five years or more with this syndrome, looking and acting very different from others. He got a lot of assistance and care. He couldn't have lived so long otherwise.

These examples might not seem like much, but when you think about the entire catalogue of fossils that we have from these ages (there are not that many) you see that the fact that we found these few suggests that compassion and caring were probably widespread.

Spikins's second category, between about 300,000 and about 100,000 years ago, has compassion extending into every aspect of human communities. She argues that there is significant archeological evidence for deep emotional investments beyond the self. She points to expanded coordinated hunting and food sharing, increased evidence for expanded caretaking, and the emergence of burials as evidence. For her final category, starting around 100,000 years ago and moving through today, she argues that the capacity for compassion goes beyond the community, beyond even the species, and can be extended to strangers, animals, objects, and even abstract concepts like "God."

But before we get overly warm and fuzzy, let's remember that the tighter you bond within your own community, the more leery you are of other communities. We know that for the history of our lineage there is a common set of options for communities that encounter one another. I like to call this the "Three Fs" (flee, fight, or fornicate). "Fornicate" is really shorthand for getting along, which often results in some degree of coupling eventually, but "Two Fs and GA" does not sound as good as "Three Fs."

For most of our history, population densities were very low, so groups were few and far between. When they did encounter one another, it was more often than not beneficial to spend some time together, collaborate, and even exchange members. They were small enough that it was not usually a case of too little food or not enough space, and mixing up the members was probably socially and certainly biologically healthy. But as communities grew and senses of identity became associated with specific places (stone-gathering sites, hunting grounds, certain river edges or coastal caves), feelings of "us" and "them" could grow stronger. Fighting between groups broke out, and we will soon get to that dark side of our story, but there is the critical step of domestication to consider first. We will do that in the next chapter.

Can We Remain Creative Within Ever Larger Communities?

In the last 200,000 years, populations of individuals looking more or less like *Homo sapiens sapiens* spread around Africa and across the globe, encountering other kinds of *Homo* who were also out there. By 15,000 to 25,000 years ago we are the only members of the genus *Homo* standing, the only *sapiens* left.

As we spread we encountered new lands and other peoples, animals, and plants. Entering new ecologies, we faced again and again the need for new ways to make a living. In a fit of creative exuberance, many populations of humans across the planet began to shape other animals and plants. Unintentionally at first, but then purposefully, we began to change the bodies and behavior of certain animals and plants and brought them into our lives, and our bodies, linking us forever to them and them to us. The expansion of our communities to the inclusion of other animals and the cultivation of crops changed the face of the planet and the way ecosystems work. In the last 10,000 to 15,000 years, our populations began to grow, climates were radically shifting, an ice age was ending, and the world as we, and every other form of life, knew it started to change. There was a perilous challenge ahead—a challenge that we had a hand in creating and one that we met head-on.

We've named ourselves the double *sapiens,* meaning we are doubly wise, or at least that we have the capacity to be so. It turns out that domestication and the building of ever larger communities is a two-way street with a lot of perilous curves, for which there is no perfect map. Are we creative enough to navigate those curves? What if we aren't?

FOOD SECURITY ACCOMPLISHED

Open a kitchen cupboard almost anywhere in the world and it is likely that every single item of food that you see did not exist for 99.9 percent of our history. Not just the packaging and processing, the actual food itself. Almost every plant or animal that we eat, and most of the ones we see around us every day, is the product of human influence and engineering. Dogs, cats, chickens, cows, horses, pigeons, hamsters, guinea pigs, rats, pigs, goats, sheep, llamas, alpacas, water buffalo, ducks, geese, rabbits, turkeys, salmon, tuna, tilapia, apples, oranges, papayas, mangos, plums, tomatoes, carrots, bananas, beans, rice, wheat, hops, potatoes, sweet potatoes, yams, onions, beets, leeks, lettuce, cabbage, peaches, nectarines, chilies, vanilla, almonds, cashews, walnuts, sunflowers, corn, zucchini, pumpkins, cucumbers, cocoa, lemons, and limes are but a small list of the animals and plants that we've created or re-created in this most recent phase of our evolution.

While nearly everything we eat today is a domestic variety of some plant or animal, in most cases the original version of that plant or animal doesn't exist anymore. But who cares? The history of human creative manipulation of plants and animals is usually far from our minds when we sit down to a family meal, stare at the contents of a refrigerator, or grab a to-go container from the neighborhood burger, curry, or taco eatery.

We want our food to do things for us. Well beyond delivering macro- and micronutrients, food has become a core part of our social and emotional lives. We want food to taste good, to be easily digestible, and to satisfy the hankerings for sweet, spicy, salty, crunchy, chewy, warm, cold, and comforting that creep into our bodies and minds. Many of us expect to have a variety of foods year-round and are upset when we walk into a grocery store and can't find the specific fruit, vegetable, cut of meat, or spice that we crave. Food stopped being simply sustenance a long time ago. For many humans it is a lifestyle. We've created food, but it also has a hand in creating us.

Today there is a debate about genetically modified foods, as people freak out when scientists insert the genes of jellyfish and bacteria into tomatoes and strawberries. But leaving aside the shock value of, and valid moral and ethical concerns about, "Frankenfruit," we have to admit that this modern laboratory manipulation, and the use of hormones, pesticides, and a whole range of other artificial contrivances to shape our food, is the direct outcome of human creativity. Our lives today, and the foods we rely on, are the products of many thousands of years of human manipulation and re-creation of the bodies and lives of other animals and plants. But that doesn't mean that the way we are currently making, distributing, consuming, and controlling food is in all of our best interests.

For most of human evolution, getting food was hard. Making it easy to get was fundamentally a process of domestication, of bringing the world around us into the social structures of our lives. The story of domestication is about more than food; it is about the creation of new lives—for us and for other species.

A Crucible

The Levant is an area of land along the eastern Mediterranean that stretches about 750 miles from what is Turkey today in the north to what is now Israel in the south and runs from the coast to 250 to 300 miles inland. In the time frame between about 17,000 and 5,000 years ago, this was a rich landscape of dense oak forests, and the antecedents of pistachio and olive spread throughout them. Seeds were readily available in the spring and early summer, and rich fruits were common from the end of the summer through the late fall. All four seasons were distinct, but not harsh. Game was abundant, with many types of gazelle, wild cattle, boar, and deer spread across the region. Even the mountainous areas had ibex and wild goats. This was a rich environment, a prime location for human communities to thrive. And to change.

Between 18,000 and about 14,000 years ago in this area, we find increasing evidence of communities using stone bowls and grinding utensils, and the remains of seeds, leaves, and fruits show a more effective exploitation of the rich plant resources. The abundance of prey animals enabled human groups to grow slightly bigger while ranging across smaller areas. By the time period between 13,000 and 12,000 years ago, a cluster of remains in the Levant region of the eastern Mediterranean indicates that some groups were sticking to the same places over many generations. These groups were intensively using the local plants and animals, and not just surviving, but flourishing. They even started building. These archeological remains are the series of sites that make up the evidence for a people we call the Natufians.

This cluster of remains is central to our understanding of one of the most significant events in the history of the human species, the shift from a life of seminomadic hunters and gatherers to that of sedentary, village-living domesticators. These Natufian peoples were not agriculturalists; they did not plant and harvest crops as we know it. But they relied on many wild crops, selectively taking some and leaving others, thus beginning to modify the plants they used. They also hunted, and we find the remains of gazelle, wild boar and cattle, turtles, small mammals and birds, and other animals at their habitation sites and in their graves. Most striking, the Natufians built houses. They constructed and maintained small buildings of stone and wood and by 10,000 years ago their villages grew to house as many as 300 to 500 people, surpassing Dunbar's proposed limit of 250 people as the maximum group size for humans.

The burials of the Natufians and many other groups across the planet of this same time period help us understand this transition. People were buried with many material items, including tools and weapons for hunting, bowls and small tools for handling and holding food, tools for collecting and processing wild plants, and the remains of the animals they domesticated. The fact that they buried animals and plants with the bodies of the dead is a visceral sign of how deeply they'd brought these other species into their lives and communities. But it is the bones of the people themselves that contain some of the richest information. These bones tell us directly about their lives and what an impact the initial move toward domestication had on being human.

Many hunter-gatherer communities had it pretty good by about 15,000 to 20,000 years ago. Their numbers were up, but not so much that they were stressed over resources. Having more of just about everything enabled greater opportunities for innovation. And once innovations showed up in one community, the likelihood of their spreading was higher as networks between communities were growing. Trade of highly valued stones and other goods moved across hundreds of miles. Finely crafted tool kits including fishhooks, needles, barbed harpoons, bone-tipped spears, sharp stone knives, stone bowls, and grinding stones found wide distribution. Human communities in particularly rich areas where the sea, forests, rivers, marshes, and grasslands lay in close proximity (as in the Levant at that time) found that with their improved tool kits they were able to extract more resources from smaller areas. For these peoples the need to wander shrank and eventually disappeared.

These increasingly sedentary communities preferred certain seeds and fruits. Hunting deer or gazelle or wild cattle, they would sometimes take only young adult males and leave the pregnant females behind, or leave certain groups of animals alone to rebuild their numbers. When hunting adult animals, they'd sometimes end up with infants, which they took back to their community to raise and eat, or not—sometimes the young animals grew up and hung around long enough to become pets. As humans began to settle for longer times in single areas, their settlements (and the garbage associated with them) began to attract other animals. Human communities like these created a new ecology, one that certain animals (pigs, dogs, birds) found quite attractive. By 5,000 to 10,000 years ago, the plants and animals surrounding humans had changed physically and behaviorally. *Domestication* is the modification of a plant or animal species such that the traits that are most beneficial to human use are accentuated. In the case of wheat or rice, it was making the seeds (the grains) larger and hindering their ability to drop off their stalks, which made them reliant on humans to propagate the next generation of plants. In the case of goats or cows, it was manipulation to develop smaller and tamer breeds that stayed in and around human settlements, learned to follow human instructions, grew fast, and provided meat, milk, bones, and horns for human use. In the case of dogs, the process is not quite so clear. Dogs and humans seemed to domesticate each other, because as it turns out, this is one of the few domestication experiments that did not start out as a human quest for food.

The products of domestication—from dairy cows and fainting goats to hairless dog breeds and turkeys with twelve-pound breasts—reflect human imaginative capacity. The cows, goats, dogs, and certainly the turkeys would not have come to those shapes, behaviors, and patterns if left to their own evolutionary paths. But domestication did not start out as intentional manipulation by humans. The earliest domestication events were unintended outcomes of the creative hunting, gathering, and building of communities that characterized the earlier parts of our history, and they went both ways: As we reshaped others, they also reshaped us. We share a deeper connection with those dairy cows, fainting goats, and hairless dogs than is comfortable to admit.

Reshaping Animals

More than 12,400 years ago, at the site of Uyun al-Hammam in what is today the country of Jordan, a group of humans dug a grave and laid two bodies in it, one on top of the other. One body was that of an adult woman and the other an adult red fox. They added a few tools and some red pigment, then covered the bodies. At around the same time at the Natufian site of Ain Mallaha, in what is today northern Israel, another group stood in a grove of oaks and pistachio trees and laid a young woman to rest in a shallow grave, placing a deceased puppy next to her head. They laid her hand on the puppy before covering them both and sealing the grave—a touching image and concrete evidence of domestication.

The archeologists Greger Larson and Dorian Fuller recently summarized the three main ways in which animal domestication happened. They call these processes the "three pathways" and label them *commensal, prey,* and *directed.*

The commensal pathway is the one that dogs took and the one in which humans and the other species of interest have the most mutualistic relationships, at least at first. There is no intentional action by humans at the start of this pathway; instead it is the other species that begins to hang around the humans. The commensal pathway begins when another species is attracted to the human niche. This starts when certain individuals or groups of a particular species begin hanging around human communities because they are attracted by something that the humans are doing. Leaving trash piles near camps that attract smaller animals, which in turn are food themselves, could blaze this pathway. Even the use of fire at night, creating a safe zone around the periphery of the human campsite, could have been attractive to some species. And when human communities started to settle in one place, all of these aspects of the human niche became amplified and very attractive to certain animals. These animals, the ones truly drawn to the human way of making a living, are called synanthropic.

The human body louse and pigeons became obligate synanthropes, meaning they have to live alongside human populations to survive. Other synanthropic animals fall into more creative relationships with people; they move from being attracted to aspects of the human niche to being habituated to human presence, and if there is a little bit of mutual shaping, domestication can result. The human-connected populations and their wilder relatives do not immediately separate; they may exchange genes for some time. But eventually the synanthropic groups become fully integrated into human communities and swap their close relationships with their wild cousins for a home by the human hearth. Which brings us back to our best friend, the pooch.

As many as 25,000 to 30,000 years ago there were two species of mammals who were doing really well across the Northern Hemisphere:

gray wolves and humans. Both were highly social animals with complex shared lives. Both had a strong sense of loyalty to their groups, communal care of the young, and a keen hunting ability. But we humans had a lot more going for us: big brains, thumbs, tools, fire, language (by this time), and even in some places (like the Levant, Northern and Southern Africa, South Asia, and Central and Eastern Europe) we'd figured out how to limit our wandering and stay more or less in one place. There were numerous times when human communities and wolf packs came into conflict, especially over kills. When humans moved into an area, the wolves would have noticed that a new top predator was in town and that they'd have to take a second seat to us. They'd have started following human hunting groups, seeking to scavenge as best they could, sometimes maybe even challenging the humans, and eating one or two if they caught a few of them alone. But most of the time they avoided the sharp spears and arrows and fire that the humans wielded.

Then things started to change. The longer the packs hung around humans, the more likely it was that a pack, or some of its members, never left the protection of the nightly human fire and the relatively easy food. We would have initially driven the wolves away with weapons and shouts, but over time the wolves remained persistent, just out of reach but always nearby. Changing their hunting patterns, the wolves began to follow the humans as they moved about, or to stick around the camps if the humans settled in for a season or two. Over many generations, the wolves' changes affected the humans, who began to tolerate their presence. These humans noted that there were a few benefits to having the wolves around. They made noises if other predators or large animals approached the camps at night; they also shadowed the humans when they hunted, sometimes driving out smaller prey that the humans could capture and eat as they moved on to find larger game. Finally, there were times when pups or young wolves ended up in human camps, abandoned or injured, and on occasion the humans tended them rather than killing them. And the true relationship began. Humans and wolves started to rely on one another as safety nets, as hunting partners, and as friends.

The young wolves in and around the human communities changed as human creativity was added to the mix. Our ancestors started to notice differences in the personalities of the pups and the eventual adults. These personality variants made a difference in how well the wolves got along with the human community, how adept they were at following human cues, and even how they interacted with human children. Some showed more attachment to humans and more responsiveness to human signals and were less likely to fight with humans over kills—even bonding tightly with certain men, women, or children, following them around and keeping watch over them. These wolves were transferring their wolf-pack allegiance to the humans, and the humans figured out a way to shape it. Before long, humans recognized that working with the pups right away produced the best companions. As our distant kin began to selectively spend time with the best and most human-friendly pups, the behavior and bodies of the wolves changed; they become dogs. By about 15,000 to 20,000 years ago, we find bones that are wolflike but show signs of domestication—smaller, less angular, and a bit more puppylike—in association with human archeological remains; it is likely that this is the first indication that wolves (*Canis lupus*) had changed enough to be called dogs (*Canis familiaris*). They were shaping us, almost as drastically, at the same time.

How do we know this? There are ample fossils of these early dogs in the Levant and Central Asia, and by 10,000 to 15,000 years ago many human communities had animals that matched in size and shape what we call domestic dogs today. The Natufian graves from earlier are not unique; similar graves and remains are found across the continents in Central and Eastern Asia and the Americas. We also know that the genetics of all living dogs ties them back to common wolf ancestors between 20,000 and 30,000 years ago, which means this is roughly when the populations of dogs and wolves began to separate as breeding clusters. Of course, wolves and dogs still can interbreed just fine and have no trouble seeing one another as mating partners. We call them different species, but they may not agree.

The process by which wolves became dogs is illustrated by a very cool experiment with foxes started in northern Russia under the former Soviet Union. It was an innovative project that demonstrates how fast and powerfully the favoring of particular pups by humans can affect the bodies and lives of canids. In 1959 the Soviet scientist Dmitry Belyaev started selecting the most friendly pups at a fox farm and separating them from the rest, letting them reproduce and live. His work was carried on by the Russian researcher Lyudmila Trut. In just forty generations (just over fifty years) they were able to get foxes that behaved, and looked, like domestic dogs. They whined and licked and cuddled, behaving in affectionate ways with the humans and one another. They also got floppy ears, curly tails, and variation in coat color. It turns out that intensive selection for certain behavioral traits has an impact on the way hormonal and developmental systems work and results in the "domestic" morphology of floppy ears and curled tails.

But it was not all about us shaping dogs. They also tapped into our community niche and used some of our own physiology to shape us. A recent spate of research in this area demonstrates that dogs have tapped into our own hormonal and psychoneuroendocrine pathways and co-opted that great capacity we have for communally caring for our young and one another. Remember the human capacity for compassion? As we were shaping the dogs, they also shaped us: They got themselves inserted into our communities and began to elicit the same kinds of compassionate, and physiological, responses that human community members elicited from one another. Work by multiple research teams demonstrates that dogs tap into the human oxytocin response system (oxytocin is a hormone in our blood and neurotransmitter in our brains that flows in moments of bonding). Some have even suggested that it was this relationship that made our direct ancestors better hunters, and maybe gave us the extra social and ecological support we needed to succeed across all the habitats that we encountered. Other groups of humans who did not contribute extensively to the modern human lineage (such as the Neanderthals) never befriended dogs—and look what happened to them! The mutually developed relationship between humans and dogs is surely one of the reasons for our success as a species.

There are a number of other animals that became domesticated via the commensal pathway: cats, of course, rats and mice, guinea pigs, chickens (descended from the red jungle fowl that started to hang around human communities in Asia more than 4,000 years ago), and even carp. But most domestication relationships did not start out as mutually beneficial; rather they started out because humans got more creative with their hunting patterns.

The prey pathway begins with human action. As populations began to settle down, even start rudimentary agriculture, they continued to hunt large and small game in the areas around their villages. However, many communities soon noticed that if they took all of any specific type of game, it became scarcer, maybe even disappeared. This meant that hunting parties had to go farther and farther away from the villages and that the return for investment in hunting decreased. Some villages, the less creative ones, kept this up and soon found themselves under serious nutritional stress. Others used our human capacities for observation, innovation, and coordination to come up with alternatives.

Most of the best prey, the wild ancestors of cattle, sheep, goats, reindeer, water buffalo, and pigs, would not have been attracted to human waste dumps and hunting remains like the wolves/dogs and other commensal pathway species (pigs might have been, but humans hunted them for food, so the attraction did not last long). These game animals would have been very wary of humans, who by 15,000 to 20,000 years ago were the top predator around. Javelins, bows and arrows, spears, and traps of all sorts made humans formidable predators in nearly every environment in which they lived. Although it took them a long time, and they did not always correct their course, many human communities noticed that indiscriminate hunting was not in their long-term benefit. So they began to manage the wild prey populations. Many predators stalk young, old, or injured animals, but they do this because those targets are easier to catch and kill, not because they have a management plan in mind. Humans, however, identified patterns between what they hunted and how the prey reacted and how scarce they were in following years. By around 10,000 to 12,000 years ago we can see evidence in the bones of consumed animals of the preferential taking of young males and the avoiding of females, especially pregnant females.

If prey were taken selectively, with an eye toward making sure that reproduction was not impacted and that the social structure of herds or groups was not totally disrupted, prey populations stayed stable or even grew.

When a community stopped hunting female wild cattle, those herds would, over time, tolerate the closer presence of humans. By watching the wild cattle, as our deep ancestors watched predators and learned about their lives, these more recent ancestors could have begun to understand the life cycle of the wild cattle and made a few risky, but creative, ventures. They started bringing a few, as youngsters, into the villages, building corrals and trying to keep them alive, and they succeeded. They'd been watching the cattle across generations—they knew about their life cycles, shared that information with one another, and collaboratively came up with ideas about raising their own cattle— and thus prey domestication was born. Once cattle, sheep, pigs, llamas, and goats were living with humans, it was a simple task to do, like with dogs, a bit of behavioral and morphological shaping via direct manipulation (for wool, milk production, or rapid growth for meat). The selection of specific individuals to breed was a first step toward modern domestic animals. And hamburgers.

The third pattern of animal domestication was the direct pathway. Between 6,000 and 10,000 years ago a large number of human communities were settled into villages and towns and had some dogs running about the cultivated areas around their dwellings. Their needs were changing: the need to carry large amounts of material items between villages, the need for extra power to turn the land for planting, the need to serve the growing demand for trading relationships, the need to resolve conflicts and a growing potential for violence . . . So humans, using what they had learned in the early domestication process, began targeting wild animals and repurposing them, intentionally shaping the animals to provide specific services. Animals such as donkeys and camels were captured, selectively bred, and trained as pack animals; the same with horses. Even honeybees were brought in and put to work making honey for the humans. Species that had been brought into human communities earlier were converted to new functions; water buffalo, sheep, alpacas, and many others were trained and shaped for labor and for growing extra wool and other products. Humans also took to capturing and domesticating smaller prey animals for more intensive food sources (such as rabbits, ducks, geese, many other birds, and fish) and as pets (hamsters, gerbils, and chinchillas).

ANIMAL DOMESTICATION

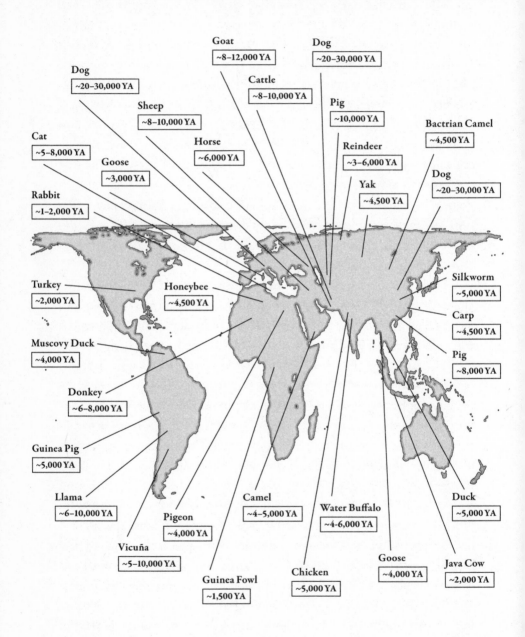

Dog
~20–30,000 YA

Goat
~8–12,000 YA

Dog
~20–30,000 YA

Cattle
~8–10,000 YA

Pig
~10,000 YA

Sheep
~8–10,000 YA

Bactrian Camel
~4,500 YA

Cat
~5–8,000 YA

Horse
~6,000 YA

Reindeer
~3–6,000 YA

Dog
~20–30,000 YA

Goose
~3,000 YA

Yak
~4,500 YA

Rabbit
~1–2,000 YA

Turkey
~2,000 YA

Honeybee
~4,500 YA

Silkworm
~5,000 YA

Carp
~4,500 YA

Muscovy Duck
~4,000 YA

Pig
~8,000 YA

Donkey
~6–8,000 YA

Guinea Pig
~5,000 YA

Llama
~6–10,000 YA

Camel
~4–5,000 YA

Water Buffalo
~4-6,000 YA

Duck
~5,000 YA

Pigeon
~4,000 YA

Vicuña
~5–10,000 YA

Goose
~4,000 YA

Java Cow
~2,000 YA

Guinea Fowl
~1,500 YA

Chicken
~5,000 YA

The domesticates we now have, whether they started out in the commensal or the prey pathway, are also the products of the directed pathway. Once we humans discovered that we could manipulate, shape, and select patterns, varieties, and behaviors, our creativity (and some would say our cruelty) took off. Think about Holstein cows, all the dog breeds, fancy show chickens, and the entire range of household pets found around the world: The domestication of animals is a global biological and ecological fact created and maintained by human action. And all in the last blink of an eye in our evolutionary history.

When Is a Forest a Garden?

To the casual observer, the rain forests of Southeast Asia about 10,000 to 12,000 years ago would have looked pretty much like the rain forests before and afterward—lots of palms and thorn-covered plants in the lower canopy, and dense trees of all shapes and sizes reaching to the sky. But to the eyes of researchers looking into the former forests via pollen analysis, digging into the soils, and reconstructing past landscapes, a pattern emerges: The plant species that make up the forests are shifting in frequency and density. Certain palms and fruiting trees and vines are becoming more common, others are moving from one type of growth pattern to another, and others are simply disappearing. One expects these types of change in forest structure as climates change and sea levels rise and drop—but these changes in Southeast Asian forests are not clearly linked to the climate. Something else started to shape the way the forests look and work. Guess who.

The genus *Homo* had been living in and around the forests of Southeast Asia for hundreds of thousands of years without changing the ecology much, but by at least 10,000 to 15,000 years ago, humans started targeting certain types of trees, favoring them and their fruits, nuts, and leaves or using their bark or their long, dense, threadlike stems (think of rattan). Moving small climbing vines or pulling out competing saplings that hindered their access to the trees opened up new space for growth and reproduction for humans' favorites. People might even have defended certain trees against other animals and kept birds out during the fruiting season.

More than 12,000 years ago, communities of humans in what is today central and northern Mexico were hunting and gathering alongside rich lakes and lush valleys. The volcanic soils provided fertile support for plant growth, and the humans were taking increasing advantage of some of those plants. The ground-growing squashes that go by the scientific name *Cucurbita pepo* were heavily exploited. Their hearty meat and ease of carrying, storing, cooking, and eating made them a perfect target for domestication—and that is why we have their descendants today: the pumpkins and summer and winter squashes. By 10,000 years ago, the human communities that were devouring them recognized the correlation between the large seeds and the plant growth fairly quickly, and they selected for replanting those squash that were larger, grew faster, and had larger seeds. Over time the majority of the squashes reflected those traits that were preferred by the humans—squashes were domesticated as a result of human creative, and selective, manipulation.

At about this same time, the most famous plant of the Americas (and for much of the world today) was also entering the reshaping relationship with humans—maize, or corn. Possibly as early as 10,000 years ago and certainly by 6,000 years ago, small, delicious cobs of corn were becoming staples of the diets of human communities. There is ample evidence that the maize of today is derived from one lineage of a kind of tall and broadleaved grass called teosinte. When the grass teosinte reproduces, it sends up stalks that have five to twelve kernels (seeds) on them, covered in a hard casing. But with some work, one can break open the ripe casing, get out the kernels, and mash or cook them, and they are a good food source—but you need a lot of teosinte to make a meal. Well before 10,000 years ago, human communities were exploiting the fields of teosinte in what is today Mexico, but they figured they could do better. As with the squash, selective gathering of the pods of teosinte and even more selective dispersal of the seeds slowly reshaped the grass's seed pods such that the kernels began to adhere to the small central core as opposed to the outer hard covering. But these human communities did not stop there; they began to focus their selection on those outer coverings, favoring the softer and easier-to-open ones, and to replant only those teosinte pods that had more kernels and not those that had fewer. Over the course of 4,000 years or so, they created maize: The first true and completely recognizable dried corn cob discovered in archeological remains dates to about 6,000 years ago (the genetics tells us it split from teosinte about 10,000 years ago).

But the new plants, the creations of human innovation and a lot of collaborations (planting and harvesting are a community-wide undertaking), did not stay put. Over the span of about 2,000 years (6,000 to 4,000 years ago), maize agriculture spread up through northern Mexico and across what is today the southwestern and southeastern United States. Humans were not content with simply creating new life and new ways of living; they also shared it across communities and across space and time.

Today one plant, *Oryza sativa,* is the staple food for nearly 50 percent of the population of earth—we know it as rice. Domesticated a number of times over the last 9,000 years across Asia, this small grain played a major role in the lives of humans and other animals (one related species, *Oryza glaberrima,* was also domesticated in Africa). Over the last 3,000 to 4,000 years, different societies have modified it into many forms, usually variants of the short-grained (now called *Oryza sativa japonica*—originated in China) or long-grained version (called *Oryza sativa indica*—originated in India). The closest wild counterpart to rice is another species in the genus *Oryza* called *Oryza rufipogon. Oryza rufipogon,* a sinewy grass that thrives in swampy areas, has hard red seeds and is edible but tough, weedy, and hard to control. So how, and why, did humans focus their ingenuity on this plant?

We know that 8,000 to 12,000 years ago human communities in what is today China were becoming more settled and developing ways to store food. Storage of the seeds of early rice, *Oryza rufipogon* grains, and acorns are found in the Pearl and Yangtze River areas. The biggest hassle with the early rice-like *Oryza rufipogon* (aside from the limited productivity of the grains) is that as the grains ripen, they fall off the grass stalk and land in the swampy water or on muddy soils and are eaten by birds and other animals or germinate, starting the life cycle again. If those grains held on to their stalk, humans could take the top of the stalk off and carry it with them to their camp or village and remove the grains by hitting the stalk against a hard surface (a process called "threshing" today). Some communities of humans began to see the variation in the *Oryza rufipogon* stalks they gathered. Some had grains that held tightly; others did not.

Groups of people living around the Pearl and Yangtze Rivers could selectively collect stalks, removing all those whose grains fell off easily ("easy shattering") and letting only the tougher ones dominate. There is genetic evidence that humans began increasing the presence of the tougher, more shatter-resistant stalks by weeding out the weaker ones. A specific genetic mutation in *Oryza* toughens the connecting tissue between the grain and the stalk and makes it very difficult for the grains to drop off; it is called "shatterproof," or *sh4* officially. It shows up naturally now and again but disappears quickly in most populations of *Oryza,* as those plants with it have trouble reproducing (dropping their grains). But by about 5,000 to 7,000 years ago, the *sh4* mutation shows up in most domesticated strains of rice—humans noticed the effects of the mutation and by favoring those plants they enabled the survival and spread of this genetic variant in rice plants. This is a great example of early genetic engineering by humans, something we do a lot of today. Pretty creative human enterprise spread a genetic variation in rice plants, changing rice forever. But this created a problem: If no grains dropped off, how did harvesting occur? Back to (collaborative) work—lots of it.

Rice prefers wet and swampy environments, and while there are many varieties of modern rice that can grow on dry land, most rice, including all the early forms, needs wet or even flooded areas to thrive. Each stalk of rice does not have many grains, so many, many stalks are required to feed humans. If these stalks are not able to reproduce by themselves, it means that humans must not only gather and thresh the rice (to get the grains) but also replant the rice each cycle (annually or even twice a year) so that new stalks will emerge and produce new grains. For a human community of even just a few hundred, we are talking thousands and thousands of rice stalks at a minimum, needing to be collected, threshed, sorted (grains for eating and those for replanting), processed (for food and for planting), and then eaten or planted. And the cycle would begin again.

This complicated seasonal process parallels the story of wheat and other cereals in the Levant and Central Eurasia. Across the planet

PLANT DOMESTICATION

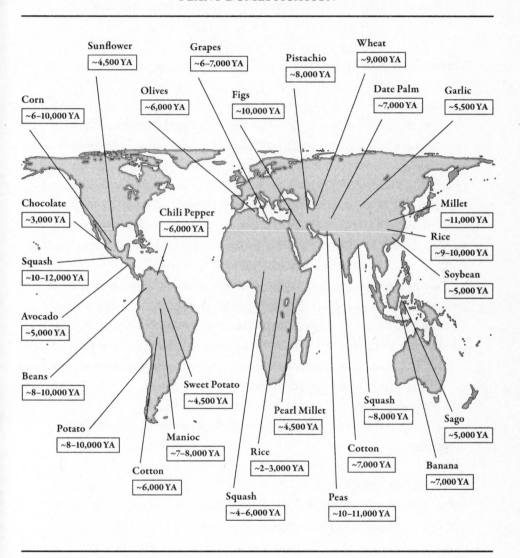

Sunflower ~4,500 YA

Grapes ~6–7,000 YA

Pistachio ~8,000 YA

Wheat ~9,000 YA

Olives ~6,000 YA

Figs ~10,000 YA

Date Palm ~7,000 YA

Garlic ~5,500 YA

Corn ~6–10,000 YA

Chocolate ~3,000 YA

Chili Pepper ~6,000 YA

Millet ~11,000 YA

Rice ~9–10,000 YA

Squash ~10–12,000 YA

Soybean ~5,000 YA

Avocado ~5,000 YA

Beans ~8–10,000 YA

Sweet Potato ~4,500 YA

Squash ~8,000 YA

Sago ~5,000 YA

Potato ~8–10,000 YA

Manioc ~7–8,000 YA

Pearl Millet ~4,500 YA

Rice ~2–3,000 YA

Cotton ~7,000 YA

Banana ~7,000 YA

Cotton ~6,000 YA

Squash ~4–6,000 YA

Peas ~10–11,000 YA

human communities engaged in similar processes with other plants: potatoes in the Andes, millet and rice in Africa, the banana in Southeast
Asia and the South Pacific, sunflowers in North America, and many,
many more.

The shape, genetics, and life cycles of the plants changed, and the effects cascaded into the ecosystem. Once again, as we shaped the lives and bodies of other species, our own were being reshaped as well.

Domesticating Ourselves

Between about 7,000 and 12,000 years ago, many human communities underwent the transition from sedentary hunter-gatherers who affect the plants and animals around them to full-blown farmers and herders, relying heavily on their crops and domestic animals. Because this was so ubiquitous and happened with so many human populations, we assume that this transition was both attractive and beneficial to the communities involved. But when we look at the archeological records of these early farming communities, we are presented with a vexing dilemma: The move to agriculture initially made human health worse.

So why did these first farmers stick with it? Right before the transition, the sedentary hunter-gatherer groups were a very healthy lot and appeared to be doing really well, among the best in the history of our species. But with the agricultural transition, their health deteriorated, social and gender inequalities show up in the archeological record, and, for the first time in our species' history, evidence of serious coordinated and large-scale violence between communities (war) erupted.

Three key reasons explain why humans stuck with agriculture, tough as it was:

- stability of food sources,
- increased populations, and
- being locked in to the land.

The first is easy to understand. Once you start growing your own food, a lot of new options become available. You can plan ahead. You know that, for example, you can plant a specific amount of wheat or rice and it will produce enough food to last a certain amount of time. If you have goats or sheep or chickens to supplement the plants, you have a double set of options for food, plus you might still gather and hunt a bit in your area.

The second and third are parts of what we might call a vicious cycle. Initially, agriculture and domestication mean that human kids get a consistent diet and can grow a little faster and moms can reliably get the nutrition they need for nursing during that critical part of early infant life. The constant availability of protein and carbohydrates and the ability to cook and mash them also mean that infants can switch to nonmilk foods much earlier than they can as part of mobile hunter-gatherer groups, so moms wean earlier. This means the time between births goes down and the overall birthrate goes up. As agriculture intensifies, women have more babies more often and the population goes up, fast.

The vicious cycle is completed with the third fact: Once you've committed to agriculture, it is almost impossible to pick up and leave. You've invested all of your time and energy in planting the crops, and they are not mobile. You've built a village and places to process and store your crops, and your community is getting larger, with many more young kids around. You can't just pack it up and move, or if you do, you lose everything and put your group at mortal risk—think of the difficulties encountered by the Pilgrims after they left their native England (and how it took assistance from local agriculturalists in North America for them to survive). Besides, if agriculture has spread in the region where you are, most of the other prime locations are likely already occupied by other communities. Where do you go if you need to move? And how do you transport all your stuff? Being sedentary, communities accumulate much more than when they were mobile. Once committed to sedentism and agriculture, human communities are in it for the long run, for better and worse. And the "worse" was pretty bad. The bones tell quite a story.

The advent of agriculture corresponds with a multiplication of cavities in human teeth. Cavities are a disease that affects the hard parts of teeth by demineralizing and wearing them away via bacterial fermentation. Ever wonder how we got along without toothpaste? The bacterial fermentation is caused primarily by carbohydrates, which are much higher in domesticated plants than in the wild versions. In studies of oral health, researchers have noted that agriculturalists have as many as four times more cavities than hunter-gatherers, especially when those agriculturalists boil their plant foods, creating mushy gruels that can hide out in the spaces between teeth and rapidly ferment (thus the advent of flossing and toothbrushing). Tooth loss during the lifetime is also higher in agricultural populations than in hunter-gatherers, suggesting that increased carbohydrates and reduced dietary diversity can also lead to periodontal disease, weakening the roots of teeth and the gums surrounding them.

The teeth also tell us about the emergence of significant gender differences that arose with agriculture. Hunter-gatherers don't show gender differences in tooth disease, but studies of agriculturalists from North America, South Asia, and Africa reveal that females had higher frequencies of cavities than males, and researchers suggest that this could be due to women having higher-carbohydrate and lower-protein diets than men in these societies. The remains of these early agriculturalists are clear physical evidence for structural gender differences in human communities.

The shift to agriculture also often involved a reduction in overall animal protein consumption and a reduction in the diversity of plant types consumed. That meant that while there may have been more overall food of a few types for the early farmers (like lots of rice grains), the range of the diet was reduced so macro- and micronutrient requirements weren't always satisfied. People seemed to get shorter. Human bodies often respond to nutrient deficiencies by slowing growth and trimming bones' growth trajectories. We know that a corn diet limits the niacin available to the body, a focus on wheat causes iron deficiencies, and an overreliance on rice can cause protein and vitamin A deficiencies. A number of studies of the bones of early farmer populations demonstrate the frequent appearance of bone disorders, like osteoarthritis, and overall declines in stature with the transition to agriculture.

The move to domestication also correlates with an increase in infectious diseases. Rarely do we have any archeological evidence of large-scale infection across nearly all of human history—until we get to communities practicing domestication (about 7,000 to 10,000 years ago). There are a few obvious reasons for this. Being sedentary means not being able to move away from diseases when they hit. Having larger groups of people living closer together (and sharing latrine spaces) creates a perfect storm for viruses and bacterial infection to develop and pass, quickly, through communities. Diseases like tuberculosis (likely evolved from the interface of human and cow mycobacterium) and treponematosis (yaws and multiple types of syphilis) appear in human communities with the advent of animal domestication.

Domestication must have had a massive impact on the human gut. The gut microbiome is the more than 100 trillion bacteria and other microbial critters that live in the digestive systems of animals. In all mammals, the microbiome plays the leading role in digesting food, in staving off illness, and even in balancing our moods (yes, throwing off the balance of critters in your gut can make you depressed). But the makeup of the microbiome is affected mostly by what one eats. While humans share general patterns as a species, each different group of people around the world has a slightly different microbiome. This is why when you go from one place on the planet to another you often get an upset stomach. Your digestive system is undergoing a migration shock and getting introduced to a new set of microbiota.

For millions of years our lineage relied wholly on uncooked plant and animal matter; then for half a million years or so we added cooked plants and animals. Then domestication changed the biology of our guts and almost everything else, rapidly. But the challenges did not wipe out most groups, and while inconvenient, they did not destroy humans' determination and creativity.

Over time the upside of agriculture began to pay off, communities grew, systems of domestication improved, nutritional balances were found, and the domesticators developed new patterns that made their system all the more attractive. Some groups began to creatively manipulate the ways in which food was stored; salting meats made them last longer and letting grains start to ferment produced all sorts of new options for nutrition and enjoyment (beer!). Over time, even the shifts in the gut microbiome began to reap benefits; the challenges to our guts resulted in new relationships with bacteria, enabling us to get even more experimental with fermented and modified foods (yogurt, cheese, kimchi). And it was the ability to use cow's milk in parts of Africa and Eurasia that enabled us to do to ourselves what we did to the rice plant: Humans bioengineered themselves to be able to drink milk.

All mammals produce the enzyme lactase early in life, as it is the critical piece the body needs to break down the key nutrients in milk. Without lactase, mammalian bodies cannot digest milk (the sugar in it is called "lactose"), get little benefit from it, and instead get intestinal distress. In most mammals the genes that regulate and produce lactase turn off as the mammal matures into an adult. In an evolutionary sense, this is understandable; when do adult mammals ever get to drink milk? The body shifts its resources elsewhere. However, the system is not particularly tight, and genetic mutations that keep lactase production turned on show up now and again in all populations. Usually they stay at a low level or disappear, and under almost all circumstances they offer no benefit to the body. However, if there is milk around and adults can consume it, then a new environment is established and the frequency of the mutation that leaves lactase production turned on becomes beneficial. Just as the intentional selection and protection of rice stalks that were more shatterproof increased the $sh4$ gene mutation in rice, the keeping of cows, goats, and sheep provided a new context in which those humans who could get benefits from drinking milk into adulthood tended to have an edge (be healthier and have slightly more children). The mutation for keeping lactase going into adulthood became more common. Here again the microbiome becomes a central player. Having the sugars and fats from milk in the gut well into adulthood enables a whole new range of bacteria and microbes to flourish, increasing the body's ability to exploit the energy and nutrition from milk and its by-products. So anyone able to get nourishment from milk as an adult today has some ancestry from one of the communities spread across Africa and Eurasia that milked their animals.

But humans able to digest lactose are still a minority today. In fact, many populations who rely heavily on milk products cannot digest raw milk either. Communities in South Asia experimented with fermentation of milk and found that treating the milk by putting it in combination with bacteria that produce lactase-like enzymes creates a new food that is digestible and very beneficial—in this case, yogurt.

As these modifications to food expanded, adding more types of bacteria and chemical landscapes to our guts, so did the action of our microbiome.

The bacteria and other microbes in our gut are central in the absorption and excretion of minerals like zinc, iodine, selenium, and cobalt. They produce a range of vitamins (like biotin) that are central to the functioning of our own genes' products, including enzymes and other proteins, which regulate our bodies' development and metabolism. These patterns are known as epigenetic processes and represent a deepening understanding that the most recent biological science is revealing. But the point for now is that what a mother eats and what an infant eats both go into shaping the child's microbiome and influence the functioning of the child's physiology, and that can be passed along across the generations.

Globally populations were using animals primarily for meat and then taking further steps to utilize their wool, feathers, eggs, and other parts. The two-way interface between animals and humans got more and more complex, and the benefits grew. With domestication, which was triggered by the securing of the human food supply, the modern chapter in the human story had begun. For better and for worse.

PART THREE

WAR AND SEX

How Humans Shaped a World

CREATING WAR (AND PEACE)

The year 2016 was rife with war, violence, and atrocities committed by humans. Violent conflicts raged in Afghanistan, Syria, Yemen, Ukraine, Israel, Libya, and the Democratic Republic of the Congo. As of the end of that year, the members of the terrorist group ISIS had beheaded, murdered, and raped thousands; there were more than three hundred mass shootings in the United States; and daily acts of violence and protests occurred in rich and poor countries alike. One cannot be faulted for taking a pretty bleak view of humanity.

Unless you actually take a look at the data. Then another picture emerges.

There are more than 7 billion humans on the planet, but only an infinitesimally small percentage of them are engaged in any of these acts of violence, terror, and warfare. Even if we listed the total amount of humans living in anything even approaching a war zone, it comes out to around 4 percent of humanity. Only about .005 percent of the population of the United States dies via homicide annually. This is not to belittle war and homicide; they are a terrible reality of being human. They are simply not as ubiquitous as we think.

The philosopher Thomas Hobbes wrote that the natural state of humanity is "war of every man against every man" and that life is "solitary, poor, nasty, brutish, and short." This assertion is popular with theorists who argue that humans evolved to be killers, or at least aggressors, and used the threat and perpetration of violence as a major advantage in evolutionary competition. The anthropologist Richard Wrangham and author Dale Peterson argue that competition between males is a core feature of human evolution. They tell us that this led males, early on, to hate and kill perceived competitors, making enemies of them, and that this is why the marks of an evolved tendency toward aggression can be found in our bodies and minds today (for example, in the way our brains and the release of hormones respond to threats, and in the fact that males have larger and more dense muscles than females—presumably for combat).

More recently, the evolutionary psychologist Steven Pinker argued in his book *The Better Angels of Our Nature* that despite the horrific nature of modern human violence, we were significantly more violent in the past due to our natural inner beasts and we became less violent as civilization advanced. He suggests that if we look at the evidence from the archeological record, the percentage of individuals killed by other humans in the past is higher than it is today. He writes, "When we look at humans' bodies and brains, we find direct signs of design for aggression. The larger size, strength, and upper-body mass of men is a zoological giveaway of an evolutionary history of violent male-male competition." Countering this tendency, he argues, modern civilization, with our laws and moral codes, is curbing our inner beasts and bringing the "better angels of our nature" to the fore. Pinker, along with Hobbes, is joined in these assertions by many political scientists, such as Azar Gat.

Often cited to support this view is the fact that while many other species aggressively hunt, capture, and eat prey, they rarely engage in intentional, lethal, and coordinated violence with members of their own species, as we do. But a few animals do engage in killing of their own. Social mammals—like primates, wolves, and big cats—can engage in lethal violence with members of their own species. A male lion might lethally injure another male in a fight over access to a group of females. Two rams might butt heads until one of them staggers away to die. Or a male baboon might repeatedly attack a female from his own group, fatally wounding her and her infant. But in these cases, the killing is not a premeditated goal. Most species don't engage in extreme violence regularly and methodically, and even when they do, it's executed without the creativity and coordination we humans bring to the task.

Humans *are* the only species with premeditated homicide and full-out war. A whopping 60 million people, more than 2.5 percent of the entire human population between 1939 and 1945, died as a result of World War II. But does the fact that we modern humans have perpetrated such concerted killing, and of course many other horrific forms of atrocities, at such large scale, actually result from being "wild at heart"— evolutionarily prone to violence, homicide, and war?

Other scholars have argued that violence and warfare are not core to our deep nature. Biologist Edward O. Wilson, prominent among them, contends that the remarkable human ability to form tight cooperative groups, involving an innate sense of morality and group loyalty, gave rise to tribes, which in turn gave rise to greater conflicts and full-blown war. Regarding the comparisons to the violent tendencies of other primates, the primatologist Frans de Waal has championed the view that empathy and altruism have deep roots in our apelike past and that rather than being naturally prone to war, humans are naturally inclined toward compassion and morality. And the anthropologists Douglas Fry and Brian Ferguson have asserted that the fossil and archeological record suggests that rather than becoming less violent as we became more civilized, it was when we began to settle in villages and towns, investing heavily in livestock and territories, and developing large-scale inequality in wealth, status, and power, that we developed (and perfected) coordinated and large-scale violence, culminating in strategic warfare. They also suggest that while homicide occurred in the deep past, and in some groups it became common, intentional and premeditated killing was not the norm across the history of our species.

The proponents of these opposing arguments have marshaled evidence they deem sufficient to support their claims. And though for much of the evolutionary record hard evidence is scarce, there is a combined body of data, from the study of human behavior and biology, from the study of other primates, and in the fossil and archeological record, that makes these core perspectives testable.

Just over 800,000 years ago, a group of *Homo antecessor*—one of the hominins that was not quite yet human—carefully cut the flesh off the bones of six children and teenagers of their own kind. We do not know for sure why, but various scenarios are proposed.

The remains of the children were found by a team of Spanish researchers at the Gran Dolina cave site in the Sierra de Atapuerca, near Burgos in northern Spain. The Gran Dolina cave is one of six important sites discovered in the area, known as the Atapuerca cave system, and Gran Dolina was the longest occupied, from approximately 800,000 to 300,000 years ago. At the time that *Homo antecessor* lived there, the area featured three rivers running through extensive valleys, with a mix of open grasslands and woodlands. Warm springs and summers turned to cold winters. Abundant animals, large and small, populated the area, including elephants and bears, many varieties of deer, bison, hyenas, foxes, small wolflike canids, monkeys, and many species of birds, snakes, and lizards. The cave where the children's remains were found also contained at least 845 worked pieces of stone and bones from fifteen different types of mammals, as well as other, unmarked, *Homo antecessor* bones. The excavation revealed that the inhabitants made stone tools both inside the cave and just outside it and used them to cut the meat from the bones and to crush the bones to get at the marrow.

The researchers on the team that studied the children's bones, led by the archeologist Eudald Carbonell, have no doubt that they are evidence of cannibalism. They display cut marks precisely in keeping with those left on the bones of bison, elephants, and other animals found alongside them in the cave garbage pits. As all were butchered in the same way, and all the bones were discarded as refuse, the wider research community has generally accepted that all must have been food. But the bones leave us with a quandary: Was this cannibalism an act of desperation due to imminent starvation? Might the children have died, and the rest of the group ate their flesh to hold off that same fate? Or, as some have suggested, was the butchering a ritual act, perhaps performed after the death of one of their own? Or was there a more devious explanation?

Another possibility, suggested by Carbonell and his colleagues, is that the cannibalism was committed as part of a conflict with another group. They posit that one group of *Homo antecessor* raided another, likely in a dispute over hunting territory, and that the cannibalism would have been a way of killing two birds with one stone. Raiding the other group was meant to ward them away from prime hunting grounds, while the children's flesh was a source of highly prized protein. Another anthropologist, Keith Otterbein, who has worked in the anthropology of warfare, proposed that the remains are the earliest evidence of that special kind of cooperative and creative mix of aggression that we call war and that the cannibalism may have been a form of psychological intimidation. Were these early members of the genus *Homo* clever—or devious—enough to perform such an act in order to instill terror in their opponents? We may never know.

The Gran Dolina case is a good example of how difficult it is to piece together the earliest history of human violence; to determine how common it was, the forms it took, and the motivations behind it. With the Gran Dolina find, all we really know is that the flesh of six young *Homo antecessor* was cut from their bones in the same manner as meat was cut from the bones of other animals at the site. But were these young from the same group that butchered and apparently ate them? Was such cannibalism common? Was it a ritual act or one of desperation?

A popular notion about the evolution of human violence, homicide, and war is that as our ancestors became better hunters they fostered an inner demon, a lust for violence—and that they took the next step and turned their increasing success as predators into the particular skill of hunting one another. In the late 1950s, the paleoanthropologist Raymond Dart proposed the modern version of this "man the hunter, man the killer" argument. He proposed that the australopithecines, the hominins before and alongside our own genus, *Homo,* were strong hunters, and the fact that many of their own fossils bear marks that can plausibly be interpreted as the result of trauma suggested that they were killers as well. Dart asserted that the marks were due to the damage from bitter aggression between our ancestors. He claimed the evidence demonstrated a natural lust for violence activated by hunting other animals—one that was quickly turned into the even more dangerous enterprise of hunting one another.

"Man the hunter leading to man the killer" is just one of many stories about the origins of the relationship between humans and violence. Other common ones suggest that men are naturally violent and coercive as part of human evolutionary heritage because it helped men attract women, defend them against other men, and defeat opponents in battles for dominance. Another notion proposes that warfare is an ancient practice, that human history is a story of conflicts between individuals and groups, with homicide and violent coordinated fighting being the norm. The advocates of these ideas argue that it is only recently, through modern civilization, that we've begun to control our violent and bestial urges.

Alternately, perhaps deep cooperation and altruism emerged from violence and war—they coevolved. Maybe conflicts between groups led to stronger within-group cooperation, enabling certain groups (the best cooperators) to get creative and successful in their fights with other groups. The proponents of this theory tell us that liking, trusting, and being willing to die for the members of your own group combined with hatred, fear, and distrust of members of other groups is pretty much how we arrived at modern humanity.

Despite the enticing ideas presented in these stories, they are all wrong, or at least severely incomplete. Though definitive conclusions about what occurred those 800,000 years ago in the Gran Dolina cave, and at a number of other sites that offer more telling clues, are elusive, a clear story of the overall trajectory of human violence does emerge, and it is different than many think.

A View from the Primates

Anyone observing a group of monkeys has inevitably seen the following: clusters of females, young and old, with their offspring nursing, playing, sleeping, and feeding on fruits and leaves. The females groom one another by running their hands through one another's fur, sometimes chattering their teeth or smacking their lips and making contented grunts. A cluster of young monkeys will roll around, grabbing each other and making smiling faces while keeping their teeth covered. They play a lot. Scattered around the area the adult males are sitting alone, or in groups of two to

three, eating, resting, and occasionally approaching females for grooming and sometimes joining the group of youngsters for some rough-and-
tumble play. If it is a particular time of year, the adults will engage in a
quick bout of sex now and then, sometimes leading to a fight and sometimes not. Eventually, if one watches for enough hours, she will hear a
scream and see a fight. A male or a cluster of females will chase a single
monkey, maybe even grabbing him or her and biting or tugging some fur
out of its back. Then everything gets calm again and the scene is as we
first encountered it.

We have to keep in mind that humans are primates too. If we can
show that there is a tendency toward violence, even war, in other
primates, then we might be able to safely assume that this pattern in
humans comes from a very deep primate evolutionary root. It might be
in our nature—whatever that means.

This way of thinking (called *phylogenetic inference*) assumes that more
closely related organisms share more ancestral traits. For example, all primates have forward-facing eyes with good depth perception and grasping
hands with thumbs, as do humans. Humans have these traits not because
we are humans, but because we are primates and the traits are part of the
evolutionary baseline of being a primate (actually part of the definition
of being a primate). As we narrow the groups by looking only at those
that are more and more closely related (say, monkeys, apes, and humans,
or even just apes and humans), we get more specific shared traits. Apes
and humans have rotating shoulders (we can swing our arms in a circle),
but other primates do not. This is a shared trait that arose just on the
lineage of apes and humans after the split with the lineages of the monkeys (about 22 million years ago).

But these examples are about physical traits, and the details that interest us are about behavior. Finding behaviorally shared ancestral traits is
a bit more difficult, but not impossible. Monkeys, apes, and humans tend
to live in groups that have multiple males and females (and young) and
complex social relationships—primate lives are a lot like soap operas.
Making and breaking friendships, being attracted to others and convincing them to have sex, competing with others in the group for social status, raising young and seeing them leave home (or stay), are all shared

aspects of being a primate. We all do these things in different ways (humans with much more complexity and enhanced creativity), but the basic patterns are all due to our being primates, in general, and not specifically human or ape or monkey.

So, if we could demonstrate that monkeys and apes, like humans, use targeted and coordinated violence toward others, especially between groups, then we could make a strong argument that warfare, or at least its underlying drive toward violence, is a very old trait indeed.

There are situations and times when serious fighting does occur in primates. But it is rare and usually doesn't do much damage. Primatologists Bob Sussman and Paul Garber asked the basic question: How much do primates use aggression, fight, and commit violence against one another? They looked across scores of published studies and found that most primates spend the vast majority of their time resting, feeding, or in positive social interactions. The most socially active of primates (capuchin, macaque, and baboon monkeys; and chimpanzees) can spend up to 20 percent of their time in (nonviolent) social interactions, and humans are even more socially active than that. Severe aggression is rare in primates. This is not to say that fighting does not occur and that in some species it occurs more than in others; it is just to note that physical violence usually makes up far less than 1 percent of all activity and even more rarely involves lethal violence.

Nonetheless, competition and low-intensity aggression are a part of daily life, much as they are around the home and office. Spend the day with a group of primates in the bush and one is likely to see a few small fights, an array of mild threats, a few slapped hands, and even a bite or two. But actual wounding and other types of severe aggression are rare. Primatologists and biologists have shown that competition is checked by networks of relationships and social alliances. Fights happen and violence is employed, but most conflicts are negotiated through getting along, breaking up, making up, and avoiding one another. Yes, sometimes a fight escalates to the point of injury, and sometimes it is even lethal, but that is not the norm, nor is it what we might call a strategy (a consistent pattern used by individuals). Individuals who fight a lot usually don't fare too well.

What about differences between males and females? In most primate species males are larger than females, often have larger canine teeth ("fangs"), and thus have a greater potential to harm females than females do to harm males (in one-on-one fights). There are researchers who argue that this pattern is reflective of an evolutionary adaption for males to use violence to control females (and that humans are a good reflection of this). While it is true that in some apes and monkeys, males do use aggression to coerce females to stay near them—or even to mate with them—there are also many other species (a majority of primate species) where males are not able to use aggression to coerce females at all. In fact, in many species, females group together to form coalitions to resist male attempts at coercion or aggression. Also, we have to keep in mind that compared to many primates, human males are not that much bigger than human females and both sexes have very small canine teeth. Within groups there is a wide range of ways in which aggression and social control are used. There is no pattern in primates to which we could point as a shared evolutionary basis for violence in humans.

So far we've looked at interactions only within groups. What about between them? Is it in the intergroup relations that other primates can show us a possible human proclivity to violence and war?

For most of early primate studies it was assumed that primates were highly territorial and that groups would fight to defend their territories. We now know that most primates are not what we would call "territorial," because areas they use overlap with areas that other groups of the same species use. But there are conflicts over space, and in most cases groups of the same species tend to avoid being in the same place at the same time (though not always). Researchers have argued that this is a way to minimize the risk of conflict and violence between groups. This is not to say that if one spends enough time watching primates she won't see two groups coming together over a contested area and putting on a big show for each other—lots of hooting and hollering and maybe even some fighting. These conflicts can result in serious injury or death but rarely do. Just as within groups, between-group conflicts are often resolved via negotiations or avoidance. Or just running away. Severe violence and aggression between groups is rare and seldom results in death.

Looking at the lives of other primates shows us that extreme violence and warfare are not ancestral traits and that these kinds of things might truly be found only in humans. This is correct—for the most part. There is a particular primate, our closest relative, that bucks this trend: the chimpanzee.

Nearly twenty years ago the anthropologist Richard Wrangham and the journalist Dale Peterson wrote, "We are apes of nature, cursed over six million years or more with a rare inheritance, a Dostoyevskyan demon. . . . The coincidence of demonic aggression in ourselves and our closest kin bespeaks its antiquity." They were referring to the idea that it is not all primates but rather apes, specifically chimpanzees and humans, who share a core evolutionary history of violence and war. They suggest that this history is written in blood and is the sign of a warrior-like past that enabled males (including humans and chimpanzees) to hone violence and coercion into a fine-tuned weapon that enabled success in a world of conflict and strife.

If there are clear and marked patterns of violence that are the same in both chimpanzees and humans, then we can assume that these appear because they reflect the specific evolutionary path of our last common ancestor (the LCA about 7 to 10 million years ago). After more than fifty years of focused study on more than eleven chimpanzee communities, there is no doubt about one thing: Chimpanzees can be really aggressive.

The main problem we run up against when looking at chimpanzees to better understand humans is that there are many communities of chimpanzees, two species (*Pan troglodytes* and *Pan paniscus*—often called the bonobo), and a lot of variation between them. *Pan troglodytes* also comes in multiple types (or subspecies) that can be roughly divided into Western, Central, and Eastern African forms. Chimpanzees are big-brained, very complex social primates. They have social traditions that vary between groups, and in captivity they can be trained to communicate with humans using rudimentary forms of sign languages.

We, and our ancestors, do share a lot with the chimpanzees.

Chimpanzees and bonobos live in large communities with many males and females and young. Most of the time the communities are broken up into smaller subgroups that range across the territory of the community. In eastern chimpanzees the whole community is rarely together in the same place at the same time. In western chimpanzees and bonobos, larger subgroups and whole-community gatherings are more common. In eastern chimpanzees, males are particularly aggressive toward females and are often able to coerce them using aggression and threats. In western chimpanzees, the males are less likely to use violence to attempt to coerce females, and when they do, they are less successful at it. In bonobos, females are dominant to males in many circumstances, and males have no luck using violent coercion on females.

Both chimpanzees and bonobos will capture, kill, and eat other animals when they can (this makes up about 5 percent of chimpanzee diets and a smaller percentage of bonobo diets). In many chimpanzee communities, hunts for monkeys high up in the trees are times of great excitement for the whole group. As noted in an earlier chapter, males do most of the chasing and capturing of the prey, which they often share with their closest allies, and sometimes with their moms or other females. Jill Pruetz and colleagues' reports from Fongoli, in Senegal, of chimpanzees using sharp sticks to jab small nocturnal primates (galagos) are the only case known where chimpanzees use tools to hunt mammalian prey. And it is not so much the males, or only the adults, that are doing it. Youngsters of both sexes are the most common hunters, and teenage females are the most successful at it. This scenario is not what the "man the hunter" hypothesis supporters had in mind.

As for violence between groups, eastern and western chimpanzee males occasionally get together and walk the boundaries of their territories in single-file lines (sometimes females join in). Researchers have called these "border patrols," and the participants are often more silent, maybe even more serious, than when they move around other parts of their territory. When these patrols encounter individuals from neighboring communities, they can act violently, hooting and jumping around, and, on occasion, they attack and the interaction can be lethal. The patrolling group generally attacks only if they outnumber the individuals from the other group. This reflects a certain amount of coordination: a male starts out toward the boundary, maybe quietly hooting, and others fall into line behind him. When they encounter another group, there is no shared conversation or sharing of overt information. Rather, one or two individuals will, if they're feeling a numerical superiority on their side, launch into the attack; then the others join in as the hooting and hollering reaches a fever pitch.

Finally, and strangely, chimpanzee males and females (primarily in eastern chimpanzees) have been observed killing infants in their own communities (maybe even their own offspring) and from other communities during border encounters. Sometimes after killing an infant the group will consume it, sharing the meat just as they would the meat of a monkey or a bushpig. Other times they just leave them on the ground with no particular recognition at all.

Is this a window into the cannibalism at Gran Dolina? Probably not. Remember that *Homo antecessor* used tools to deflesh the bones and extract the marrow, a much more consistent and intentional act. In the chimpanzees there is no clear pattern as to when they eat, or discard, the carcasses of infants. Interestingly and confusingly, bonobos do not engage in border patrols, lethal intercommunity violence, or infanticide.

So, what do chimpanzees tell us about the evolution of human violence? Unfortunately, not much.

Humans are equally related to the two species of chimpanzees, and those two species are very different when it comes to the types and patterns of aggression they display. On the one hand, *Pan troglodytes* males can be really aggressive to females, but *Pan paniscus* males rarely start fights with females (and when they do, they often lose); both of these instances show up in human societies. The eastern and western chimpanzee border patrols and intercommunity lethal violence might be similar in some ways to human behavior. Human males can, and do, form groups and attack other groups of humans in many different circumstances, occasionally involving severe and lethal violence. But human feuding, homicide, and war, with their political, economic, historical, and social underpinnings, are not directly comparable to the eastern and western chimpanzees' behaviors.

While some researchers continue to argue that the chimpanzees give us insight into evolutionary origins of war, most anthropologists and biologists don't see sufficient justification in taking the comparison to that conclusion. The evidence suggests that humans, chimpanzees, and bonobos share the potential for social coordination above and beyond that of other primates. Severe violence between groups and male coercion of females can develop, but so can female dominance as well as peaceful intra- and intergroup lives. All are possibilities in our shared heritage. Humans and chimpanzees are complex, socially dynamic primates who have the capacities to use tools, to coordinate with other individuals a bit more than other primates do, and to use different social strategies to negotiate our daily lives. The key point is the wide variation with which they take place. This variation happens because of a shared creative spark—one that we, and not the chimpanzees, have expanded on.

Violence in Our Bodies

Other primates do not wage war, but we do—so it's worth asking if there is something distinctive in our genetic makeup that makes us organize and coordinate groups to fight one another. Violent behavior is directly affected by the nervous system, brain, and hormones.

It's pretty clear which parts of the brain (the prefrontal cortex, the dorsal anterior cingulated cortex, the amygdala, and the hypothalamus) are centrally involved with the expression of aggression and violence. It's not that these areas "cause" aggression, but rather that when we are aggressive many of them are involved in particular ways. In general, these parts of the brain receive inputs (vision, smell, touch, pain, sound, memory, language, etc.) and then interact to stimulate other bodily systems (the hormones, neurotransmitters, blood circulation, and muscles) into action. These particular systems in the brain are involved in actions like introspection, regulation of emotions, detection of conflict situations, and the regulation of responses to anger, pain, and social rejection, and they are involved in behavioral action. There is also a suite of molecules produced by the body that directly interact with these regions of the brain. These molecules include serotonin, dopamine, monoamine oxidase A, and a variety of steroid hormones such as testosterone, other androgens, and estrogen. Much has been revealed about the workings of our bodies.

Here is an example of this system: When you are walking alone in a dark alley at night and you hear footsteps rapidly approaching behind you, your experience (knowing, or assuming, that being alone in a dark place can be dangerous) combines with your inputs (hearing footsteps behind you, having limited vision due to darkness, and seeing limited areas to move due to being in an alley) and kick-starts a series of actions by your brain and nervous system, which communicate to your hormones and facilitate changes in your muscles and blood flow, vision, and rate of breathing. You are in what researchers call fight-or-flight mode, and you spring into action. Which actions you take vary depending on the situation and your past experience, but getting out of there quickly and turning to confront the person behind you are two of the most common responses, and your body is ready for either. You may opt for violence. You may not.

Adding other people into the scenario makes it less predictable. But none of what we know about these systems suggests that they were shaped over evolutionary time to serve a function specifically for violence, even though they are almost always part of a violent response. All of these systems have many other functions. While they are components in the expression of aggression and violence, they are also wholly tied to, and shaped by, the lived history, social context, health, and daily lives of our bodies.

No biological system in the body can be distinctly identified as "for violence."

Not even testosterone. We all know that testosterone stimulates or enhances aggression and violence, especially in males—right? No. Testosterone courses through both male and female bodies. On average, males have higher circulating levels than females, but that does not mean what most people think it means. Having more testosterone does not automatically cause one to be more violent. There is no patterned increase in aggression at puberty, when human males undergo a significant increase in the production of testosterone, and even when given extra testosterone, adults' aggression does not tend to increase.

What the evidence supports is that in competitive or acute-stress situations (like a fight), humans (both males and females) can rapidly respond by increasing the production of testosterone. The increase can enhance muscle activity and efficiency and might also result in lower sensitivity to pain (again in both men and women). This might help make individuals adept in aggressive competition, especially most males, who are starting at a higher level of circulating testosterone than most females, but it does not cause or even control the pattern of violent behavior.

More than the manners in which our bodies produce violence and aggression, it is the ways in which we creatively use, and restrict, that violence that are at the heart of understanding humanity. Our ability to make peace is more complicated and valuable than our ability to make war.

Extreme Violence—Ancient or Modern?

Living in small foraging groups characterized the vast majority of human history. It is only in the last 5,000 to 20,000 years—out of a 2-million-year history of the genus *Homo*—that some groups of humans began to settle down, live in larger clusters, build villages, and start farms. Because the "forager group structure" is one of the most common ways to think about understanding the human past, many researchers study those few remaining human groups who live (or until recently had lived) in this lifestyle. There are a few problems with this approach. Looking at contemporary foragers is not a window into the past—they do not live in isolation from other nonforager groups, and they certainly did not stop evolving while other groups of humans continued to do so.

But this does not mean that the modern foragers can't tell us something important about the social patterns of small-scale societies and of living in a foraging ecology. Both of these patterns are extremely rare in human communities today yet were very common in the past. Looking at them is not a measure of what our ancestors did, but it can offer insight into some of the ways that humans work in these kinds of communities.

Both sides of the debate over whether warfare is an ancient trait or a recent one cite these modern small-scale groups. There are many who argue that foragers are especially violent and warlike and that it's the larger-scale civilizations that have made us a more peaceful lot in the last few centuries. Then there are those who disagree.

The anthropologist Doug Fry and the psychologist Patrik Söderberg looked extensively at violence in modern mobile forager societies. They were able to get excellent-quality data on twenty-one societies and found 148 instances of lethal violence. A stunning 69 of the 148 came from the Tiwi people of Melville and Bathurst Islands off the coast of Australia. Fifty-five percent of the events were one killer and one victim; 23 percent had more than one person participating in the killing of a single individual; and 22 percent of the events had multiple people involved on both sides. Interestingly, nearly half of the societies sampled (ten of twenty-one) had no lethal events perpetrated by two or more persons, and three societies had no lethal events at all.

What were the reasons behind the lethal events? More than 50 percent were between two individuals in the same group due to a perceived slight or insult, revenge, spousal abuse, or a fight over a man or a woman. Of the 33 percent between-group deaths, the majority resulted from two different clans seeking revenge on each other or a disagreement between close groups or clans. The majority of all these lethal events between groups occurred just in the Tiwi, who have some of the richest and most extensive ceremonial practices associated with death and burials. The rest of the total events are made up of small percentages of feuding between families, killing someone outside the society (killing missionaries, for example), and accidents (more than 4 percent), and, interestingly given the Gran Dolina evidence, about 1.4 percent were from starvation cannibalism.

What do Fry and Söderberg conclude? "When all cases are examined . . . most incidents of lethal aggression can aptly be called homicides, a few others feud, and only a minority warfare. The actual reasons for lethal aggression are most often interpersonal, and consequently, the particulars of most of the lethal events in these societies do not conform to the usual conceptualization of war." Yes, lethal events happen in modern forager groups, but they are almost never warfare. Being a big-brained, socially complex, highly creative primate with access to tools (and weapons) can be dangerous. But such societies have ways of handling such danger.

The anthropologist Christopher Boehm looked at fifty intensively studied forager societies and found that when individuals are overaggressive or stingy, stealing or cheating, bullying or unpredictably killing others, the group they belong to reacts firmly. Active social sanctioning ranging from public shaming or condemnation, to invoking supernatural punishment, to kicking the offender out of the group, is used to control behavior. Boehm discovered that in most of these societies adult men often positively reinforce nonaggressive traits. A preference for positive social relationships, and working as a group to maintain them, is widespread across societies, not just in foragers. It is not that modern humans are always peaceful or that men are not aggressive, but that we see constraints on aggression and a favoring of positive social interactions almost everywhere we look.

It is a common assumption that, although we value pleasant, nonaggressive males, those males who are more assertive, aggressive, and "dominant" will do better in society and be more attractive to women (like Wrangham and Peterson said for chimpanzees). Everyone knows that "nice guys finish last." But is that true?

The evolutionary psychologists Margo Wilson and Martin Daly stated that "certainly, it is easy to envision circumstances in which a man's capacity to use violence effectively might enhance his attractiveness to women . . . even where sexual harassment and assault are prevalent, a husband with a fierce reputation can be a social asset." This assumption suggests that aggression toward women by men enables an evolutionary advantage for the males and gets them more resources and more offspring. It assumes that females might even prefer to mate with those men who are more aggressive because they are the best providers or because by mating with them the women (and their offspring) are protected from other aggressive actions by men. Sounds plausible, but are violent guys more popular with the ladies?

Given the attention this idea has received, there are surprisingly few studies that strive to answer the question: Do aggressive males do better? A study of the Yanomamö, a small-scale society in the Amazonian region on the borders of Brazil and Venezuela, is held up to support the assertions that male aggression is an evolved strategy, demonstrating its longterm success. The study is often said to settle the matter.

The Yanomamö live in villages associated with territories and gardens. They occasionally raid other villages, sometimes abducting females during the raid. The Yanomamö engage in relatively high rates of aggression, and violence breaks out within and between villages, sometimes resulting in death. If a Yanomamö man is involved in a killing, he must undergo a purification ritual during which he becomes an *unokai*. Only a minority (about 30 percent) of men become *unokai* (that is, actually kill someone); however, it has been claimed that *unokai* have, on average, 2.5 more wives and three times the number of children than do non-*unokai* men. This difference appears to indicate an evolved relationship between lethal aggression and reproductive success in human males.

However, there is a problem. While *unokai* do have, on average, more offspring, they are not being compared with a group of men who are of the same age. We know from studying the other primates that age can affect dominance and reproductive success. Doug Fry's reanalysis of the original Yanomamö data set shows that *unokai* are on average 10.4 years older than non-*unokai*. It is not surprising that, on average, men who are ten years older have more wives and children (this is common in many small-scale societies). Having more kids, for the Yanomamö, is as much about being older as it is about being more violent.

Adding to this story are the data available for the Waorani, another much-studied South American small-scale society known for their aggressiveness and who have the highest rate of homicide of any small-scale society studied. The anthropologist Stephen Beckerman and colleagues interviewed and examined the genealogies of 121 Waorani elders and collected complete raiding histories of 85 warriors. They studied raiding histories, marital records, and the number of kids per man and discovered that "more aggressive men, no matter how defined, do not acquire more wives than milder men, nor do they have more children, nor do their wives and children survive longer." They also found that more aggressive men had fewer children who survived to have kids themselves.

It turns out that aggressive males do not "do better" in an evolutionary sense in either of the two well-known, and well-studied, examples of hyperaggressive small-scale societies where reproductive success was actually measured. We see that in modern forager groups, most lethal violence is not warlike; it is most often the result of disagreements, grudges, and feuds within groups. We also see that the majority of these societies value friendliness and cooperation more than aggression and violence (just like in most other primates) and use social interactions to control aggression.

So violence happens, in some societies more than others, and getting along via complex social ways of living together is common across all primates, including humans. But the rarity (or absence) of war in other primates and in contemporary small-scale human societies doesn't tell us why war seems to be a central part of the human experience today. We know that war happens and sometimes it happens a lot. The question remains: When did this pattern of warfare start, and why?

Creating War

First, is there any link between the development of hunting and the emergence of a drive to violence or "bloodlust"? The hard evidence available is scant for much of the time before the emergence of the *Homo* line and only a little better after that. The probable earliest types of weapons, such as thrown rocks and crude tree-branch clubs, don't help, because rocks were used for many purposes and tree-branch clubs weren't preserved.

Nonetheless, the evidence we do have provides the basis for a much more compelling argument. As plausible as the "man the hunter becomes man the killer" argument may seem, what we find from the analysis of the fossil and archeological record is that the timing is all wrong. We now know that the damage done to the bones of australopithecines, and many members of early *Homo*, was the result not of their being hunters or predators, but rather of their being hunted by the range of large and dangerous predators all around them. As for their descendants (our ancestors), who learned to hunt, they became top-tier hunters well before anything like warfare, or even frequent homicide, shows up in the fossil and archeological record.

Bones tell us a lot, but there are limits. Studies of how and where violence occurs in modern peoples from around the world, and those of populations from the recent past for which we have written and oral records, in addition to bones, give us good insight into the sorts of marks to look for. Damage often associated with lethal violence includes dented or shattered skulls and faces, crushed rib cages, and what we call "parry fractures," breaks in the forelimbs, such as the ulna, radius, wrists, and hands, which result when someone shields himself from a blow with his arms. One might think interpreting how violent our ancestors were is a simple enterprise, requiring measuring the frequency of bones with such marks. But all of these kinds of damage can also be caused by accidental falls, which might have happened while engaged in hunting, for example. As we've seen, hunts often involved chasing animals through treacherous terrain. And recall that for a long time, our ancestors hunted some really large creatures with nothing more than short pointy sticks and a whole lot of optimism.

Consider two scenarios:

- It is 500,000 years ago and a member of the genus *Homo* is carrying an armload of juicy roots and some fruits and is walking back to the place above the valley where his group has been sleeping for the past dry season. Out of nowhere a member of another group—a rival group that lives on the other side of the valley—jumps from behind a boulder swinging a large wooden club. Our protagonist drops the roots and fruits and raises his arms just as the heavy wood connects with a cracking thud. He falls hard against the sloping ground and rolls down the steep embankment, broken and bloody, fatally wounded.

- It is 500,000 years ago and a member of the genus *Homo* is carrying an armload of juicy roots and some fruits and is walking back to the place above the valley where his group has been sleeping for the past dry season. As he carefully steps along the slim ledge of the cliff face he is dreaming about the warm feeling of a full belly and the humming and dancing around the fire that will follow the feast. Failing to notice a small area of loose rock in his path, he steps onto a ledge that gives way and plummets face-first down the steep embankment, spilling the roots and fruits and smashing his forearms. He lies broken and bloody at the bottom of the embankment, fatally wounded.

The fossil remains we recover 500,000 years later would look similar. Had this been an attack by a human much later in time, after tipped spears and arrows had been created, the remains of a spearhead or arrowhead might be found with those of the skeleton, or even embedded in a bone, which we find plenty of later in the record. But in an attack with one of the earliest forms of weapon, such as simple thrown rocks, or a stout tree-branch club, the impact on the bones might be extremely similar to that from a fall. This makes interpretation of the possible signs of lethal violence in the deep past especially difficult.

What about indications of coordinated group killing or of larger-scale warfare? What would constitute evidence for that? It is often impossible to determine whether remains that show clear signs of intentional trauma, such as parry fractures or even a stone tip from a spear embedded in bone, are from a one-off fight between two members of a group, or several members of different groups, or if they should be considered indications of larger-scale, coordinated conflict. But if we find a number of bodies together, all or most with evidence of trauma, and especially with evidence of mutilation, such as limbs removed, or when the evidence indicates that the violence perpetrated required multiple participants in coordinated action, then we have something.

Let's return to the Gran Dolina site, which, due to the apparent evidence of cannibalism, some have interpreted as an instance of premeditated lethal violence, and maybe even of warfare. We could make a better case for the interpretations of cannibalism if we had a number of other sites revealing clear signs of cannibalism that also clearly indicate that coordinated violence of some kind had occurred. Alas, the only other evidence we have offers no such support. A site known as Bodo in Ethiopia produced a *Homo* fossil skull showing similar butchering marks from about 600,000 years ago. According to paleoanthropologist Tim White, who has studied the fossil cranium, it likely belonged to a member of the *Homo erectus* line. It displays clear signs of cut marks, indicating that a sharp-edged stone was used to cut the flesh away from the bone at various locations on the skull, and as with the bones at Gran Dolina, the cut marks are identical to those on animal bones found at the site. But no more evidence was found here than at Gran Dolina about who did the cutting and why, nor what they did with the meat.

Another location where remains have been found that many researchers have argued provides evidence of cannibalism in the early *Homo* species is a site in China called Zhoukoudian, first discovered in 1921. Located about thirty miles southwest of Beijing, the site is a treasure chest of fossils from between 600,000 and 300,000 years ago. The remains of as many as forty-five *Homo erectus* have been found there, as well as thousands of stone tools and animal bones. The early excavators of the site included the anatomist Davidson Black, paleontologist and priest Pierre Teilhard de Chardin, archeologist Henri Breuil, and the paleoanthropologist Franz Weidenreich, who all suggested that some of the *Homo* bones looked as though they were processed and crushed much in the same way as many animal bones, and that this indicated cannibalism by their comrades. However, more recent work, conducted in the 1990s and 2000s by biological anthropologists Noel Boaz and Russell Ciochon, demonstrates that the damage to the *Homo erectus* bones, and to many of the other bones at the site, was actually perpetrated by giant hyenas, called *Pachycrocuta*, which are now extinct. These giant hyenas captured all sorts of animals and dragged them to the caves, including *Homo erectus*, and proceeded to chomp, crush, and otherwise maul the bones as they consumed their kills. Fascinatingly, over the thousands of years at the site, there were many periods when the hyenas stopped using the cave, and in those periods small bands of *Homo erectus* actually moved in, making the caves their own living spaces (while they could). It would not be everyone's idea of a dream home.

Another set of remains in the fossil record that might be interpreted as indicating cannibalism are those of Neanderthals found at a site called Krapina, in Croatia, which dates to much later, about 130,000 years ago, and a few younger sites in Europe and China that also produced fossil bones of *Homo sapiens* with indications that they were butchered after death. But in these cases the evidence is often that of cut marks on the bones that are not in the places one would expect if butchering for meat and thus not clearly associated with cannibalism. It is often interpreted as a funerary behavior, marking the dead—but no one is arguing that it was from murder or warfare.

What about the record of the other kinds of violent trauma? Here we have a good deal more data to work with. For the Pleistocene period, from about 2 million years ago through to about 10,000 to 15,000 years ago, which encompasses most of the history of the genus *Homo,* we have remains of *Homo sapiens* and of other members of the genus *Homo* from more than 400 sites in Africa and across Eurasia. And for the periods thereafter, the Holocene and the Anthropocene, we have thousands of examples from around the world. They provide a relatively clear picture of the emergence of war.

To appreciate the clear pattern that arises out of the data, it's important to survey the collective evidence over the full time span. For the Pleistocene data, we have a wonderful analysis performed by the anthropologists Marc Kissel and Matthew Piscitelli. They scoured published resources to create a database of 447 fossil sites from around the globe that have skeletal remains from *Homo sapiens* dating earlier than 10,000 years ago. They chose this cutoff date because it is the official end point of the Pleistocene period, which is demarcated as such because the end of the last glacial period occurred at this time, coinciding roughly with the emergence of domestication and agriculture. As we've seen earlier, human life began to change dramatically in many ways, and at increasing speed, at this rough juncture. The data show that increased perpetration of violence was one of the many aspects of this change.

From this sample, only 11 of the 447 sites, or about 2.5 percent, have fossils that show any evidence of trauma. The overall database includes the remains of at least 2,605 individuals (most are not complete skeletons), and of these only 58, or approximately 2 percent, show any evidence of traumatic violent injury. To put it in another way, approximately 98 percent of all the sites for which we have hard fossil evidence over the nearly 2 million years of human life up until 10,000 years ago show no signs of traumatic violence.

The kinds of violent trauma we do see can be dramatic, like the cranium from Sima de los Huesos (a site in the Atapuerca region of Spain, next to Gran Dolina) from about 430,000 years ago. Cranium 17 is the only one of twenty-eight individuals found at the site with any trauma that might be due to interpersonal conflict: two dents on the forehead. The researchers at the site thought two whacks to the head produced them, which likely resulted in the individual's death. This example, combined with two others, the Shanidar 3 Neanderthal, from what is today Iraq, with a cut rib, and the Upper Paleolithic *Homo sapiens* individual from Sunghir 1, from what is today Russia, with a damaged neck vertebra, are the clearest examples of interpersonal violence we have in the Pleistocene fossil record (about 2 million to 14,000 years ago). There are a few more fossils, Maba 1 (from China) and Dolní Věstonice 11/12 (in Moravia in the Czech Republic), with healed damage to the frontal bone, that also might be good examples of interpersonal violence. There are more fossils with some trauma, but these three (or five) are the ones that most agree are due to interpersonal violence. At best we have five examples of interpersonal aggressions (with three resulting in homicide) over a span of hundreds of thousands of years and thousands of fossils.

Combining these data with the best available data from the period from about 14,000 years ago up to 5,000 years ago—the beginning of the historical record—we find the following:

- From about 2 million to 14,000 years ago, approximately 2 percent of all fossils have signs of violent trauma and very few sites have any evidence of such violence.
- From approximately 14,000 to 7,500 years ago, as many as 4 percent of all human skeletal remains show signs of violent trauma, and while sites with such remains are still not common, significantly more have been found.
- From 7,500 to 5,000 years ago, up to 7 percent of all human skeletal remains have signs of violent trauma, and many of these come from a few sites where there are high percentages of damaged remains, real signs of organized and lethal conflict between groups.

The overall story, then, is one of little evidence for regular or frequent violent interpersonal trauma for the vast majority of the history of the genus *Homo* and almost no sites with multiple instances of trauma, and then large upticks in the period from 14,000 to 7,500 years ago and again at 7,500 to 5,000 years ago. This leads us to focus not on the deep past to explain our current patterns of organized and lethal violence, but rather on the more recent past.

But can the lack of evidence for lethal violence be taken as clear evidence that little such violence actually occurred? The absence of hard evidence on its own might be considered inconclusive, but the overall pattern in the data, and the other findings at the later sites showing clear signs of homicide and large-scale conflict, allows a strong case to be made about why our level of violence began to increase. To appreciate how strong the argument for this later emergence of increased violence and warfare is, we must take an up-close look at the sites that best record the change.

It is at these sites, the anthropologist Brian Ferguson points out, that distinctive signs of coordinated group violence begin to appear, though they are still quite rare by comparison to the total number of sites found for the same time periods. The earliest of these, called Jebel Sahaba, is situated along the Nile River in northern Sudan, where it approaches the modern border with Egypt. The occupation of the site by people dates to between 14,000 and 12,000 years ago. Based on the tools used and the kinds of plant and animal remains at the site, we can tell the people at Jebel Sahaba were foragers and they had found a prime spot. At that time Jebel Sahaba, and the area just around it, was an oasis of bountiful savannah, dotted with large numbers of antelope and goatlike herbivores, and rich in fishing resources. But the region was undergoing rapid climate change, becoming drier, and harsher conditions led to lower food supplies in the surrounding environs, which were hit harder earlier. Jebel Sahaba was a haven that would have been much desired by outsiders.

The remains of what appears to be a cemetery were found there in an excavation in the early 1960s by a team led by the American archeologist Fred Wendorf. Fifty-nine bodies were uncovered, comprising forty-six adults and thirteen children, whose remains now reside in the British

Museum. Out of them, twenty-four, or roughly 40 percent, revealed evidence of traumatic violence. Some featured stone points from arrows and stone flakes situated in and around the rib cages, while others displayed parry fractures, and in some, stone points were embedded in bones. The sheer number of skeletons with indications of traumatic violence is a robust indication that coordinated and violent conflict occurred here. This is the oldest, and clearest, evidence of large-scale interpersonal violence in the human fossil record—and it stands alone in this time period in the intensity of its violence. The leading interpretation is that the violence reflects competition for the ecological richness at the site, with the residents defending against incursion.

The site of another cemetery nearby, just across the Nile, which dates from the slightly more recent time of approximately 12,000 years ago, raises some interesting questions about what Jebel Sahaba tells us. Of thirty-nine skeletons unearthed there, none showed any sign of violence. This suggests that the people in the area were not engaging in consistent coordinated violence, as might be an interpretation if we looked only at the Jebel Sahaba site. Brian Ferguson asserts that the record of intense violence at Jebel Sahaba was likely due to a concentrated burst of conflict, perhaps a small-scale war, and that over the long term, there is little indication of continuous conflict in the region.

At Nataruk, a site west of Lake Turkana (Kenya) dating to about 9,000 to 10,000 years ago, the first example of a massacre is found. Twenty-seven individuals, including twelve full bodies, were discovered, half buried in what would have been the mud in the shallows of the water's edge. Ten of the twelve complete skeletons clearly died from violent trauma at the hands of other humans, and it is likely that many of the others did as well. There are parry factures, crushed skulls, chopped-off hands, and indications that some were bound by their hands and feet before being slaughtered. All were killed or died around the same time. The Nataruk landscape was a particularly fertile area during this time period, probably sustaining a large population of many communities of foragers. They had pottery and storage, and likely a complicated set of relationships. Maybe they also had the beginnings of ideas about territory, property, and even jealousy. Or maybe this was just an encounter between two groups, one of whom was particularly violent. We have no way of knowing specifically, but placed in context, this is the first and largest evidence of the human capacity for massive and organized cruelty.

The next oldest possible indication of warfare in the record comes from the Ukraine and the sites of Voloshkoe and Vasilyevka, alongside the Dnieper River, which date to approximately 12,000 to 10,000 years ago. The people who lived at these sites were also foragers, practicing fishing as well as gathering in the rich bounty of animal and plant life of the wider ecosystem. Interestingly, both sites also date to a period of rapid climate change, just as with Jebel Sahaba. Again survival pressure and an inequality in access to the best locales and resources may have led local groups into conflict.

A cemetery was found at each site. At Voloshkoe the remains of five of the nineteen individuals buried either displayed embedded stone points or were missing body parts. One skeleton, that of a man, was buried away from the others, and a stone point was embedded in the back of his neck, with two other points in his rib cage. The researchers who analyzed the remains conjectured that he may have been executed. The lower arms of another male skeleton had clearly been cut off, and the hands of yet another male had been cut off, as well as the legs below the knee. While these finds do not seem to be indications of coordinated attacks, they might be reflective of punishment, or the treatment of captives resulting from coordinated attacks between groups. What is quite clear is that they constitute evidence of intentional, even creatively conducted, homicide.

At nearby Vasilyevka, five of forty-four skeletons were found with stone points either embedded in bones or adjacent to them. A female whose age is estimated at between eighteen and twenty-two years old had an arrowhead embedded in one of her ribs, and another female of around twenty-five was found with arrowheads right next to her rib cage. A man in his late twenties had a stone point rammed deep into his backbone. The archeologist Malcolm Lillie and colleagues argue that this site shows a focus on younger individuals as targets of violence, which they assert might have been due to their being the strongest, and therefore best able to defend the resources of the group, and prime targets for raiders.

A particularly interesting find at this site is that skeletons show indications of slightly higher levels of protein consumption by the males than the females, so the site might also provide early evidence of gender hierarchies—some of the earliest signs of gender inequality.

Sites including clear indication of lethal violence become more prevalent in Northern Africa and Europe starting in the period between 8,000 and 6,000 years ago, though they are still rare by comparison to the total number of sites. At these excavations the percentages of remains showing clear signs of lethal violence range from approximately 3 percent to 18 percent. Out of the remains of sixty individuals buried at the site known as Calumnata, in Algeria, which dates to between 8,300 and 7,350 years ago, two, or 3 percent, showed signs of death by violence. At Bogebakken/Vedbaek, in Denmark, and at Skateholm in Sweden, both from approximately 6,800 to 6,400 years ago, the ratio is four out of sixty people, or 6 percent. And at Brittany/Île Téviec in France, the number is three of sixteen, or 18 percent.

Turning to sites in the Americas, the earliest fossils date to approximately 12,000 to 9,000 years ago, and at least two of them have arrow or spear points embedded in their bones. But the number of skeletons is so small that drawing useful conclusions about the nature of aggression from these early American remains is not possible. By approximately 6,000 years ago, as in other parts of the world, the rates increase in the Americas. At the Windover site in Florida, dating to 6,400 years ago, nine of sixty-eight remains, or 13 percent, show signs of violence, while at Indian Knoll in Kentucky, dated to between 6,100 and 4,500 years ago, the number is much smaller, at 48 of 880 individuals, or 5 percent, which have either arrow points embedded in them or were mutilated, or both. We have less data for Asia and Africa, but the trends seem to be similar.

So we see that up until the period of about 7,500 years ago, clear evidence of lethal violence between humans is still relatively rare, and it's unclear in most of the cases whether the violence is indicative of warfare. But starting around 6,000 to 7,000 years ago we begin to find more examples of unambiguous evidence of coordinated large-scale killing.

At the sites of Talheim and Herxheim in Germany, which date to around 6,000 to 7,000 years ago, and Schletz in Austria, from the same period, mass graves were excavated in the early 1980s and mid-1990s. Talheim was an early farming settlement in what is today southern Germany. At a nearby site, referred to as the "Death Pit," the remains of thirty-four individuals were uncovered, and many of their skulls showed signs of violent trauma, such as fractures and punctures. Many bodies were lying facedown, others in unusual twisted postures, and many skeletal parts were mixed together, which suggests the bodies were unceremoniously dumped in the pit at, or very near, the same time. Interestingly, no remains of children younger than four years old were found, leading to the conjecture that perhaps the victors in an apparent conflict took the youngest children as spoils.

At Schletz, another mixed early farming and foraging settlement, with what appears to be some earthen fortification built around it, as many as 200 individuals were buried in one grave, apparent evidence of a mass slaughter. Many of the bodies had missing limbs and some of the skeletons showed clear indications of traumatic violence, again including crushed and punctured skulls. Remains of fewer young females than would be expected if the deaths were due to natural causes were found, which may be an indication that the perpetrators of this slaughter took some of the young females with them. It appears that this massacre also signaled the end of the settlement at Schletz.

At Herxheim, a grave of up to 500 individuals was found, many with cut marks on their bones. Strangely, many of the skulls were detached from the bodies and piled together. Many limb bones were mixed into clusters with other animals' bones.

Sites with remains of mass killings are found increasingly all around the globe starting around 6,000 to 7,000 years ago. But it is vital to emphasize that for each of the sites described here, many, many more from the same time period, and even in the same areas, show no signs of organized violence.

The best conclusion, both from this detailed data at each site with evidence of coordinated violence, and from the collective data of all sites over the span of time, is that for most of our evolutionary history, human culture was not characterized by a high incidence of either homicide or warfare compared to the modern era. However, over the last 5,000 to

10,000 years, the pace and intensity of this type of violence markedly increased.

This analysis is directly opposed to those who, like Steven Pinker, argue that human nature is violent from its very origins. Pinker, Azar Gat, and other supporters of this view rely almost exclusively on previously published reviews by the archeologist Lawrence Keeley and the behavioral economist Samuel Bowles. They suggested that as many as 15 percent of humans in the past died from violence—a death rate unparalleled in even the bloodiest episodes in recent history. But these assertions are highly contested. Brian Ferguson and Douglas Fry, among others, point out that Keeley and Bowles rely heavily on a limited set of archeological data and on living forager peoples and recent tribal societies for their data on warfare and killing. This is a problem for many reasons, the primary one being that recent connections to larger economies and political systems change the ways in which violence plays out. The remaining forager peoples are a tiny subset of all of the forager societies that used to be common and thus are poor representatives of the ranges of behavior in such societies. Keeley and Bowles (and thereby Pinker and Gat) also often combine homicides and revenge deaths with larger-scale coordinated aggression, giving the sense that warfare and coordinated violence are much more common than the actual record reflects.

But most important, these researchers ignore pretty much all fossil data older than approximately 14,000 years ago and focus primarily on the few archeological sites where we do see violence in the last 14,000 years as representative of all human evolutionary history. This is an unnecessarily narrow view.

Brian Ferguson, after extensively reviewing the details and published reports for the sites in depth, calls the data they use a "selective compilation of highly unusual cases, grossly distorting war's antiquity and lethality." We know that with more than 400 sites having provided more than 2,500 remains from before the 14,000-years-ago cutoff, we do in fact have a significant record, and that record suggests that there was less interpersonal violence, not more, in that earlier period.

The fallacy in the "deep roots of warfare" reading of the record of violence is brought into bold relief when we also consider the timeline of the wider range of early human behavior. If you were to plot all of the data about the course of human evolution that we considered in chapters 1 through 6 on a curve over time and then compare that timeline with the timeline of signs of increased violence and of warfare, a much more compelling understanding of the origins and nature of our violence emerges. What stands boldly out is the coincidence of the emergence of more complex societies and sedentism with the rise of coordinated lethal violence and war. Broadly, the rise in economic, political, and social inequality correlates with the rise of war.

Of course, coincidence is not an adequate basis for any argument, so we have to consider the reasons underlying the pattern. Fundamentally, the relative bounty enjoyed by groups settled in areas relatively rich in resources, as well as areas that offered protection from the elements and from predators (such as Jebel Sahaba), incentivized other, less fortunate groups to raid them. This period is when we begin to see that the acumen we developed in strategic hunting methods was apparently turned on our own. But again, perhaps the more striking deduction is that even with the incentive to attack, for most of the time that the settlement of Jebel Sahaba thrived, the community was apparently able to avoid such conflict with surrounding groups. A good indication of this state of peacefulness is that while at some later sites, such as Schletz (from about 7,000 years ago), we find defensive structures like earthen walls or caches of weapons, which are clear signs of anticipated violence, none of these is found at the earlier sites. The record from this earlier period, despite an uptick in violence, is characterized predominantly by what we refer to as broad-scale peace—most communities got along fine.

A key component of the ratcheting up of this complexity in human communities was storage. Once foods can be stored, there need to be systems of maintenance, management, and oversight of the storage. Storage then produces the concept of "ownership" of control over the items being stored and over the locations and structures used for storage. Individuals in most foraging societies have some limited personal ownership—a bow or some pottery or jewelry—but not much, and treat most community goods in a shared manner. Avarice and envy do occur, but most day-to-day interactions over goods in forager societies are more

HUMAN CREATIVITY

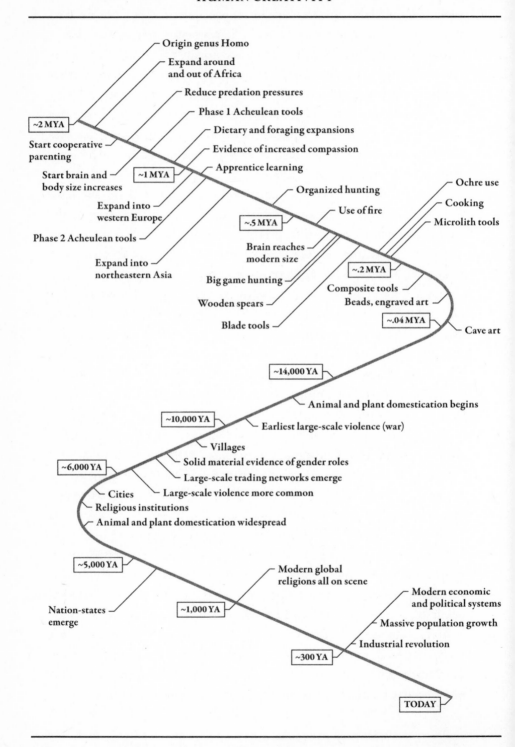

~2 MYA

Origin genus Homo

Expand around
and out of Africa

Reduce predation pressures

Phase 1 Acheulean tools

Dietary and foraging expansions

Evidence of increased compassion

Start cooperative
parenting

Apprentice learning

Start brain and
body size increases

~1 MYA

Organized hunting

Expand into
western Europe

Use of fire

Ochre use

Cooking

Microlith tools

~.5 MYA

Phase 2 Acheulean tools

Brain reaches
modern size

Expand into
northeastern Asia

Big game hunting

~.2 MYA

Composite tools

Wooden spears

Beads, engraved art

Blade tools

~.04 MYA

Cave art

~14,000 YA

Animal and plant domestication begins

~10,000 YA

Earliest large-scale violence (war)

Villages

Solid material evidence of gender roles

~6,000 YA

Large-scale trading networks emerge

Cities

Large-scale violence more common

Religious institutions

Animal and plant domestication widespread

~5,000 YA

Modern global
religions all on scene

Modern economic
and political systems

Nation-states
emerge

~1,000 YA

Massive population growth

Industrial revolution

~300 YA

TODAY

egalitarian and/or shared than in sedentary agriculturalist communities, where ownership of items and property is a key aspect of everyday life.

We take the idea of property for granted today, but prior to early sedentary groups, this was likely not a clearly defined or utilized concept. Mobile communities of foragers had areas they used and in some cases areas that they would defend from other communities. However, once people were settled into a village and practicing agriculture, property became a stark reality. The investment in reshaping the land and the plants and the community's utmost reliance on both of those things for nutrition create a strong relationship between the land and the community. The building of a village, with permanent houses and sheds and corrals for animals, the planting of crops, and the managing of the storage of those crops, creates a new way of looking at the land: It becomes something that the community created, built with their own hands; it is "theirs."

The researchers Samuel Bowles and Jung-Kyoo Choi point out that for the early village-living agriculturalists, "crops, dwellings, and animals—could be unambiguously demarcated and defended," and they were tangible products of human action—they were there because people created them. This new way of relating to the world meant that places and items could belong to communities, and even to individuals—a new shift in seeing the world.

Storage, property, and the division of people into multiple roles in a society change both how members of a community interact with one another and how they interact with other communities—they increase the possibility of intergroup conflict. These processes become quite creatively, and lethally, developed over the most recent four or five millennia of human history.

We know that at approximately the same time that larger settlements show up in the archeological record, agriculture emerged, as did the domestication of herds to tend. Many changes that were then set in motion created larger groups with increasingly strong senses of group identity, more storage, greater devotion and obligation to places, and increased inequality—all creating more opportunities and incentive for violence. Rich resources in a local area are best exploited by dividing up labor into specialties. Agriculture and domestication require the planning of sowing and harvesting; processing, caring for, and protecting animals; and butchering and preparing their meat. The increasing need for these diverse skills presented a stellar opportunity for human creativity and cooperation to shine as we divided up responsibilities, and rewards, in ways that were acceptable to the group as a whole. But the hierarchies in status, wealth, and power that went hand in hand with the management of larger surpluses of food and the division of land and other resources also created increased incentives for conflict, greed, distrust, and even cruelty.

Just as today some jobs are better than others, so would they have been in these early societies with their blossoming towns and eventually cities, with some roles more dangerous and some having more plentiful access to food or other resources. The archeological record shows that soon after the appearance of towns, agriculture, and surpluses, some burials start to look different from others. Some individuals are buried with more precious goods (metals, weapons, and maybe even art), some are in group graves and some by themselves, and still others don't even seem to warrant actual burials. The bones from the burials start to show us differences as well—chemical and isotope analyses of teeth and long bones reveal that some members of groups were getting more protein or minerals than others; some have more evidence of diseases and greater physical injuries from their labors. Early on these differences are small, but by 5,000 to 7,000 years ago they are becoming quite pronounced. Once a society is divided in these ways, once inequality becomes introduced, its forms and outcomes from creativity can expand, inequality can increase, and the sources of potential conflict multiply, both within groups and between them.

How does a community maintain a sense of cohesion with such stratification and inequality emerging? One mechanism is to develop symbols and rituals that reinforce the group identity. The importance of being in a group and the sense of community identity is likely very old in the human lineage given the core role that cooperation has played in every aspect of our evolution, as we've seen in the prior chapters. But when we start to see increasing role differentiation in communities, we also see the signs of the formal development of clans and lineages and of the creation of stories and beliefs that bind them together. The creation of such connections enables larger and larger groups to work together, and to engage in peaceful relationships. And, of course, these same associations and beliefs may help to separate them from others. This is a critical juncture in human history, one where divisions between individuals in communities and between communities themselves start to take on central roles in day-to-day life. It is the institutionalization of these differences within and between communities that is core to the emergence of coordinated violence and warfare.

The larger clans became, the more impressive the collaboration both within them and between them we find indication of, in construction, defense, agriculture, and trading (of goods, people, ideas, and ideologies). These developments also created stronger incentives for large-scale violence. Surpluses of food and other goods, trade relationships, strong community identities, larger and denser communities, and social hierarchies within and between communities all added fuel, and options, to the motives and possibilities for serious conflict. A community that managed to accumulate surpluses of food, for example, would be a prime target for confrontation by less fortunate (or less skilled) communities, especially during times of drought or series of floods, and especially if the different groups had created distinct identities, forming clans. Long-distance trade, and the creation and distribution of prestige goods such as precious metals or shells or highly sought-after foods, favors those who create the goods, who often hoard them, or who live along the trade routes controlling the movement of the goods. And the larger and wealthier settlements became, the greater the payoffs for winning conflicts became. Some humans turned the skills that enabled mass peaceful collaboration to the task of mass violent collaboration. For most of human history, lethal violence took the form of relatively rare homicides: revenge killings, deaths from fights over mates, and domestic disputes. However, the development of clans, and then greater political entities, provided both the incentive and the justification for one community to attack another without identifying specific individuals as the targets. Humans made the mental shift from individual-on-individual violence to thinking of a whole group or cluster of groups as "the enemy": We creatively dehumanized other humans.

War and peace must be seen as two sides of one coin of human creativity and part of the contemporary human niche. As we came to master survival via intensive cooperation, collaboration, and creativity, those same skills also enabled us to master new forms of conflict and destruction. The fossil and archeological record combined with a comparative examination of the other primates and of human biology does not support the argument for a deep root to human warfare and organized violence. Rather, these data combine to powerfully *refute* the notion that our proclivity to organized violence and to waging war was a core, and early, adaptive outcome of human evolution. The capacity for war emerged from the capacity for peace, our knack for innovating, getting along, and jointly tackling the challenges the world throws at us. Both war and peace are part and parcel of the creative modes of collaborative cooperation that humanity used and uses in meeting the challenges of living and succeeding over the last 2 million years.

And while the ways humans have used this capacity in regard to war and peace are complex, when it comes to sex, gender, and sexuality, the whole ball game moves to a new stadium. Let's go see that game.

CREATIVE SEX

Googling "sex" in 2016 yields approximately 3.34 billion results in 0.29 seconds. That's nearly four times as many hits as one gets when Googling "religion," three times as many as "politics," and about 50 percent more than "death." But slightly less than "food." If representation on the Internet tells us anything about what matters to humans, then sex and food are pretty darned important. But we don't need Google to tell us that. Food and sex are the basic goals of life for most organisms, not just humans.

As far as sex is concerned, animals generally come in two variants: female and male. We call these the "sexes" and they are the two complementary manifestations of animal biology necessary for reproduction. In most cases, one of each sex is needed to get together and physically exchange gametes (either egg or sperm, which is how we classify biological "female" or "male") to produce an offspring. To state the obvious, this physical exchange is at the heart of species' ability to successfully leave descendants. Because sex is so important, sexually reproducing animals have physiological systems that reward them for engaging in it. Sex feels good.

And because it feels good, many mammals take it up a notch—they have sex more often than is necessary to reproduce. We call this "social sex" and it comes with costs. Those animals that have more social sex also have more sexually transmitted infections (STIs). Increased sexual activity means taking on more risks to health—a choice we might think would soon become extinct given the fundamental evolutionary cost, even if it does feel good. But in highly social animals (like canids, whales, and primates), more sex is apparently worth the STI risk, and social sex is common. The fact that some groups of animals so gladly take the risks of increased sexual activity leads many researchers to believe that there is more than just pleasure behind social sex. Primates are among the social sex champions of the animal kingdom, so it should come as no surprise that they are also the STI champions of the animal world. It should be even less surprising that humans are the STI champions of the primates. We, as a species, have lots of sex. That means it must be really important. But humans don't just have more sex; we take it to a whole new level. The author Jared Diamond in his aptly titled book *Why Is Sex Fun? The Evolution of Human Sexuality* states it best: "Human sexuality is . . . bizarrely unusual by the standards of other animal species."

Humans also have sex in many different ways. For men and women ages twenty-five to forty-four, 98 percent have had heterosexual genital-genital sex, 90 percent have had oral sex, 36 to 44 percent have had anal sex, and 6 to 12 percent have had homosexual sex. These numbers make most other species on the planet look like prudes. By age twenty-four, one in three sexually active people have at least one non-HIV STI, and more than 19 million new sexually transmitted infections occur each year in the United States alone. Bottom line: Humans have more STIs than other organisms because humans have more sex, and more kinds of sex, and more contexts for, and issues with, sex than any other animal. We are crazy about it.

Sex is more than just an act, a goal, or a biological pattern; it's a central part of our lives. We write about sex, we think about sex, we talk about sex, we have prohibitions about sex, laws, ideologies, and assumptions about sex. We watch sex we are not participating in; we pay for sex; we use sex as a tool, a weapon, and a healing practice. We are so creative with sex that we've even developed a distinctively human category to mess with the basic biology of sex: gender.

"Gender" is a catchall term for the roles, assumptions, and expectations humans have for the biological sexes, and it creates a problem when analyzing human sexuality. When humans say "male" or "female," they are almost always referring to gender as opposed to biological sex—the two are not the same. Any specific human's gender behavior profile is not simply determined by their biological sex or their patterns of sexual activity. This makes human sexuality (the "who, how, and why" of having sex) especially challenging to understand and explain.

There are important differences between the sexes: Women give birth and lactate, men are usually larger and more muscular, and the levels and patterns of some hormones vary between the sexes. There are also important similarities: Our reproductive organs come from the same embryonic tissues; our bodies are made of the same material and structures; our hormones and brains are the same; we are the same species. Humans have a unique sex/gender muddle that it is both wonderful and a giant pain.

How Sex Works

The combining of gametes from two parents to produce an offspring, sexual reproduction, evolved hundreds of millions of years ago from asexual organisms that reproduced by splitting in half or by budding off copies of themselves. Sex evolved (most likely) as a response to dealing with changing environments. Reproducing by sex creates new variation by combining genetic data from two parents, providing the offspring with more options.

Imagine a simple organism living in a pond. Let's say this amoeba-like thing filters water to get food. It might do just fine copying itself as long as the water temperature stays more or less constant, but what if things warm up? The filtering system it uses might not be able to accommodate the new temperatures. But maybe there are lots of similar organisms in the pond and each is a little different from the others in its ability to deal with temperature fluctuation. Blending with another similar but slightly different organism could be a good option, as it can give the resulting offspring more flexibility and thus a higher chance of getting both parents' DNA into subsequent generations than either had reproducing asexually. But not all new variants do better. In fact, some do worse. Such is the risk of sex. It is the overall payoff that matters: As long as some offspring do better in comparison with the asexual reproducers, the system (sex) has a chance of catching on. Added variation needs to work out in favor of organisms only on average to keep sexual reproduction in a system. This is a good thing, thank goodness; otherwise we'd all be asexual reproducers and the world would be a lot less interesting.

Sex is a biological way to generate more variation for organisms in order for them to have better chances to meet the challenges the world throws at them. It is a risky venture. Given that, one would think that most organisms would be conservative about sex, thereby minimizing the chances for problems. For many insects, fish, and reptiles, sexual reproduction is reasonably straightforward. There is a specific time in life when their reproductive biology turns on, and they go for it: Males and females exchange gametes. One, both, or neither sex takes care of the resulting fertilized eggs until the young hatch and they are on their own. Then the reproduction biology turns off and the animals go back to their regular, nonsexual lives, or they die.

Mammals (like us) are a bit different. Mammals have internal fertilization and gestation. The gametes need to get together inside the female's body and stay there as they develop into the embryo and then fetus. Then the female gives live birth, and has to nurse the offspring until it, or they, are ready to fend for themselves food-wise. This type of sexual system adds certain aspects to mammalian bodies and behavior. Females have mammary glands and nipples for lactation and particularly structured genitals and reproductive tracts to facilitate both sexual intercourse and live birth via the same vaginal pathway. Males have complementary genitals to the females' and tend to have external testicles and often an external penis (unlike most animals), leaving male mammals' genitals more exposed than those of other animals.

Humans are strange-looking mammals. We are primates, and primate females have mammary glands like other mammals, but monkeys, apes, and humans have only one pair, whereas most mammals have between three and five pairs. In humans that one pair is also surrounded by a lot of fatty tissue that develops at puberty. Humans also stand upright, so that one pair of mammary glands surrounded by fatty tissue takes on a distinctive look: Women have breasts. Men, unlike most other mammals, have a penis that lacks a bone to assist in erection. The human penis relies on a complicated blood hydraulic system to become erect and useful for sexual activity. It is also shaped by the structure of the female genitals, which serve in both sexual and birthing roles, which results in humans having the thickest relative penises of the primates. Humans also walk on two legs. This leads to the realignment of a set of muscles called the gluteus maximus and minimus to help with the propulsion stride (pushing our bodies forward when we walk or run). These muscles wrap around the back of the pelvic girdle (the cluster of bones that make up your midsection, connecting your upper and lower body), giving us a large bulge where other animals have none, one that is often also a location for storing fat: Humans have butts. We are also relatively hairless, which is very atypical for a land-based nonburrowing mammal.

Breasts, butts, relatively hairless bodies, and atypical male penises. Humans are weird.

Sex for mammals, including humans, is tied to complex bodies, behavior, and physiology and to the raising of young (for females and in many cases for males as well). This means that sex is a lot more than the physical act of copulation. While most mammals stay reasonably conservative in their sexual systems, sex is anything but boring. Many mammals have certain times of the year when their reproductive tracts "turn on." These mating seasons are referred to as "being in heat" or "rutting" or "estrous," and you'd better not get in the way when they arrive. Mammals' bodies, including their genitals, become primed with hormonal and sensory floods, and they want sex. We know that for mammals sex feels especially good. Both males and females can have orgasms and are usually capable of many copulation events in the "turned on" time period. Mammalian sex is characterized by a lot of running around and behavioral and physical negotiations by males and females. Once the mating season is completed, the sex drive turns down (or off) and most mammals go back to their daily lives.

Some mammals don't "turn on" sexually for only brief windows in the calendar; their sexual biology functions across the year. In such cases both males and females can engage in sexual activity even when they are not seeking to reproduce. This is where things get interesting and our role as primates becomes informative.

In most macaque species there are one or two peak times of the year for mating. At those times most females go through a variety of physiological changes. The skin around the females' vaginas and anuses can become slightly swollen (massively so in some species) such that any male can notice. These females also undergo behavioral shifts, causing them to spend more than the usual amount of time following males and presenting their rear ends to those males in invitation to have sex. If the males do not respond well, females will shake their heads in front of the male's face, sometimes grabbing his facial fur for emphasis. If that fails, they might grab the male's genitals as a last-ditch effort.

Males also undergo change during this time, largely in response to the females. They spend more energy trying to get near the females who are sexually active to sniff their rear ends, copulate, and groom with them. Females usually mate with many males, but they also exert choice, denying some males and favoring others. Males do occasionally try to force females to have sex with them but, in most macaque species, have little luck (females who really do not want to have sex either sit down or walk away). During this time there are also a lot of scuffles between males, as many of them try to gain access to the same female, sometimes disregarding the established social hierarchies. Sex, or the possibility of it, often influences macaques to rebel against the established social norms.

But not all macaque sex happens exclusively in those mating periods or in reproductive contexts. Younger males will sometimes hang out with one another and manipulate one another's genitals, sometimes mounting one another, and occasionally copulating. Adult females, especially in certain macaque species (like the Japanese macaque), will also participate in homosexual sexual activity, mounting one another and behaving like they do when copulating with males. Males also masturbate, sometimes often, and occasionally females do as well, but not nearly as much. Most important, aspects of sexual behavior like mounting and touching and massaging of genitals show up in a lot of noncopulatory situations—after fights, in moments of stress, and sometimes in quiet moments between two good friends. Macaques use aspects of sexual behavior as part of their social networking, not just for reproduction.

Chimpanzees have even more complicated sexual lives than macaques. Female chimpanzees have large swellings around their genitals that peak during ovulation, indicating their fertility status. Needless to say, male chimpanzees, especially high-ranking ones, take this very seriously and spend a lot of time next to those females, copulating frequently with them or at least giving it the college try. Chimpanzee females do not always want to copulate with those males. In the eastern chimpanzees, this reluctance can result in a lot of fighting. Males will attack females, sometimes ganging up on them in efforts to coerce them into sex. Other times, the male and female not only want to be together, but will actually leave the other members of the community behind and go spend up to a few days together, feeding, grooming, and having lots of sex, just the two of them.

Outside of these mating contexts, chimps use a lot of social sex. Males, especially those who are good friends and allies, often seek each other out during times of stress and fondle one another's genitals as a bonding and stress-reducing behavior. Females also engage in some homosexual touching interactions. Sex in chimpanzees, like in macaques, can be a social tool.

Bonobos (the chimpanzee species *Pan paniscus*) are the apes that have lots of sex. Bonobos are chimpanzees, so they have the same types of swellings and issues around sex that other chimps do. However, there are several differences. Females are usually dominant to males, so no males are able to coerce females into having sex, but in bonobos it is rare that they would have to. In bonobo society males and females of all ages use sexual activity (homosexual and heterosexual) as a social tool. When they see each other after a long absence, they have a brief bout of sex by way of a greeting. When they fight over a big chunk of fruit, they will often resolve the conflict by having sex. Bonobos use sexual activity as a type of social glue. This does not mean that they always have sex, that they don't fight, or that sex is all they do. However, bonobos are at the high end of the nonhuman primates as far as frequency of sexual activity.

Human females do not have the swelling around the genitals like some of the other primates, nor do they have specific mating cycles or massive behavioral shifts like we see in macaque females. Human females, like all mammals, have menstrual cycles but typically have a larger blood flow associated with the cycle than other mammals. Both males and females, if in good health, are capable of sexual activity year-round. Humans, like other primates, seek one another out for sexual activity and have lots of social sex. But here is where many of the similarities cease.

Our sexuality is tied to the societies we live in; the rules and laws and belief systems we participate in; the partnerships, bonds, and alliances we form, rupture, and create anew. Humans are the only mammalian species we know of where a percentage of the species has a consistent homosexual sexual orientation, and we are the only species to take vows of chastity (and sometimes maintain them). We are very rare among primates in that we often form long-term bonds between two individuals that can be related to sex and reproduction. We are unique in having sets of symbolic associations between sex, age, ethics, morality, and behavior: For humans, when, how, where, and with whom we have sex matters a great deal, not just to the individuals having sex but to their communities and the society as a whole. Humans have an enormous range of sexual tastes, desires, and habits, many of which veer very, very far from anything having to do with reproduction. Humans have taken the basic mammalian package associated with sex, and the primate twists on that package, and created a whole new way to have, think about, represent, regulate, and embody sex.

To understand how we got so creative with sex, there are three main aspects of the human story to understand: parenting and bonding, gender, and the fact that for humans, sex is never just sex.

Creative Parenting

No sexually reproducing species survives without a good parenting plan. Ensuring that one's offspring make it into adulthood (or to a point where they can fend for themselves) is a critical aspect of the social lives of mammals. In most cases it is the mom who does the bulk of this work.

But, as we noted earlier in the book, in many highly social mammals, including many primates, having allomothers—group members aside from Mom helping raise the young—is common. These extra caretakers aren't always just other females; in fact, our ancestors created a whole community of caretakers.

If we venture back to the early Pleistocene, about 1.5 million years ago, and focus on a group of human ancestors, we would see that their solution to the "baby problem" (remember chapter 5) is a group caretaking endeavor that the anthropologist Sarah Hrdy calls "mothers and others." In a group of fifteen or twenty early *Homo* there might be two or three infants. These infants would not be exclusively carried and cared for by their mother. Rather, they'd make the rounds, being held, carried, and attended to by other members, young and old, of the group. This holding of infants is simultaneous with their moving across the landscape, locating stone sources, making tools, and carrying them. This caretaking strategy is also happening right alongside their power scavenging of kills by saber-toothed cats, hyenas, and other big carnivores and carrying chunks of meat to safer locations (and avoiding other large predators).

Imagine what this group looked like at the end of the day moving to their safe sleeping places along the cliffs of a small ravine: All twenty or so would be spread across about forty or fifty feet. A few adults and teenagers in front and back would carry sharpened stone flakes or a sturdy piece of wood. But most of the group would be carrying armloads of stones or chunks of meat or clusters of fruit or tubers. A few would have infants on their sides or cradled in front of them. Once they got to the sleeping site, the infants would be passed to the mothers and nursed. Afterward the moms might hold on to them while the group shared the food, and many other members would coo at the infants and maybe groom them while they nestled in Mom's arms. Or maybe older siblings or other group members would take the infants while the moms socialized and even moved away from the group to spend some "alone time" with certain group members.

The bottom line is that many, if not all, of the members of these early *Homo* groups likely took on substantial aspects of the care and development of children. This system of multiple caretakers enabled the mothers to participate in many of the group activities. In chapter 5 I noted that some researchers argue that this shared caretaking role is one of the reasons that human females, unlike all other primates, undergo menopause, where females live long after their reproductive cycling shuts down. It's clear that groups of early *Homo,* from at least *Homo erectus* on, began to coordinate different actions, responsibilities, even roles, with one another in order to contribute to the survival of the infants as they built that particular niche that we call the human community.

What does this have to do with sex? Early *Homo* began the practice that we still see extensively today, of separating reproduction and sex. By developing a community approach to parenting, our genus was able to set up a system wherein larger-brained and more helpless infants were possible. Such developments would not have been possible if the standard mammalian pattern of Mom alone raising the kids held. Human children are basically helpless for years. The only way to enable such a system is to share the parenting responsibilities across multiple individuals. But such sharing also means that the biology of reproduction, and thus that of sex, is not limited in the way it is for most mammals. Because of the costs of reproducing, most mammals have a limit on sexual activity: The system turns on and off appropriately. Humans, on the other hand, are essentially capable of sex all the time. So the system of communal parenting, of mothers and others, removed the necessary link between sex and parenting. Obviously, the two remain tied—no sex = no offspring—but the limits on sexual behavior tied to the high costs of raising young were relaxed.

This brings us to the flip side of this system. Sex can happen more often, and because we as primates have a basal pattern of at least some social sex, our ancestors were able to ratchet up that pattern and make sex a regular and important part of the social landscape. But having sex as a regular part of the social agenda presents two interesting quandaries:

1. Humans don't have sex all the time and they don't have sex with just anyone.
2. We are quite particular about sex and tend to form long-term and very strong sexual relationships with one or a few individuals across our lifetimes. In fact, a large number of humans are relatively monogamous (most of the time).

Today we place great emphasis on building pair-bonds and the system of legal and religious agreements we call marriage. How did that arise from a lineage practicing communal parenting and frequent social sex?

For most of the past fifty years the standard line for the evolution of human monogamy and marriage has been as follows: Human infants are costly, so human females need help raising them. Over the course of the evolution of the genus *Homo,* females needed to find ways to buck the basic mammalian pattern of dads leaving moms to do all the caretaking work. As such, they evolved a hidden ovulation (no external signs, like perigenital swellings and such) and had sex with multiple males to confuse paternity. The lack of overt ovulation signals made males unsure of their possible reproductive success and so they spent more time trying to be with a female as long, and as exclusively, as possible to guarantee paternity. Females then chose those males who contributed to parenting, or at least protected them and provided them with food and other goodies to assist in the raising of the offspring. This pattern, over evolutionary time, gave rise to the pattern of pair-bonding and relatively common monogamy we see today in humans.

Nice story, but it's wrong.

We know that most primates don't have big signals of their ovulation, only a few do, so nothing new there in humans. We also know that communal parenting had to be early on in the evolution of the genus *Homo.* Otherwise those helpless, increasingly large-brained infants would not have survived. So the image of early *Homo* moms all by themselves trying to land that one ideal male is not accurate. We also have good evidence that from early on, sharing of food, predator defense, toolmaking, and other key aspects of life were central to the success of our genus. Otherwise these fangless, clawless, small, and pretty unthreatening little hominins would not have persisted and become us (remember chapters 2 through 5). So the idea of an early *Homo* female waiting for a single male to provision her with the nutrition and support needed to raise their kids is not supported.

Also, a pair-bond is a strong and deep long-term social relationship and may, or may not, involve a sexual relationship. Pair-bonds are not necessarily associated with marriage or with monogamy or even with the production of children, but they can be. There are many reasons why the myth of the nuclear family (man, woman, and their kids) as being deep in our history is strong, but that does not make it true.

Only about 3 percent of all mammalian species are monogamous. There are a cluster of primate species that live in small groups made up of one female, one male, plus young, and pair-bonds come in a number of different types across primates. But pair-bonds do not equal monogamy. In fact, it's clear that there are two types of pair-bonds: social pair-bonds and sexual pair-bonds.

A social pair-bond is strong and different in physiological and emotional terms from other friendships. A sexual pair-bond is a pair-bond that has a sexual attraction component such that the members of the sexual pair-bond prefer to mate with each other over other mating options. In many mammals pair-bonds develop and are maintained via social behavior combined with the physiology of neurotransmitters and the hormones oxytocin, vasopressin, dopamine, corticosterone, and others. In the few mammals where the biology of pair-bonds has been studied, social and sexual pair-bonds are often interconnected, but in humans this is not the case. Humans have diverse types of sexual pair-bonds, probably more than any other species. Humans also have social pair-bonds with relatives and close friends, with same-sex individuals and different-sex individuals, individuals of the same age and individuals of different ages. Humans are also distinctive among most mammals in having sexual pair-bonds both heterosexually and homosexually.

Pair-bonds, with or without sex, are not the same as marriage and are not necessarily connected to monogamy: They don't explain marriage and the nuclear family. Pair-bonds, both social and sexual, in humans are part of the complex cooperative and collaborative networks that emerged as a core pattern in human evolution. Of course pair-bonds can involve sexual attachments and are at the root of what we experience with romantic love.

There is an extensive body of research looking into the history and structure of marriage systems throughout the world. Basically, anthropologists, historians, and sociologists agree that, in general, marriage (in both secular and religious systems) is best seen as a way of structuring the inheritance of property, as control and regulation of sexual activity, and recently, as the culturally sanctioned outcome of romantic love. This is also an important way in which cultures can officially recognize and sanction sexual pair-bonds and the resulting offspring.

The idea that romantic love and marriage are connected and that marriage is the ultimate outcome for a couple in love began to emerge in the sixteenth century; it spread rapidly across much of the Western world and now extends over much of the globe. However, in many societies still today, there is no necessary connection between romantic love and marriage. While most people would identify marriage as a natural goal for humans and would also equate monogamy and marriage, there are substantial differences separating marriage, mating, and sexual activity. While long-term monogamy is rare among animals and is not the only mating pattern in humans, it is the expected cultural norm in many human societies. Why?

In thinking about this topic we often miss the key point that marriage is not necessarily about pair-bonds. Rather, it is an outcome of human creativity in dealing with the complexities introduced by the evolutionarily recent innovations of property, inequality, towns, cities, gender, and importantly, organized religion. For example, in Europe until the 1500s most marriages were based on verbal agreements between the participants (and/or their families) and not necessarily sanctioned by any religious organization. Modern Western forms of legal marriage have early roots in Roman common law regarding property and inheritance but were not officially or legally sanctioned until more recently. It was not until the sixteenth century that the Roman Catholic Church officially required marriage to be sanctioned by a priest, and it is around this same time that nonreligious official marriage registries emerged in Europe. The husband-wife relationship that is the mainstay of modern Western marriage was famously promulgated by the Protestant theologian Martin Luther. Luther, after forty years of celibacy, turned into a vehement proponent of the nuclear family and husband-wife structure that now typifies much of the world. The system spread and grew markedly in the sixteenth century, with the state playing a more significant role. Legal systems became active in structuring and regulating marriage at the same time that more options for property ownership, small business practices, and government by representation became increasingly common. The marriage systems we see today are part and parcel of the emergence of the modern political nation-state over the last four centuries. Sanctioning of offspring in regard to ownership, inheritance, and social hierarchy has become a very important aspect of the human niche.

Understanding parenting, pair-bonding, and even marriage helps us understand a bit about sex, but not much about sexuality. How, why, and whom we have sex with, aside from reproduction and some social bonding, are not really explained by realizing that humans pair-bond a lot and are communal caretakers. But understanding gender can help us get a bit deeper into the landscape in which human sexuality operates.

Creating Gender

Most people, and many researchers, use the words *gender* and *sex* interchangeably. Which is a mistake.

Looking across a crowded room, one can usually pick out the males and the females. We like to think that we use good biological characteristics, such as body shape, presence of breasts, and face and head form, to do so. But we don't. We primarily use details like clothing, hair and makeup styles, posture, ways of speaking and walking, and how people "hold" themselves. For humans, gender is what matters. *Gender* refers to the social, cultural, and psychological constructions that are imposed on the biological differences of sex. Unlike all other sexually reproducing organisms, we embed the fact of biological sex into a complex web of gender. It's never just about our sex. Sex is biology, male or female, based on chromosomes and whether or not one produces a sperm or an egg. Gender is much more than biology. The formation of gender is the process by which males and females develop the expected psychological and behavioral characteristics that equip them for the tasks that their sex typically performs in the societies in which they grow up.

We tend to think of gender as binary—male or female—but it does not work like that. In most but not all societies, there's more of a spectrum between masculine and feminine. At one extreme we have total femininity and at the other end total masculinity, with most people falling in between those points. In our society, we expect sex-females to fall largely toward the behaviorally feminine side and sex-males to be mostly toward the masculine side. Behaviors we culturally associate with masculinity, such as assertiveness, aggression, and intense interest in athletics, are seen as normal for the male sex. So when women exhibit these behaviors, we see them as behaving like men on the gender spectrum.

The gender roles of any given society reflect a division where sex-females are expected to fill particular roles and sex-males other ones. There is usually a good deal of overlap, but the expectations of difference are telling. This is especially true for important social behavior. For example, in US society the male is supposed to propose marriage to the female, or when it comes to public displays of sympathetic emotion, females can cry at a sad movie, but men are supposed to be stoic and comfort the females. Gender is prominent in the way we divide up society's roles as well. Think of jobs we consider female (secretaries, librarians, nurses) and those we think of as male (construction workers, business managers, airline pilots). What do you imagine when you picture each one of those jobs? There are many jobs in which both sexes participate, but we see them through gender-based filters due to our deeply gendered lives and expectations. Picture a lawyer; now picture a female lawyer and now a male lawyer. In the first and third instances most likely you pictured a man, and in the second a woman. But are they dressed the same? What about hair and accessories? What are they carrying and what kind of shoes do they have on? How would you expect them to behave in the courtroom? The point is that we have specific expectations of how the genders should look and act and what roles they should fill in society. This pattern of expectations is a central part of all human cultures, but the specifics of gender are not always the same.

In regard to sex, we expect one partner in a sexual relationship to act feminine and one to act masculine; we expect gender complementarity in sexual interactions. Same-sex couples may challenge social expectations because so many of us tightly associate gender with biological sex and expect behavior to follow gendered assumptions about heterosexual reproductive patterns, even when many in our species don't.

Our views of such divergent, and necessarily complementary, roles and expectations for gender cloud our ability to actually see that genders are not nearly as different as we think.

The psychologist Janet Shibley Hyde proposed the gender similarities hypothesis more than a decade ago. This hypothesis holds that males and females are similar on most, but not all, psychological variables. That is, men and women, as well as boys and girls, are more alike than they are different. And the hypothesis is supported by the available data.

A combination of the most recent overviews of gender similarities and differences in the psychological literature reveals massive similarity, much more than most people think. And there are some small but important differences. Unfortunately, most of the data we are working with come from modern Western nations (North America and Europe), and although there are some multinational studies, we do have a more limited true understanding of species-wide gender patterns. We have to be careful interpreting these data because gender patterns that characterize the developed "West" today are the main ones that emerge in these analyses and may not reflect accurately the patterns for our whole species. Having said that, there are some key gender differences that emerge across all tests, such as muscle size and strength, throwing ability, and a few other anatomical differences, basically those tied to biological sex. But we already know about size dimorphism and such; it's very deep in the history of our genus. It is the few psychological variables that show up as differences between males and females (as genders) that are more enticing. There are differences in impulsiveness (males exhibit more), the people/things dimension (females report being more drawn to the social and males to the material), and sexuality (males report higher sex drives, higher interests in pornography, and more likelihood of committing sexual violence) that are far more interesting.

Gender matters because it's a core part of the social fabric in which all humans develop the way they see and interpret the world. Gender also matters because it shapes our biology, even at the level of our brains. Substantial research demonstrates that there are very limited biological structural differences between male and female brains. In fact, there is much more variation across all human brains than there is between male and female ones, so research into brain variation is often best done not on the male versus female level but at the level of variation among individuals and in populations. We can identify some patterns of difference between adult male and adult female brains that appear to be rooted in biological sex differences, but they are very nuanced and usually represented by changes in densities of neurons or patterns of connectivity between very specific small areas of the brain. If one held a brain in one's hand, there would be no way to tell for sure if it was male or female by just looking at it. In children, it is very difficult to find any differences in the functioning or structure of male and female brains. But here's the surprise: There are patterns in adult brain function that help you to sort them by gender. As a human develops, the patterns of connections the brain develops are influenced by the individual's experience as he or she acquires gender. The process by which humans acquire gender shapes our neurobiology.

Our gender shapes our experiences and expectations, which in turn shape our behavior and bodies, in regard to sexuality and more. But the gender differences we see now are those of humans today. What about in the past? When and how do we see gender in human evolutionary history?

Excavating Gender

Differences in body size and costly infants are the only clues we have to possible gender differences in our human ancestors between about 2 million and about 50,000 years ago.

In the early hominin, pre-*Homo* fossils, males tend to be larger than females. That pattern (called *sexual dimorphism*) gets reduced a bit in our own lineage, but males of our genus are still, on average, about 10 to 15 percent larger than females. That means we can assume males had slightly higher muscle mass and density and greater upper-body strength than females (as they often do today). We can also assume that females might have been constrained in their activity at the very end of pregnancy (the ninth month or so) and by the need to be able to breast-feed the infants often in the first year or so of their lives. That means, like today, the energy needs of a female go up at the very end of pregnancy and in the earliest part of infant care, and that the female and the infant need to be near each other most of the time in the early part of the infant's life. The anthropologist Leslie Aiello and colleagues demonstrated that this uptick in energetic costs for female *Homo* started around 1.5 to 2 million years ago and, as we discussed in earlier chapters, pushed our ancestors to get more creative with the kinds of foods they acquired and how they processed them and to develop more cooperative parenting options.

That's it. Males are a bit stronger and bigger (on average), and females have some specific constraints due to our big-brained, costly infants. Nothing else in the fossil or archeological record before about 30,000 to 50,000 years ago gives us any real clues to gender.

But what about hunting? Males are bigger, so we should expect that they were the hunters and females stayed back at base camp waiting to process the food, right? Wrong. Early members of the genus *Homo* were power scavengers long before they were hunters, and there is no reason to expect differences in scavenging ability based on small differences in body size or sex. Plus, we have good evidence that it was cooperation by the whole group that enabled successful power scavenging. The earliest hunting is of small game, so the small differences in size are not important or constraining. The earliest evidence of a kind of hunting that involves heavy upper-body strength, like the use of handheld spears to stab the prey, is at around 300,000 years ago, but the evidence that is available (not much) suggests that both males and females participated in hunts (both sexes were a lot more robust than either is today). We do not see good fossil or archeological evidence of gendered hunting differences until relatively recent times (the last 10,000 to 20,000 years or so).

We do have some evidence that while males and females hunted together, they may have differed in their roles in the posthunt processing of foods and hides. We know that earlier humans, especially the Neanderthals, used their teeth extensively as part of their tool kit. A recent overview of Neanderthal teeth from three different sites and of both males and females shows there were slightly different wear patterns between the sexes and that tooth chipping happened for males more on the upper teeth and for females more on the lower teeth. While this is not much to go on, it suggests that males and females were doing slightly different things with their teeth in the processing of meat and hides. What these differences could be is hard to determine, but the fact that the patterns are there in the fossil teeth suggests that gender roles differed. They just weren't the same gender differences we see today.

As for toolmaking, that's a different story. Picture an early *Homo* group making stone tools—striking the hammer stone on a cobble, sending flakes flying, and shaping a beautiful hand ax. Who did you picture doing the actual toolmaking? Probably a male. Almost all depictions of stone toolmaking we see in books, on the web, or in museums have males doing the toolmaking—and they are probably 50 percent right. The other 50 percent were female. There is absolutely no evidence to suggest that toolmaking for nearly the entire 2-million-year history of our genus was gender biased. None. Every bit of information we have about the tools, how they were made and used, suggests that there is no sex or gender pattern at all. The modern gender assumptions about men and tools and men and hunting are really, really recent. But why?

We impose our current perceptions of how the world is onto the past. Think of all the books we read growing up, the television shows we watched and the stories we were told. Why is Tarzan the toolmaker and hunter in the jungle, not Jane? Why does nearly every image of cavemen include males holding clubs or stone tools and women holding babies? Representations of the deep past almost always have men doing the things we associate with masculinity (toolmaking and hunting) and women doing the feminine things (cooking and caring for young) because that is the way we see the world (or expect it to be). We assume that men do the tool-related work (mechanics, plumbers, carpenters) because they are better at it than women. This is a gender assumption, not a biological or social fact. For hundreds of pages I have reviewed the data that demonstrate that both males and females were involved in toolmaking, most hunting (except for maybe the largest-game hunting), and infant caretaking. Most men have greater upper-body strength than most women, but they are not intrinsically more skilled at tool-based labor. During 1940–1945 (World War II) in the United States and Europe, hundreds of thousands of women took over the labor and construction jobs of the men who went off to war. And they did so amazingly well. Our modern experience of gender roles emerged hand in hand with the changes in our societies, religions, and economies over the last four to five centuries that have increasingly favored greater role differentiation between males and females. Our gendered lives make it difficult to see the past as different from today, regardless of the data.

Art is another area where the re-creations show us men painting caves and carving figurines. Here we have very little evidence of any gendered patterns, except one recent survey of cave art. One of the most common forms of cave art is that of the outline of a hand. Starting about 40,000 years ago, humans would venture into caves and rock shelters, chew some pigments and berries to create a paint, and place their hands on the cave wall. They'd spit the pigment across their hands, and when they pulled their hands away the outline of their hands remained, stenciled onto the rock. These are among the earliest evidence of painting we have, and they continue right through the modern day. These works of art are beneficial for our quest to see sex and/or gender in the past, as hands are parts of our physical bodies and they reflect dimorphism (size differences) of both sex and age. The archeologist Dean Snow looked at thirty-two of these hand images from eight different cave art sites. He calculated whether the hands were most likely male or female, those of adults or of youths. Twenty-four of the thirty-two were female. Seventy-five percent of the hand stencils were done by females, and five of the eight male hands appeared to be those of teenage boys: Women and children were doing most of the hand stencils, at least in parts of Europe between about 35,000 and 15,000 years ago. However, it is not at all clear what this tells us about gender in the broader sense.

We have very little evidence of gender roles in the deep past, and even when we do, they rarely correspond to our assumptions about gender today. By more recent times, the last 10,000 to 15,000 years or so, especially after the advent of agriculture and settlements but including more recent forager peoples, gender roles become clearer. We start to see differences in the bone and tooth chemistry between males and females, suggesting slight differences in nutritional status; we also start to see differences in the muscle scars and wear marks on the bones, suggesting slightly different lifestyles or work patterns. And we also see an uptick in the birth rates, suggesting that women were spending more time being pregnant and in the early infancy caretaking and feeding roles. All of these patterns could be reflecting gender. Grave goods and burial patterns also start to show some status and gender differences around this same time (in some cases males and females are buried with different items). As we noted in previous chapters, heightened social and material complexity, inequality, and gender all start showing up hand in hand in this most recent phase of human evolution. Males and females always overlap a lot, but the closer in time we come to the present, the more we see evident differences in their roles in the acquisition and processing of food, in the caretaking of young, in the production of art, in the social hierarchies of societies, and in their sexuality.

And it is now, having a good idea of what sex and gender look like in the human past, that we can turn to the very interesting, admittedly speculative, and yet surprisingly creative evolution of human sexuality.

Ordinary, Everyday Creative Sexuality

Deep in our primate lineage, sexual activity expanded slightly beyond an exclusive allegiance to reproduction. Social sex became an important part of social interaction in our apelike ancestors and likely even more so in our recent hominin ancestors. Human bodies evolved to be physiologically capable of engaging in sex year-round and across most of their lives. Humans developed caretaking systems that lessened the constraints imposed by the energetic costs of reproduction. We evolved a system that freed sex from a direct link to physiology and parenting and enabled its use more broadly as a social tool. Then we got really creative.

Humans evolved the capacity to form tight and lasting bonds between individuals that create physiological and emotional ties that are forged, broken, and remade in part via sexual activity. Humans created gender, where males and females adopted differing roles in society and the concomitant expectations for how to behave. Gender created a complexity in how, with whom, and when humans have sex. Today sexual activity, or even the possibility of sexual activity, can be about pleasure, politics, power, or even just fun. The bottom line is that humans don't just have sex; they have "sexuality."

The biologist Anne Fausto-Sterling tells us that "sexuality is a somatic fact created by cultural effect"; our bodies and desires are shaped by our distinctively human creativity. Day to day, or perhaps night to night, humans have a hand in creating their sexual landscape.

Our desires, attractions, and passions for engaging in sexual activity are the most dynamic in the animal kingdom. Humans can be physically attracted to one sex, both sexes, or one or both genders, and can even alternate back and forth. We are the only mammals we know of that have a consistent percentage of individuals who have exclusive same-sex attractions across the species. Humans also develop preferences for specific traits that activate their sexual desire: blondes, brunettes, humorous partners, reckless bad boys/girls, romantic gestures, patent leather heels, washboard abs, and on and on. To top it off, humans have all sorts of consensual sexual activity beyond genital stimulation. We hold hands, flirt, kiss, fondle, hug, massage, spank, tie up, and engage in all sorts of other sexual interactions that do not involve genitals. The dark side to this dynamism is the fact that we also have all sorts of nonconsensual violent and coercive sexual activity, using sex to abuse, coerce, torture, and demoralize.

Many researchers have tried to simplify this amazingly complex human sexuality to equate it with the sexual system of other mammals. They argue that all the diversity in sexuality is just a covering for the underlying basic mammalian evolutionary patterns of trying to get as many copies of your DNA into the next generation as possible. For females, the pattern is wanting to successfully raise costly young by getting good males to "stand by" them or at least invest in them and their offsprings' support. For males the pattern is wanting to inseminate as many females as possible to get their DNA into the next generation. Most of these researchers will agree that humans have added a lot of complexity, but they steadfastly stick to this paradigm of evolutionary pressures as the best basis for understanding human sexuality.

This traditional argument matches the commonly held popular assumptions about human sexuality and relationships: Our bodies are wired to find mates. Following this line of reasoning, once the best biological mate is found, the brain and hormones kick in to create a particular kind of attachment drive that leads to the monogamous pair-bond (which may or may not last), offspring, and the nuclear family unit—a man, a woman, and their children. When one finds her or his perfect mate, the evolved chemical cascade will lead one toward a pair-bond relationship. Most then argue that the bonded male-female pair (with offspring) is the evolved, or natural, unit of the human family; that marriage is part of human nature; and that there is a specific pair-bond partner out there for everyone. Moving songs and stories continue to perpetuate this perspective.

Other evolutionary biologists and anthropologists have challenged this perspective and offered another extreme, that males and females are naturally at odds, with males wanting to have as many sexual encounters as possible and females usually only wanting good (or potentially good) fathers. A lot of assumptions about the whys and hows of male and female sexuality accompany these views.

However, there is no robust anthropological, biological, or psychological support for either of these positions. They are too simple and do not jibe with what we know about human evolution. Over the last 1.5 million years or so, the genus *Homo* developed a parenting system that radically shifted the costs from a single female to a wider range of individuals. Such a system makes the argument that a female is focused on getting one good male for paternal investment not relevant. There is almost no evidence for the nuclear family as the core residence and social unit in the archeological record until very, very recently (sometime between the last few thousand years and the last few centuries). While there is substantial evolutionary evidence that humans do seek pair-bonds (socially and physiologically), these bonds do not necessarily involve sex, marriage, exclusivity, or even heterosexuality. So the assumption that human pair-bond sex reflects the basic evolutionary goal of reproduction is too narrow. Finally, these traditional explanations avoid the issue of gender altogether.

Humans have created a set of expectations for how people should behave based on cultural assumptions about their biological sex. But these assumptions often rely on incorrect or at least overgeneralized notions about what being male or female means biologically. And because of this, many humans feel at odds with their culture's gender assumptions. This is not to say that all connections between gender and sex are wrong—they are not—it is just to note that over time, gender roles and patterns change, much more rapidly and widely than the actual biology of being male or female. That means gender is not a static thing; it changes just like all other cultural patterns and processes. Thus, the sexuality associated with one's gender will, like just about everything else, change across time.

To top it all off, humans are strange-looking mammals with an amazing creative capacity for imagination and symbol. In addition to all the complexities that our parenting, pair-bonding, and gender systems bring to sexuality, we also take aspects of the human body and connect them to our sexuality. For example, recently in many societies (initially Western ones, but now spreading), female breasts have been strongly associated with sexuality, and entire subcultures of attraction, and politics, are built up around them. There is even a whole area of surgery devoted to altering breast size and shape in regard to social patterns. In a purely biological sense, this is bizarre, given that breasts are primarily associated with lactation and feeding of infants, but in humans, due to our standing upright and fatty deposits around them, breasts stand out much more than in any other animals. During sexual arousal, breasts can become highly sensitive due to the ring of nerve tissue around the nipple (there due to the feedback system developed for breast-feeding), and thus for many women their breasts can play a part in heightening the physical enjoyment of sexual activity. But so can hands, neck, groin, feet, and many of the other parts of the body that have clusters of highly sensitive nerves; indeed, much of the skin covering our bodies fits that category.

It is partially due to their being a major visible component of female anatomy that breasts have received so much attention. Some researchers have argued that this is an evolved sexual signal giving men information about a female's sexual state . . . an absurd notion. What signal do breasts send? There is no correlation between breast size or shape and the ability to lactate, so merely having breasts basically lets everyone know that the female human has mammary glands and can lactate. Others argue that breasts signal the onset of the capacity to become pregnant, which may be true, as females' breasts develop at puberty, but once they are present, there is nothing more to signal . . . so why post-puberty should there be so much attention on breasts and their size and shape? This weird focus on breasts emerges because some cultures have created an association with this part of female anatomy and what we call desire. Desire is a strong longing or sense of want and hope for acquiring someone or something. Much in contemporary human sexuality is built around desire.

This web of desires is part of human cultural diversity. For as many societies that see the breast as sexually attractive, there are others that do not. The ancient Greeks, for example, spent a lot of their time thinking about the penis (what they called the *phallos*), which also seems to have come back in vogue in the United States of late (at least as measured by penis jokes in films and the constant barrage of penis- and erectile-enhancement advertisements). Some societies cover most of the body, seeing the show of skin as sexual, and others cover almost none, seeing little sexuality in simple exposed flesh. Some see sexual activity of all types as normal for youngsters but mandate that once an individual becomes an adult he or she must limit himself/herself to only certain types of sexual behavior. We have co-opted many parts of the body, many types of clothing and adornment, and many behaviors into this web of desire, and we've also created a whole landscape of sexuality in which to place it. Human societies even categorize different types of sexual activity as different things. Some label genital-genital contact as sex and other types of sexual activity as something else. Others label all heterosexual touching as sexual. Some are accepting about the wide range of human sexual attraction and activities, and others are harshly against anything but reproductive heterosexual intercourse. There is no one pattern that characterizes all human societies when it comes to their views, politics, and expression of sexual behavior.

Once we throw together gender, language, cultural diversity, and the human body, we create a template for human sexuality that is wide open to innovation, to alteration, and to limitation. Human sexuality is not fixed to reproductive sex, so we can exploit the physical sensations associated with sex in a variety of ways—for fun. This enables humans to make sex a part of many different aspects of daily life and manipulate that sexuality for social, political, and even economic ends. How much retail activity has nothing to do with sexuality? From shampoo and yogurt to clothing and cars, advertisements and packaging stimulate desires that have little to do with the products' practical use.

Sex can help us create amazingly close connections. But it can also be used to break those connections; sexual closeness, jealousy, trust, and betrayal are powerful aspects of the human experience. Sexual activity itself can then become a symbol for many things, used in both positive and negative ways. On the worst end of this continuum, sexuality and desire can be used as a tool of power to control females or males, to abuse them and to coerce them. On the better end, sexuality can be used as a way to facilitate openness and trust via acceptance of the diverse range of human experiences. Most contemporary societies fall somewhere in between these extremes.

Without a time machine, we have no exact way of knowing how our ancestors behaved sexually. But we know what humans do today, and we have bits of evidence from our bodies and the record of our evolution that help us assemble a good outline. As the scientist Rebecca Jordan-Young says, "we are not blank slates, but we are also not pink and blue notepads." Our brains are not made "male" or "female" but develop via interactions between the external world and our own sensory apparatus; our bodily systems show important differences between the sexes, but they are more similar than they are different. Gendered behavior and gender relations change over time as our social and structural contexts shift; our worldviews and experiences change accordingly. As a species we've created human sexuality, and the interplay between our creativity and the way we shape the world as it shapes us is a dynamic and ongoing process. A take-home message about the creativity inherent in sexuality is that it is essentially collaborative. Even if one does it on one's own, others will loom large in one's imagination. As with all creativity, it takes more than one to do it best.

In the next three chapters we expand on this imagination and collaboration via a focus on three of the most distinctive ways human creativity went beyond our everyday world to grasp the ineffable, the transcendent, the cosmological. It's no exaggeration to say religion, art, and science created the universe humans now perceive.

PART FOUR

THE GREAT WORKS

How Humans Made the Universe

RELIGIOUS FOUNDATIONS

Religion is a profound part of the human experience. Few would dispute that religious belief has defined core parts of the human existential universe for millennia. Some argue it does so better than anything else.

There are 5.8 billion people who identify as religiously affiliated around the globe today, which is 83 percent of the world's population of about 7 billion. Religious experience of some sort or another is a daily activity for most human beings, and religion is woven into the societies in which we all live. Many nations see religion as central in their heritage, others have lists of which religions are legal to practice within their borders, and some even try to forbid religions entirely (without much success). Most societies on the planet observe multiple religious holidays and have religious leaders influencing, if not making, governmental policy. In nearly every year of the twenty-first century so far there have been violent religious-affiliated conflicts on five of the seven continents. At the same time, religiously affiliated organizations provide a lion's share of the assistance to the wounded, homeless, and impoverished around the world. In the United States today, 76 percent of the population self-defines as religious, 3 percent as atheist, 4 percent as agnostic, and 17 percent as nothing in particular. Where one falls in that range of affiliation makes a difference to oneself and one's neighbors. In 2016, 42 percent of potential voters polled in the United States stated they would not vote for an atheist for president. Forty percent stated they would not vote for a Muslim.

Humans take their religion seriously.

Just under 4,000 years ago Judaism, the first of the Abrahamic religions, was established in the southeastern Mediterranean region. Shortly after the death of its fabled founder, Jesus, some 2,000 years ago, an offshoot from Judaism began its climb to become the largest organized religion on the planet, Christianity. The last of the three main Abrahamic monotheistic traditions, Islam, emerged about 1,300 years ago as a major component of the lives of those in the Arabian Peninsula and across the southeastern Mediterranean region. Starting nearly 1,000 years ago some Christian and Muslim societies began their expansions, bringing their religions, often forcefully, to new areas of the planet. Conflicts between the three major Abrahamic religions have ebbed and flowed for more than 1,000 years, often taking center stage in much of the world's political landscape.

As recently as 2016 an Islamic offshoot fundamentalist group calling themselves the Islamic State was battling with nations representing all three Abrahamic faiths in the border regions between Iraq, Syria, and Turkey, a leading presidential candidate in the United States was calling for banning Muslims from entering the country, and people of multiple faiths were attentively listening to one particular Christian (the leader of the Catholics, Pope Francis) as he called for peace and tolerance. And this brief overview does not even mention the more than 40 percent of the earth's population who are not part of the three main Abrahamic faiths (most peoples of India and China, for example).

According to the Pew-Templeton Global Religious Futures Project, the current distribution of the world's religions looks like this: There are about 2.2 billion Christians (32 percent of the world's population), 1.6 billion Muslims (23 percent), 1 billion Hindus (15 percent), 500 million Buddhists (7 percent), 405 million people (6 percent) practicing various folk or traditional religions, 14 million Jews (0.2 percent), and an estimated 58 million people (just under 1 percent) belonging to a range of other religions, including Baha'i, Jainism, Sikhism, Shintoism, Taoism, Tenrikyo, Wicca, and Zoroastrianism (and others).

Many people don't realize just how recently formed the current religious landscape is. The majority of the religions practiced today are no older than a few thousand years, and none have clearly identifiable roots older than about 6,000 to 8,000 years ago (Hinduism is the oldest we know of at present). This means that for most of our history as a genus (*Homo*) and as a species (*Homo sapiens*), the world of organized religion, that thing that is so central to humanity's everyday existence today, was either very different or not here at all.

Religion, like so many other parts of the distinctive human existence, evolved over time, and investigating that process is what this chapter is about.

THE WORLD'S RELIGIONS

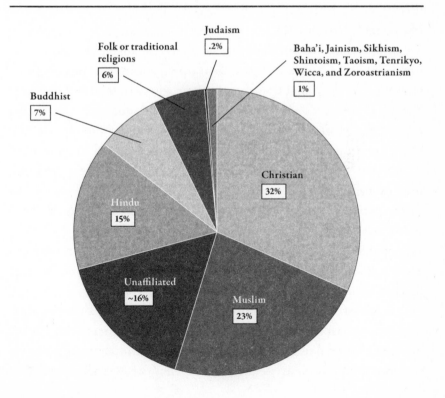

The tricky part in this process is to specifically define what "religion" actually is and to determine what evidence of it would look like in the fossil and archeological record. In the past few thousand years we find churches, temples, written records, icons, and a huge array of art and symbols that point to specific religious traditions, practices, and beliefs. But going back past these, back to the early settlements, back past agriculture and domestication, back into the lives of the foraging peoples of 20,000, 80,000, 300,000, even 800,000 years ago, we want to ask and answer the questions: Where and when did religion show up, and what does it come from?

As you may have guessed, the answers reveal that religion is a uniquely human characteristic and it is possibly one of the most fascinating examples of just how creative our species is.

What Is "Religious"?

Most people refer to themselves as religious, but not everyone agrees on what that means. To call someone "religious" usually means they have a particular set of beliefs in regard to a specific ultimate reality and/or a deity or deities and that these beliefs come with a suite of practices. Today it might mean belonging to an established religion, or not being aligned with a specific religion but believing in a god or gods, or even being someone who accepts a spiritual or transcendental component of life but does not subscribe to a specific set of beliefs. On the other hand, a wide range of people do not believe in the existence of a god or gods but do participate in specific religious traditions, holidays, and rituals (such as "secular Jews" or what are often called "lapsed Catholics"). There is also a cluster of people who are staunchly opposed to the possibility of a god or gods and who maintain an antagonistic relationship with organized religion of any sort (usually called "affirmed atheists").

Regardless of how we classify them, most humans regularly behave as if there were a transcendent or supernatural reality whether they explicitly believe in one or not. People around the world have superstitions connected to everyday behavior, and they display them without considering their origin or validity. Knocking on wood, avoiding the evil eye, carrying a charm for luck, believing certain things about certain dates, particular animals, and appropriate behavior around the dead, are all examples. These actions assume that there is an element of the supernatural at play, even if the assumption is subconscious. The most important and ubiquitous aspect of this human investment in the transcendent is that of wishing and hope.

Wishing and hope reflect the human ability to generate expectations of future outcomes by using more than what is predictable based on one's surroundings or based on what one has experienced. Many species use basic predictability when they decide to search for food, have sex, fight, make up, or perform just about any task in their day-to-day lives. But that is all based on some material reality available to the individuals (like knowledge of where fruit is or the size of an opponent) or experiences they have had (there was fruit in a particular location in the past or they were able to beat this other individual in a fight before). The "hope" and "wishing" that humans do rely on the use of imagination to provide individuals and communities with a justification to undertake risky or unpredictable actions—actions that under normal conditions of predictability could be interpreted as leading to failure, danger, or even death. When a small group of soldiers tries to fend off a larger army, when a team that is down by three scores in the last few minutes of the game rallies, when natural disasters destroy a crop or a village and the community vows to persevere, they all share one thing in common. Hope. Against all odds and evidence they wish—they believe—they can succeed, and thus they try in spite of the material reality laid out in front of them. Other animals might occasionally perform risky or unpredictable behavior, but humans regularly hope and wish for outcomes that seem beyond our capacities, and we try to achieve them, as individuals and as communities. This is a regular part of human existence.

When taking a test or watching a sporting match, most humans have an internal dialogue wherein they hope or wish for a specific outcome, not based on how much they studied or what the statistics tell them about the two opposing teams, but rather as a request to a deity, some supernatural element, or even to nothing in particular, but a hope nonetheless. It's very likely this ability to hope and wish preceded, and formed a baseline for, the capacity to be religious today.

The anthropologist Maurice Bloch, in an article entitled "Why Religion Is Nothing Special but Is Central," points out that one of the most distinctive aspects of humanity is that, over our evolutionary history, we've gone from being transactional beings to being transactional *and* transcendent beings. "Transactional beings" are those whose range of experience is based on interactions between individuals and between groups and their experiences in those interactions. Such beings can have complex lives and dynamic social networks. Macaque monkeys or chimpanzees, for example, with dominance hierarchies, friendships and fights, histories and complex suites of learned behavior necessary to effectively "be" in one's group, are complex, transactional beings. Humans are too. But we also have a transcendent component to our lives. We have roles, rules, and interactions that are based on more than strict experience and material reality; these roles and rules are created by our individual and communal imaginations and made real. Much of what characterizes the roles of "professor" or "priest" or "great-aunt" or "ancestor" comes from more than just the biology of relatedness to your great-aunt, the training or experiences of the priest or professor, or the reality of the life of the individuals you consider ancestors. The rituals we perform and the expectations we have in regard to genders, nations, religions, and economic systems are all part of this package. Humans are both transactional and transcendent beings, and that pattern shows up sometime in our evolutionary history, most likely during the evolution of our own genus, *Homo.* This process is almost certainly tied to the emergence of what we call "religion."

But finding a physical record of religion in the deep past is extremely difficult, if not impossible—first and foremost because we might not know what we are looking for. All of the present religions are recent, so the material things that characterize them are not likely to be found in the deep past. There is an old joke among archeologists that whenever you are digging up a site that is older than 4,000 to 5,000 years and you find an item that does not clearly have a function (such as for cooking, hunting, or storage), then you call the item either "art" or "religious." This comment is sort of tongue in cheek, not to mention a little irresponsible. Much of what we have as far as the material record of religion in human evolution is simply things that don't seem to have any other function, and thus become "religious" by default. This is not particularly good science.

Maurice Bloch points out a second problem when he tells us that "anthropologists have, after countless fruitless attempts, found it impossible to usefully and convincingly cross-culturally isolate or define a distinct phenomenon that can analytically be labelled 'religion.'" It is, even today, challenging to develop one definition that encompasses all known religions. It's easier to identify someone as religious than it is to comprehensively define religion. So defining items and patterns in the past as part of a religion is exceptionally difficult. But it's worth a shot if we are to understand the human creative spark.

The Sense of Identity

Anthropologists Candace Alcorta and Richard Sosis give us a list of four key patterns that appear in most, if not all, practices-and-beliefs sets that we usually call religion.

- First, they argue that religions are characterized by a belief in supernatural agents and counterintuitive concepts. Belief in "supernatural agents" means, as we noted earlier, that humans actively perceive transcendent things, forces, and beings that exist beyond the realm of normally perceivable reality and that these forces or beings are relevant to human life: They can potentially affect us and the natural world in which we exist. Examples of these agents include shamanic trances; spirits and spirit position; angels, demons, and other such beings; and incorporeal god(s) capable of being everywhere and knowing everything. In each of these cases the existence of the supernatural agent(s) disrupts or challenges the "natural" ways we have of perceiving the world, indicating that there is more than the natural world at play in the lives of humans. The belief in supernatural agents also creates the possibility of what Alcorta and Sosis call "counterintuitive concepts," such as talking animals, bleeding statues, virgin births, resurrections, and a range of what one might call "miracles."

- The second characteristic is communal participation in religious ritual. Many animal species perform what we could call ritualized behavior. The dancing and singing of male birds to attract mates, the bared teeth displays in macaque monkeys that signal submission, and the nuzzling and exposing of one's belly as a greeting that wolves do are all ritualized behavior. Human religious ritual follows some of the same structural patterns but differs in two key ways: It relies on symbols, and the rituals themselves act to reinforce or increase the effect of the belief in supernatural agents. A reliance on symbol means that the core items in a religious ritual are not things that, by themselves, out of context, mean anything. The word "God" has a very specific and central meaning to Christians, as does the word "Allah" for Muslims. The sign of the cross, the concept of reincarnation, the drinking of wine as blood and consuming a wafer as flesh, and many other aspects of religious ritual across different religions are all steeped in symbolic actions. The capacity to create symbols and to have them enable connections to the supernatural or transcendent is a distinctively human creative skill.

- The acceptance of the supernatural and a reliance on symbolic ritual lead to the third category: a separation of the sacred and the secular. The anthropologist Roy Rappaport tells us that "ritual does not merely identify that which is sacred; it creates the sacred." Alcorta and Sosis use the example of holy water to demonstrate this. Water when blessed by a priest (a symbolic ritual) becomes a new entity (it is transformed) by that ritual and is imbued with a connection to, or even embodiment of, the supernatural: It becomes sacred. Regular water (secular water) has chemical composition and is used for drinking, washing, and so forth. It is secular and "natural." Holy water has symbolic meaning and transcendent powers and is a separate entity from secular water. There are countless examples of this across all religions. Religious behavior involves connection between humans and the supernatural, and that works only if there is an ability to, at least in some ways, differentiate what is sacred and what is not.

- Finally, Alcorta and Sosis suggest that all of this knowledge—the religious system and the behavior, beliefs, and patterns associated with it—has to be learned. They argue that the key time for this teaching and learning is adolescence.

The historian and former president of the American Academy of Religion Thomas Tweed develops a strong argument that religions label and transform how humans experience emotions and other aspects of life. At the center of most religions is some form of "transformative experience." Tweed discusses how such experiences provide members with the language and framework of meaning that help explain "the way the world is and the way it should be." If this is the case, then the capacity for religious behavior and thought over the course of human evolution has major implications for how humans develop their sense of identity and for how people and groups understand who they are. Religious communities today use symbolic items along with ritual sounds and gestures in building a shared picture of how they see, and experience, the world.

Religions are characterized by a belief in supernatural agents and counterintuitive concepts, involve symbolic ritual that helps develop a shared experience of the world, and cultivate a differentiation of the sacred and the profane, and much in religious systems is transmitted during childhood.

How does this help us when looking back into human evolutionary history?

Evidence of Religious Experience?

It might be argued that direct evidence of such ineffable experience is an impossibility; however, if symbolic ritual is critical to making and maintaining religious meaning, then we can look into the fossil and archeological record and try to identify when material records of symbolic behavior show up. It is evidence that the basic material tools (and the cognitive skills required to make them) for religious experience exist in humans. The presence of symbolic materials in the archeological record act as a marker telling us that religious belief may have been present.

Once we have evidence of symbolic materials, we can look for evidence of ritual behavior that incorporates symbolic items, which could be evidence that religious ritual was occurring. And of course we want to look for evidence of learning (and teaching) focusing on the young as setting up a system wherein transmission of religious behavior and belief could occur. Finally, we'd want to ask when and where we see any firm evidence of a split between sacred and secular in the evolutionary record of the genus *Homo*.

Recently, the biological anthropologist Marc Kissel and I compiled and analyzed a database of all the published examples of items made or shaped by the genus *Homo* that might be considered symbolic between the dates of 2 million and 40,000 years ago. The earliest items date to around 300,000 to 500,000 years ago and include modified bits of ochre (a mineral pigment), a clamshell with a zigzag pattern carved into it by someone using something sharp (the researchers suggested it might have been a shark's tooth), a rock that looks like a person naturally but was then modified with stone tools to look more like a person, and some beads. More items, like bones with carvings on them (including one that looks like a stick figure of a human) and more examples of modified ochre, including the possibility that the ochre was being used as a body pigment, emerge between 200,000 and 300,000 years ago. But between 100,000 and 200,000 years ago items that are likely symbolic become more common (ochre use, shell and stone beads, engraved stones and bones) and between 40,000 and 100,000 years ago they become more diversified and downright complex. Ochre use and all sorts of pigments show up, as do carved ostrich shells, more elaborate figurines, and lots of trinkets that could be interpreted as body ornamentation (necklaces and other strung jewelry, feathers modified to be worn, and modified bone items). In the last 40,000 years of human history, symbolic items become ubiquitous—cave paintings and other graphic art, figurines, bone carvings, and a whole range of items that are undeniably symbolic. What these items symbolized to the people who made them is not so clear.

Are these items religious? I wish I knew.

It's not until the last 10,000 to 20,000 years that we have any contexts that we might be able to reliably identify as possibly religious meaning for any of these items. Hence it is very difficult, if not impossible, to assess what they were used for. For example, there are some amazing paintings that date to nearly 40,000 years ago found in deep caves, completely dark and dangerous to get in and out of. To paint them one human or a group of humans intentionally crawled into the small opening of a dark, dank cave and began to descend. Crawling over sharp rocks and slippery surfaces, with only a gourd full of animal fat smokily lighting the way, these individuals carried a bunch of pigments and took great risks. Once they found the right spot, they spent a long time—hours, maybe days— cramped and sixty feet underground, creating a painting that no one could see unless they performed that exact same awkward and dangerous crawl into the cave with some form of light.

One could easily make an argument that this was a religious ritual, and it would be convincing. Such elaborate activity, with the danger involved, the need for a group of people working together, the likelihood that the images of animals and geometric shapes and human handprints had deep symbolic meaning, and the fact that pretty much no one but the group who did the painting (or whoever they took into the cave) would ever see these things, all seem like good evidence that this fits the key criteria for being something that is transcendent, and maybe even reflects an intentional religious activity. But there is no way to demonstrate if such argument is right or not.

All of these early symbolic (or symbol-like) items tell us that the capacity for symbolic and possibly religious thought and behavior appears at least 300,000 to 500,000 years ago, sporadically across the range of populations of the genus *Homo*. By 100,000 to 200,000 years ago, symbolic materials are found in more places and are more complex when we find them. Symbolic items become common in all human populations over the last 100,000 years. The presence of symbolic items does not tell us when religion emerges (as we now know it), but it does tell us that our ancestors began to develop symbols and to use them for multiple purposes increasingly over the last half million years. Such items today are integral to religious practice and/or involved as part of religious experiences, and thus it is highly likely that certainly by the last 100,000 years we might expect religious capacities to develop into the kinds of religious practices we see today, possibly using the symbolic items we find in the archeological record.

There is another line of evidence as well: the intense cooperation that characterizes our lineage. Two of Alcorta and Sosis's four characteristics of religion (communal ritual and learning during childhood), when combined with the key item mentioned by Tweed, the "transformative experience," point out that we need to perform an intensive kind of communication and collaboration in order to do what we consider religion today. What if a group of early *Homo* had an experience that felt transcendent, that felt outside of the world as they were used to experiencing it—a lunar eclipse, a blood moon, an earthquake, a massive wildfire or flash flood. To coordinate agreement on what the meaning of a particular transformative experience was and to share that sensation with others and then to celebrate it as a group requires a level of shared intentionality (all consciously agreeing on the same cognitive and emotional interpretation) not found (to our knowledge) in other animals. And we know that this capacity has very deep roots in our lineage.

By a million years ago our ancestors were coordinating on power scavenging, cooperative child rearing, and stone toolmaking. Each of these three processes involves some kind of teaching, a lot of flexibility in learning, and considerable group coordination. These processes imply some pretty complex level of information sharing—but not language as we know it. By 300,000 to 500,000 years ago, many groups of *Homo* were using fire, were coordinating hunts, and were making more complex tools of stone and wood. They probably also had something closer to language, possibly a system of gestures and sounds, that helped them convey and exchange more and more information. It is the increasing use and diversification of sounds as part of the communication system that many researchers suggest might be a critical point in the development of the capacity for symbolic behavior. At this time period we start to get a convergence of increasing capacity for cooperation and coordination, improved ability to convey information and sensation (to explain things to one another rather than just showing things to one another), and fire, which gave our ancestors more time at night to work, to process foods and shape tools, and to gather in close space and communicate. They began to communicate about the ideas behind the day-to-day facts of making a living. It's not surprising that at this point in time we see the earliest symbol-like items. Our ancestors began to experiment with making meaning.

Once the process of making meaning had begun, it is not a giant leap to see what we might call "figurative language," a system of sounds and gestures that enables the emergence of metaphor. The use of gestures and sounds to represent something else—an experience, a thought, a hope, or some other facet of the imagination . . . our ancestors were developing the capacity to share what was in their minds, to imagine and to share their imaginings. They were developing the capacity for a central facet of all human lives: the ability to tell stories. This capacity is the last key item needed to set the stage for the emergence of religion.

But what about the sacred versus the secular? That key aspect of Alcorta and Sosis's characteristics of religion does not show up clearly in the evolutionary record until very, very recently. Throughout our history as a genus, even when we have what look to be clearly symbolic items like beads, cave paintings, carved figurines, and the like, we still do not have absolute evidence of any division between the sacred and the secular. Many academics have argued that the cave paintings were such spaces, that the caves were sacred areas and the living spaces were secular areas, but as noted earlier, we have no way to support such a claim (even if it does sound right).

The evidence of burials is one place where we might see this division of sacred and secular, but the patterns of the early burials (or things that we think are burials) are inconsistent, and they are often in the living spaces of the peoples who buried the dead. The two earliest possible burials consist of bodies being deposited in hard-to-reach caverns, one at Sima de Los Huesos in Spain about 400,000 years ago and another associated with the find of *Homo naledi* in South Africa from maybe 1 or 2 million years ago. The one in South Africa has no symbolic items associated with it, but the one in Spain has one finely carved and never-used stone tool associated with the bodies. Some have suggested that this was a tool used as a symbol associated with the burial. Tantalizing possibility, but these two are outliers and there's very little evidence of intentional burials until much more recently. Between 50,000 and 150,000 years ago at sites in Croatia, Israel, France, and Iraq, we find intentional burials in which the dead were interned in pits or depressions, often in the same spaces where people were living. These burials often had items such as antlers, shells, and sometimes stones placed over the bodies or parts of the bodies. But again, these are few examples and burials are not ubiquitous at all sites where we find members of our genus, even as recently at 50,000 years ago. It is not until the last 10,000 to 14,000 years ago that we find burials regularly at archeological sites and sometimes clustered separate from living spaces (the first graveyards).

By the time we see early villages and towns (starting around 8,000 to 14,000 years ago), however, we see direct evidence that items are being used in symbolic ways, reflecting a religious ritual or function. But still they are often in the living spaces. At early town sites like Çatalhöyük (about 8,000 to 9,000 years ago) in what is today Turkey there are strong indications of symbolic spaces, with bulls' heads, carvings, and forms of art assembled in what have been called shrines or altars. These clearly form some type of acknowledgment of the supernatural and/or transcendent, and there is good evidence that they were used for ritual functions. However, the majority of these shrines are in living spaces, demonstrated by the archeological evidence of daily and mundane (secular) activities going on in and around them. In these early cases the secular and sacred were not differentiated, at least spatially. If the differentiation between the two need not be spatial, then it's next to impossible to identify such a split in the fossil and archeological record, and it might be that this characteristic is one that is common in some contemporary religions, but not a requirement for religious belief or practice. In fact, in many small-scale-society religions practiced up until recently, the differentiation between sacred and secular is one based on the shared meaning and/or the potential for transformative experience and interpretation instead of the physical location or form of an item or place.

We have very little material evidence that transcendent experiences and a recognition of the supernatural were prominent in the lives of our ancestors for the first 75 percent of our evolutionary history. But over the last 25 percent of the history of *Homo* we see increasing evidence of symbolic meaning and the potential material evidence of transcendent experiences in the lives of our ancestors. Today there is no doubt that humans participate in religious experiences and most humans associate themselves with some form of religious tradition if not a specific religion. Thus, the capacity to be religious emerged over our evolutionary history, and religion eventually became a fixture of human identity.

But why?

The Road to the Big God(s)

Theologian Wentzel van Huyssteen tells us that "humans are, first of all, embodied beings, and as such what we do, think, and feel is conditioned by the materiality of our embodiment. . . . There is a 'naturalness' to religious imagination and the human quest for meaning."

Anthropologist Richard Sosis proposes that to understand religion, "analyses must focus on the functional effects of the religious system, the coalescence of independent parts that constitute the fabric of religion. . . . These traits derive from pre-human ritual systems and were selected for in early hominin populations. . . . By fostering cooperation and extending the communication and coordination of social relations across time and space . . . the religious system . . . is an exquisite, complex adaptation that serves to support extensive human cooperation and coordination, and social life as we know it."

Both make a similar assertion, that the capacity to be religious is a central part of the human experience, but they are making slightly different arguments for why that is the case. While there are countless explanations for why humans are religious, as this book is about our evolution, I will focus only on those that attempt to connect the emergence of religion to our evolutionary histories. It's important to note that the vast majority of scientific explanations avoid, discount, or remain agnostic to the possibility that the supernatural is something that exists. That, in and of itself, tells you a little bit about what might be a shortcoming in these explanations.

There are many scientific researchers who argue that it is the evolution of complex cognitive capacities, hypercooperation, shared intentionality, and the emergence of full-blown language that enabled the ubiquitous presence of religiosity in humans. Their main point is that ritual behavior becomes common and central in the human experience and that it precedes, and enables, the emergence of religion. Some point out that stone tool production affected the neurological structures associated with prelanguage communication and skill transfer and suggest that ritualized behavior (like that needed for stone tool production) has played (and still plays) a core role in human evolution. They suggest that such processes are what set the stage for the emergence of ritual, which enabled the rise of religion. There is good evidence that ritualistic behavior is integrally associated with toolmaking and other aspects of the social lives and ecological landscapes of early humans. Basically the argument is that by 500,000 to 300,000 years ago, members of the genus *Homo* were constructing stone tools, distributing them across the environment, and utilizing them in ways that suggest an increased capacity for communication and the sharing of meaning. This leads to the expansion of ritualized behavior and the possibility that a new skill of making meaning emerged.

In this vein, Alcorta and Sosis propose that the critical element in the differentiation of religious from regular ritual was the emergence of emotionally charged symbols. They argue that religious ritual is different from the ritual associated with stone toolmaking or hunting (or even ritual behavior in other organisms) in that it imbues the experience with particular emotions and sets up the possibility of a more meaningful and potentially transcendent experience. They suggest that the brain plasticity and the seriously extended human childhood (remember from earlier chapters) are what set us (humans) up to be highly susceptible to emotional priming, especially when we come to be involved in the creation of and participation in symbolic systems. They, along with the biologist Pete Richerson and anthropologist Rob Boyd, make the assertion that the "symbolic systems of religious ritual in early human populations solved an ecological problem by fostering cooperation and extending the communication and coordination of social relations across time and space." In this case, religion emerges from human capacities for ritual, symbol, and expansive emotional experience co-opted by evolutionary processes to solve the problem of obtaining the highest possible levels of cooperation.

There is another suite of scientific approaches that seek to explain the presence and patterns of religious actions, belief, and institutions as specific adaptations to particular challenges in human evolution. Some biologists and psychologists propose that the origin of religion and religious belief are adaptations generated via natural (or cultural) selection to help humans organize large groups and facilitate cooperation. Others posit that the patterns and structures of religious belief are both generated and constrained by the normal functioning of the human cognitive system (our minds). They argue that religion is best seen as sets of beliefs and that there are underlying psychological mechanisms that enable humans to conceive of supernatural agents and believe in them. These researchers are especially interested in these underlying psychological mechanisms. Researchers in this approach argue that the evolved human cognitive complex—that we are self-aware and have the ability to attribute mental states (beliefs, imaginings, desires, knowledge, etc.) to ourselves and others and to know that these things in others can be different from our own—produces mechanisms and processes that promote supernatural agency detection: the creation of mental impressions that there are supernatural agents at play underlying many observed or perceived phenomena. Once we have the belief in supernatural agents, then it is not a big jump to see the development and elaboration of a range of religious practices. But how do such explanations get us the organized world religions that dominate humanity today?

Most anthropologists and archeologists see large-scale, hierarchical religions as part of the social complexity emerging from the increasingly stratified social systems and material cultures of the past 5,000 to 7,000 years. The psychologist Ara Norenzayan proposes that the particular "Big God(s)" religions (like those in the modern-day Abrahamic faiths of Judaism, Christianity, and Islam) emerged alongside those initial increases in social complexity and coordination just after the transition to domestication and agriculture (in the last 10,000 years or so). As populations became more complex, with larger towns and increasing inequality of wealth and activity, their gods became more moralizing (setting standards for behavior), interventionist (having the potential to have direct effects on human lives), and powerful. Norenzayan then argues that it was the belief-ritual complexes (basically the religion) associated with these gods that facilitated the large-scale hypercooperation and coordination that enabled the emergence of large-scale, complex societies (like nations and states). As Norenzayan puts it, Big God religions are responsible for "Big Groups"—modern human hypercomplex societies, including large-scale intragroup coordination (civil society) and, importantly, large-scale intergroup warfare. He has a point; the archeological record does show us that these things do all appear more or less in unison.

Other scientists, such as Dominic Johnson and Jesse Bering, proposed similar explanations for the emergence of Big Gods, but they focus on the role of supernatural punishment as the key way to achieve hypercooperation in human groups and to cause conflict between them (again tying warfare and centralized-control societies to the emergence of big religions). Johnson and Bering argue that these major religions and their strong tendency toward moral policing and punishing god(s) are the direct product of evolution by natural selection for specific cognitive (neurological and perceptual) characteristics. Basically they argue that we evolved mental capacities to create religions featuring big and punishing god(s) in order to be able to coordinate larger and larger social groups. Norenzayan's argument is a bit different in that he contends that the process of human cultural evolution has resulted in a system that links our sociality, morality, ritual, and "deep commitment" to what he terms "Big Gods," who are powerful, interventionist, and punishing, and who demand commitment. He goes on to argue that, because of these characteristics, the Big God(s) religions ended up outcompeting other religions and that is why they are dominant today.

The arguments for big and punishing god(s) have become very popular, and they seem to make a lot of sense. But there are a few problems with these hypotheses.

The big and punishing god(s) scenarios overemphasize the need for human communities to develop new methods of coordinating cooperative interactions at larger scales. We know that intensive cooperation was already in place well before the advent of full-blown agriculture, sedentism, gender, and social inequality. The Big God(s) story overlooks the possibility that much of the infrastructure the scenarios assume (hypercooperation, complex communication, symbol use, etc.) was already in place by at least 100,000 years ago (or even earlier) and certainly well before the 5,000-to-7,000-years-ago time frame in which the current Big God(s) religions appear. Why didn't such religions emerge earlier? It is a good argument to connect domestication, agriculture, and increasing inequality over the last 12,000 to 15,000 years with the emergence of particular religious systems typified by Big God(s). But it is a more tenuous assertion to make the case that Big God(s) religions evolved to be the key structural factor that facilitated the emergence of large-scale civil societies, even if they did play major roles in structuring and expanding some of them.

Unfortunately, we end up with a "chicken and egg" scenario with the Big God(s) hypotheses. It's pretty clear from the timeline that the presence and structure of Big God(s) religions are outcomes of the initial moves toward increasing social complexity and material inequality, but they are also likely driving forces behind the fostering of civil control, punishment, and intergroup conflict (such as warfare). It's not so much that the Big God(s) story is wrong; it is more that it is incomplete and not a really good explanation of religiosity or religious experience. Rather, it's an explanation about the rise of particular kinds of religion and religious institutions. Besides, to get the rise of such complex and coordinated religions, you'd need to have the religious experience already firmly as part of the human landscape.

I don't think we can assess whether or not religion in general, and Big God(s) specifically, can be clearly identified as a driving force separate from the other forms of social complexity that ratchet up as groups get

bigger and socially and materially more complex in our recent evolutionary history. Economic, political, and ecological systems become more
and more complex even before the emergence of towns, cities, and states.
So we probably don't need to invoke a supernatural threat of punishment
and control to develop and maintain large-scale societies. This is not to
say that these elements do not help facilitate or maintain such societies,
just that they are not the only (or even best) explanation for them.

One critical point missing from many of the scientific explanations of
religion is the religious experience. We have established that transcendent and possibly transformative experiences are the core of the individual believer's experience of what it means to be "religious." The
cognitive, physiological, and perceptual realities of people who believe in
Big God(s) religions vary (a lot), and in that variation there might be a
relevant complexity that is missed when we focus our explanation on
what religion "does" as opposed to what it "is" for believers.

For example, the God of the Abrahamic faiths is the prime example
of a Big God, and what these researchers have called "a punishing and
moralizing" one at that. One can certainly make the argument that these
factors enabled the religions to expand and exert control. However, those
are fairly simplistic overviews of very general aspects of the religions. For
many believers practicing the faiths (Judaism, Christianity, Islam), specific core values, such as caring, love, and compassion, outweigh the punishment and control elements (prohibitions, penance, sin, gender
inequity, clerical mandates, etc.) in everyday life and in their interpretation of the meaning of the religion. While not being naïve about the
history of how religious institutions have manipulated and impacted
societies, we do need to recognize the significant variation in how individuals and communities experience and respond to the edicts, values,
and structures of Big God(s) (and other) religions. The focus solely on the
overarching punishment and enforcement structure of religions as a
functional entity can blind researchers to the very important diversity
and dynamism of experience and practice of belief at the individual level.
The experience at the level of the individual can be extremely relevant if
we are attempting to model patterns of behavior that have direct impacts
in both cultural and biological evolutionary processes.

My point is that we have to more seriously ask if we can disregard the lived experience of religious people in favor of providing overarching structural and evolutionary explanations for religions. It's highly likely that the religious experience for humans over the millennia is (and has been) more interesting than that. The idea that being a "religious" human is basically the result of the structure of a given religion is a very shallow way to think about the human experience. Our models and hypotheses need to keep this in mind.

Imagination, Faith, and Hope Came First

Well before the first appearance of modern humans there is ample evidence that our ancestors were developing increasingly complex substantial cognitive and behavioral responses to ecological and social challenges. Everything we know about the human past suggests that it was this behavioral and cognitive agility combined with increasing social cooperation and coordination, and the development of and experimentation with symbolic thought, that enabled humans to create our modern capacity for extensive shared intentionality, metacoordination, and language. At the heart of these innovations is the ability to create meaning in ways that are distinctive.

The study of how organisms approach meanings and patterns in the world is called "semiosis" (literally "to mark," the process of identifying signs and meaning). At some point in our evolution humans developed a new kind of semiosis—the use and creation of symbol. For most animals, and likely our earlier relatives, using and reading indexical signs (signs correlated with or otherwise affected by what they represent, like dark clouds meaning rain is coming) and iconic signs (which physically resemble what they mean) are common. In both these types of signs the "signifier" (the physical thing itself—the sign) and the "signified" (what the sign means) have a direct relationship. For iconic signs, the signified looks just like the signifier; for indexical signs the signified is correlated with the signifier (rain usually happens when dark clouds appear). Symbolic signs, however, have no necessary physical or even correlational link between the signifier and the signified. A symbolic sign means what it means only because those using it have agreed on that meaning. The US flag is a cloth with patterns and colors on it and is meaningless without a cluster of people getting together, assigning a meaning to it, and applying that meaning. Language is a system of symbolic signs: Every word you just read is a meaningless cluster of marks (and sounds in your head) that we (humans) have agreed mean certain things and sound certain ways. Full-blown language is impossible without symbolic signs.

Humans today are deeply immersed in a symbolic system where imagination and hope, and the symbols associated with them, can maintain stability and meaning and provide the infrastructure for faith. The ideals of morality and fairness, the expectation of how people should behave, how we want the world to be, and so on are good examples. The capacity to think like this is facilitated by our symbolic abilities and is not necessarily tied to any of the actual details of the physical world around us at any given time. But it is influenced by the symbolic and meaning-laden experiences that enculturate us from childhood on. This is a key to understanding religious thought. The way we interpret the world arises from the interactions of many elements (bodies, brains, senses, perceptions, experiences, other humans and animals, etc.). Humans, both as individuals and as communities, are embedded in a world of dense symbolic landscapes, and much of that is religious.

Perception, meaning, and experience are as central in human history as are muscles, bones, and hormones (at least over the last few hundred thousand years). How humans see the world—or better put, how humans perceive the world to be—is a major part of our evolutionary story. The manner in which symbols are generated, perceived, and utilized by humans structures perceptions and behavior and creates a human ecology where the material world (the physical environment) is never without semiotic (including symbolic) markings; we, in part, create the world we live in. The human perception of the world structures how we interact with it—belief matters in an evolutionary sense.

Maybe understanding of the emergence and evolution of religious belief and institutions is more complicated than simply explaining what religions "do" for (and to) human populations. Maybe the human tendency to be religious is not best explained as an adaptation produced via natural selection, like our remarkably helpful thumbs, or the wider birth canal, or the shape of our gluteus muscles to assist in our capacity to walk and run on two legs (and give us a butt). Maybe religious experience is a key outcome of the human niche, the way humans "are" in the world.

Across our evolution, humans developed a niche where the imagination and symbol became central facets of our ecology. In niche construction the interaction between organisms and their environment acts as a core process that affects the evolutionary pressures in shaping bodies and landscapes. In humans the ability to imagine responses to both material and perceived pressures, and to convert those imaginings into material items or actions, became a major tool in our success. This evolutionary benefit to having and deploying an imagination results in increasing use of the imaginative reaction to a diverse set of challenges, social and ecological. One way in which the imagination is deployed in humans is in religious ritual, structures, and institutions.

This is not an argument that the origin of religion fulfilled a specific trajectory of the human lineage, or for any particular adaptive function of religiosity. It is not an argument that "religion" is what enabled humans to become fully human, or allowed us to survive when all other human-like lineages went extinct. This argument just assumes that in an evolutionary context, neither religion nor religiosity can appear full-blown, just as we assume that any other core facet of the human body and niche cannot appear in its modern form without having a series of precursors (remember chapters 1 through 6). Therefore, religious belief and practice, and the deep history of the religious experience, are not actually explained via current practices of religion. We have to identify the kinds of structures, behaviors, and cognitive processes that might have enhanced the role that human symbol creation and use, and the human imagination, had in the initial appearances of religious experience, belief, ritual, and their associated institutions, in our archeological past.

This approach seeks to provide a more open landscape to diverse points of inquiry about human religious experience and does not automatically assume that people who "believe" in a particular religious tradition are wrong in what they believe to have been revealed to them through the practice of their religion. If having an imagination is a central part of the human niche, and this imagination is a basal element necessary for the development of a perception of the world that includes the supernatural, one could construct both evolutionary and religious perspectives as part of the explanations for how or why humans engage in religious practice and belief. In the evolutionary explanations, this way of viewing human niche construction and the emergence of religion provides space for arguments for the development of the functional structures (cognitive and behavioral) that those arguing for religion as a functional adaptation propose. However, there is also resonance between this niche-construction-and-religion approach for the possibility of a form of revelatory experience that coincides with the kind of perspectives proposed by theologians and scientists seeking to connect faith and the divine with the patterns in human evolution.

For example, the emergence and increasing use of symbolic representation in the human lineage, especially over the last 200,000 to 300,000 years, represents a significant expansion and reworking of how humans live in the world. Scientists (including myself) have argued that this reflects the full-blown development of the distinctive human niche and is thus a critical moment in the appearance of what we would call the "modern" humans in a cognitive sense as well as a morphological one. While scientists invoke a particular suite of evolutionary processes, plus a form of cognitive ratcheting (increases in neurological complexity), to explain this process, a theologian could add in her or his own context. It is possible to conceptualize this transition to the modern human niche as part of the process of revelation, wherein revelation from God or gods enables humans to develop a form of reflection and a supernatural orientation, eventually leading to religious belief. That is, the reality of the fossil and archeological record cannot be negated or ignored, but for the religious individual, the assumption of a supernatural engagement as part of the emergence of the symbolic in the human evolutionary record makes a lot of sense.

The approach I outline above can work as long as one is not a fundamentalist or literalist regarding religious tradition. Religion, just like every other human institution, has changed since its earliest forms and will continue to change. One cannot scientifically or otherwise assume that anything written in a book or books, or handed down verbally, across generations of individuals using multiple languages, can maintain consistency or be resistant to modification. All religions have been changing since their inceptions and still are. Anyone who cannot accept that and asserts that their version of a given religion, exactly as it stands, is both unchanged and the one true human religion is wrong. There is abundant evidence that humans were religious long before any of the modern-day religions existed.

Religious, Religions, and Humans

It is highly likely that, as the theologian Wentzel van Huyssteen suggests, there is a naturalness to the human religious imagination and that it is part of the processes that facilitated human evolutionary success over the past few hundred thousand years. If this is indeed the case, an important part of reconstructing the path to humanity has to include the possible roles that imagination, belief, and even religious activity have played and continue to play for humans around the planet.

Most humans identify as religious, so anyone who argues against religion being an important aspect of humanity is either overlooking a huge component of the human experience or simply choosing not to recognize how deep and widespread religion is. Regardless of anyone's individual feelings about any specific religion, religiousness is not about to disappear from the landscape, so engaging with it and understanding it is worthwhile. However, being upset with actions by religions and religious institutions is not the same thing as being against religiousness. This is especially important over the last thousand years or so, as a few major religions have come to dominate. Nation-states, economies, and war and other forms of violence are often related to passionate religious feelings. Understanding the distinctions between a human being religious, engaging in religious practice, the teachings and ideals of any particular faith, and the ways in which the institutions of any given religion function and act has often been a matter of life or death.

Not being part of any specific religion or identifying as not being religious is absolutely fine for humans—this is how we existed for most of our history. Abundant research shows that those who argue that being religious or belonging to a religion makes one a better moral or altruistic person are wrong. Anyone who believes that all humans must be part of their particular worldview has a myopic view of human history. There are many, many ways to be successfully human, and while we all have much in common as a species, human cultural diversity has been around for hundreds of thousands of years, is one of the hallmarks of humanity, and is not going away anytime soon. All humans are immersed in a deeply symbolic and meaning-laden world, and most of us behave, at least sometimes, as if the supernatural exists. That is a universal human transcendent reality that no other being shares.

10

ARTISTIC FLIGHTS

I ducked under the large stalactite and wedged myself beside a slimy stalagmite about sixty feet down into the cave outside of Lisbon in Portugal. Holding the light close to the cave wall, I could just make out the shape of the horse and the aurochs (giant extinct European oxen), in reddish-brown pigments, mapping to the contours on the wall, using the natural shapes to help define the bodies, heads, and legs. The two animals almost seemed alive, in motion. Then it struck me: I was probably in the exact position the artist(s) who painted these images wanted . . . I think I saw what the artist(s) created in the way she or he meant it to be seen. For a split second I felt connected across space and time. The artist(s) lived about 27,000 years ago, and for that brief moment I had a time machine.

Humans don't just live in a deeply symbolic and meaning-laden world; they create one. Art is a core creative outcome of the transcendent nature of being human. Art is much more than a product, an activity, or a process; it is a way of being in the world that essentially rises above practical worldly concerns. Art is transformative. It is, of course, best experienced in person.

Academic analyses of art are all well and good, but visceral and personal experiences of art, like the one I had in the cave in Portugal, better convey the power of art in the human story. Let me offer three more of my own experiences as illustrations.

- Standing in Madrid's Museo del Prado staring at Hieronymus Bosch's painting *The Garden of Earthly Delights* makes my head spin. I've been back multiple times, years apart, and it happens each time. The giant, three-paneled, intricately chaotic masterpiece feels as real, fantastical, terrifying, dizzying, and alluring as the best high-tech special effects in a movie or video game. Painted by a fifty-year-old Dutchman around AD 1500, it retains its power across the centuries because it speaks to us with powerful imagery, colors, aesthetic sense, and a good splash of bedlam. This one painting deals with religion, sex, gender, human-animal relationships, politics, biology, geography, and much more. It is spectacular, even 500 years after its creation.
- Seeing the *Pietà* by Michelangelo brought tears to my eyes. It is a sculpture of Mary holding the body of Jesus in her lap after the crucifixion. But the theme was not what caused my tears; it was the form. Carved from a block of marble, the sculpture flows as if it were alive and looks nothing like stone. The curves, edges, folds of cloth, the shape of the hands, necks, and faces, the position of the bodies, freeze you in a moment with this woman and this man, and give you the sense that in the next one they will move and you will move with them. This is just a rock shaped by a human, but its beauty and power are devastating. It is believed to be the only work that Michelangelo ever signed.
- Sitting on the dusty ground in a clearing outside the temple south of the Balinese village of Campuhan, I was transported as soon as the first tones of the gamelan orchestra reached my ears. Cascading melodies from the bamboo and metal instruments were woven together by the haunting rhythms of the flutes and drums. At the height of the wave of music, the dancers emerged in the center of the clearing, three young women

in brightly colored, intricately woven costumes, with shining metal headdresses and sheaths of jewelry. Their eyes, hands, fingers, and toes all performed intricate motions as their bodies moved in unison to the dense, melodic, and cacophonic music. And this was only the opening, "welcome" dance.

Art has steadily contributed to the human experience of creativity, and it continues to do so. Impractical as it may be, it has nevertheless played a special role in the story of our evolution.

Beyond Practicality

Oxford Dictionaries defines art as "the expression or application of human creative skill and imagination, typically in a visual form such as painting or sculpture, producing works to be appreciated primarily for their beauty or emotional power." The Merriam-Webster dictionary defines it as "something that is created with imagination and skill and that is beautiful or that expresses important ideas or feelings." These two definitions jibe with what many of us usually think of when we hear the word *art,* but both stress the functional aspect of art—what art is and does. We all agree that paintings, music, dance, and sculpture are forms of art, and most would agree that these products fill some aesthetic or pleasing function. But is that all there is to art? We refer to that cluster of things as "the arts" and tend to think of art in opposition to practicality, to productive effort, or to items or objects that work for us and for society, like computers, airplanes, and garbage disposals. But "art" in the human story is actually a lot more than just the creation of artifacts. Art goes well beyond just an appeal to aesthetics or the crafting of objects of whimsy, imagination, and dreams.

The author Maria Popova opens her collection of definitions of art with a phrase from the American philosopher and founder of a famous Arts and Crafts community Elbert Hubbard: "Art is not a thing—it is a way." She then goes on to lay out definitions of "art" from philosophers, artists, architects, and authors, ending with her own quote on the power of art, telling us it has "the power to transcend our own self-interest, our solipsistic zoom-lens on life, and relate to the world and each other with more integrity, more curiosity, more wholeheartedness." Art reaches beyond self-interest, that principle that has long blinkered the study of human motivation.

The artists Mat Schwarzman, Keith Knight, and colleagues tell us that art is "human behavior that involves the intense interpretation of life through language, dance, painting, music and numerous culturally specific forms." They tell us that "creativity is a muscle" built into humans at the most basic level, such that being creative, and making art, is so natural that few people even notice when they are doing it. Rather than simply leaving art for specialists we call "artists," they urge us to recognize that we hone our creative muscles all the time by engaging in a huge range of artistic endeavors. The art that we engage with is also information that we generate, use, and revise, and it forms a vital part of the human story.

As archeologist Steven Mithen tells us, "Modern humans are dramatically more creative in their behavior than any other living species." But do other species create "art"?

Years ago I had the pleasure of conducting research with a group of famous sign-language-using chimpanzees at the Chimpanzee and Human Communication Institute (CHCI) at Central Washington University in Ellensburg, Washington. My interests were not so much in their signing, but more in how these chimps, with their world overlapping so extensively with that of people, lived and behaved. The most famous, and the matriarch of the group, was Washoe, who when she died in 2007 received an obituary in *The New York Times*. She was a very unusual ape, a chimp who was raised by humans, taught a series of modified American Sign Language signs to communicate with them, and eventually ended up in a group of five signing chimps at the CHCI. Washoe was also, according to her human caretakers, an artist. She painted with watercolors, drew with crayons, and arranged items about her in particular ways. Roger Fouts, the researcher who worked with her the longest, argued that what Washoe, and many other apes (but not all), did when she was asked to paint or draw was a form of art. It was less representational, to our eyes, but as Fouts noted, it was consistent and patterned, and she greatly enjoyed the opportunity to do it. Washoe in particular showed a knack for multicolored paintings that have a strong sense of vibrancy and movement. I have to agree that her paintings are interesting, even fun, to look at, as are the paintings by some elephants and other apes, all in captivity. No noncaptive ape or elephant paints or arranges items in manners that look like "art" to us in the wild, but some do paint or draw when given the human tools (and a little bit of instruction and reward). Some of their products, if hung in a gallery and labeled as avant-garde art by a human, might even sell well. What is absolutely certain is that some animals in captivity, when given the right training and equipment, can produce images that please human aesthetic sensibilities.

Interestingly, this also happens in the wild, not with apes or elephants, but with birds. Bowerbirds are a group of birds found in Australia and New Guinea that spend a good deal of time investing in something we might call art. Bowerbird males build elaborate displays to attract females and encourage them to mate. The males collect bright and shiny objects (shells, beads, bits of glass and plastic, leaves, sticks, even chewing gum wrappers, sad to say) and arrange them around burrows or ground nests in amazingly patterned and intricate ways. They also do a dance around the display when the female arrives. The whole performance certainly looks artistic to the human eye (and in the ideal world for the bowerbird male it is also attractive to the female's eye). Recent work demonstrates that bowerbirds are able to create what is called "forced perspective" (an optical illusion to make objects appear farther away, closer, larger, or smaller than they actually are) for the female viewer to enhance their displays. There is even correlation with what we would call a more aesthetic arrangement and male mating success.

There is a similar overlap in what humans might see as aesthetically pleasing (even beautiful) and the plumage colors and mating dances of many other bird species. Such aesthetic patterns also hold true for many of the colors we see in mammals' coats. The body colors and facial markings of many animals strike us as both beautiful and potentially information laden (the coat of a skunk, the patterns on a killer whale, a zebra, mandrills, snowshoe hares, and red foxes). It seems as though humans share a certain aesthetic sense with other animals.

Aesthetics is the sense of beauty and intrinsic sensation that something is structurally or sensually attractive or pleasing. This appears to be a necessary precursor to being able to create art, but it is not the same as art, at least not human art. Maybe the human aesthetic sense is one area where our deep evolutionary connectedness to the rest of the animal kingdom shows. If our aesthetic sense is truly quite old, then we'd expect evolutionary histories to have produced a range of animals that take advantage of the aesthetic sense and elaborate on it (like bowerbirds). However, do these aesthetic senses go beyond just pleasing colors and displays? Is there any evidence that other animals extend their sense of aesthetics to a broader contemplative context? This is a context that is very common in human visual arts, but it is really tough to actually observe and measure in other animals in the wild. Many animals, especially primates, show signs of prolonged and intense staring "off" in captivity, but this is likely a by-product of being captive and its intense boredom, more of an aberrant behavior than a contemplative one. However, I have had a few experiences in the wild that suggest that maybe some other primates do contemplate beauty.

The Rock of Gibraltar is a giant limestone minimountain that juts up from land extending into the Mediterranean at the southern tip of the Iberian Peninsula. On a sunny day you can stand almost anywhere up on "the rock" (now a nature reserve) and look across the strait and see Gibraltar's sister mountain (Jebel Musa) along the coast of Morocco (the northern tip of the continent of Africa). It is a majestic sight: two continents, a sea, and a horizon of deep blues, greens, browns, and reds. When I began conducting research watching the monkeys on the Rock of Gibraltar, I often stopped and marveled at the awe-inspiring scene. To my surprise, so did the monkeys. It is quite common for one to come across an adult female or male Barbary macaque (the monkey species in Gibraltar) sitting atop one of the centuries-old walls and looking, gazing, out across the strait toward Morocco. At first I did not make much of this, but when I followed their gaze, it would lead me to a highly aesthetic view. But maybe this was just happenstance or the monkeys picking up on human behavior. I had an opportunity to test this.

Working with the National Geographic Crittercam team, we placed HD cameras on a few of the adult monkeys one summer (on collars such that the camera was right below the head of the macaque and the lens captured what the monkey was looking at). These cameras allowed us to get footage of the macaques in areas we could not go, the sheer cliff faces and the dense trees and undergrowth around the rock.

Reviewing the footage, we noticed that one female had set up a near perfect image for us. She was looking out across the strait, and the image of the Mediterranean and the mountains of Morocco in the distance was really striking; we all commented on it. But she was not still; she fidgeted a bit and shifted the frame slightly (basically adjusted her head and upper body), and the new image was so stunning that we all stopped breathing for a few seconds. The monkey had just captured the best view any of us had seen from atop the Rock of Gibraltar. And she stayed there, doing nothing but looking for a few minutes. So did we. This pattern, of a monkey framing an aesthetically pleasing picture (reflecting what they were looking at), showed up a few more times during our Crittercam work in Gibraltar and also with another species of monkey in Singapore. I am still not sure what this means, but I have little doubt that other primates and humans can agree on some things as aesthetic. Maybe the capacity to sense and enjoy aesthetic beauty is shared across the primates. But it is what humans do with that sense of beauty, where we take it, that differs. There is more to art than aesthetics.

We assign meaning to patterns and processes of aesthetic or even anti-aesthetic designs, images, items, and behaviors. The capacity to create and manipulate aesthetic qualities is how humans go beyond other organisms and make the creation of art, the manipulation of the aesthetic senses, a core part of who we are.

Humans today have a vast array of capacities for image creation and manipulation: painting, drawing, photography, videography, carving, sculpture, collages . . . From very early on in their lives, human children use items to create representations, aesthetic images, scribbles, lines, zig-zags, and doodles. These actions can be purposeful and directed (the desire to paint or draw something, to represent a person, an idea, a goal), or they can emerge when we are bored, nervous, or excited, with no specific intent behind them. The creation of visual imagery is only one of the many ways we engage the aesthetic sense. We also dance. The movement of bodies in rhythmic, and sometimes arrhythmic, fashion has a huge impact on our moods and on information sharing and can be used to relieve stress, to flirt, to reinforce social bonds, and to tell stories. Dance is common around the planet, as is music, and is one of the most powerful of the human arts. The creation of melodic sound and the collection of diverse sounds into sound narratives are a central part of the human experience. Other animals use sound for communication, and some, like many birds and the apes called gibbons, do so with melodic beauty and complexity. But humans create whole soundscapes of meaning, moving beyond just aesthetics and direct communication to create symbolic landscapes with sound (like your favorite symphony, jazz tune, rock song, or folk ballad). We also throw language into the mix. Our rich symbolic communication system can infuse sounds with an explosion of sensations, passions, and meanings via a human voice singing a melody. The final category is one that connects almost everything we label as art: stories. In storytelling we take our capacity to create and develop symbols and information and to share their meanings across space and time and fold it all into some form of narrative. Stories told around the fire, passed through the ages, reproduced and re-created through novels, theater, and films, are the singularly most distinctive of all the human arts. They have shaped how we experience the world and continue to do so.

So when did all of these categories of human art show up? And what might that tell us about our history and future as a creative species?

An Elegant Stone Tool in a Noisy World of Color and Line

Contrary to popular belief, the first human art was neither paintings nor carvings nor melodies. It came in the form of shaped pieces of stone. The philosopher of biology Kim Sterelny and the archeologist Peter Hiscock recently reviewed what the production of early stone tools meant for our ancestors, and they conclude that "stone tools were material symbols long before the ochre and jewelry of behavioral modernity."

We know that the shaping of pebbles into choppers and cutting implements was among the earliest and most important modifications of the world by our ancestors and that this ability to make tools radically reshaped the human niche. But what we've not considered are the actual shapes and forms of those tools, and what the process of tool creation might have meant to early humans in the context of art.

The shaping of tools from stones requires a degree of imagination, co-ordination, and collaboration we don't see in other animals. It also sets the stage for a kind of creativity that opens the doors for art, such as in the earliest Oldowan-type stone tools. The cobbles were shaped into chopping tools and the flakes were used to cut through meat and hides. The process involved creating sharp edges, turning the stones around at multiple an-gles, and envisioning a set of shapes that might not have been obvious from the original cobble. The goal was to create something that could be used, but the imagining and the working of one shape into another set the cognitive template—shaped our brains—to be able to see shapes in our minds and translate them into a new reality using hard, durable material in the world. We can easily imagine that groups of early humans, while sitting together shaping rocks into stone tools, accidentally or intention-ally messed with their technique now and then and came up with a new flake or a particular angle that struck them as aesthetic (remember, the aesthetic taste, a sense of beauty, is at least in its rudimentary form found in many primates and thus was there in our ancestors). Maybe they'd look at it for a while and show it to the others in the group. Possibly they set it aside to look at or just tossed it out after a while. Regardless of whether or not they tried to make the same thing again, we know that the process of stone toolmaking sets up the possibility for early humans to experiment with creating shapes and forms from stone and that their aesthetic sense might have influenced what they were doing. The line to Michelangelo's *Pietà* begins to make more sense as we imagine our early ancestors' inces-sant hammering of stones together.

By the more recent stages in human evolution (the last 300,000 to 500,000 years or so), we start to find more tools made than were used, and tools that were made with a level of craft and symmetry that went well beyond what was needed for them to be effective as knives, hammers, and grinding stones. These stone tools of what we call the late Acheulean tradition start looking more and more elaborate, more and more like art. Researchers have discovered what they call the "golden section" or "golden ratio" for a type of Acheulean tool called a biface (a stone shaped on both sides to create sharp edges and a point). This golden ratio is a shape that, while not necessarily more effective than other shapes in regard to cutting and chopping, seems to have an aesthetic appeal. When the archeologist Matthew Pope and colleagues looked at 148 assemblages comprising more than 8,000 bifaces from across the Acheulean record of Europe, Africa, the Near East, and India, they found that the vast majority fit in the range of the golden ratio. This is almost 100 percent impossible via pure chance. The members of the genus *Homo,* across vast distances, were making tools that were aesthetically pleasing, as well as good for using. Aesthetic taste had an impact on stone toolmaking. We see this in other evidence as well. Regional and local stone tool styles emerge clearly by this time, some sites even having idiosyncratic shapes and styles suggesting that at least sometimes one or more individuals in a group developed a specific toolmaking style, noticeably different from others—maybe for aesthetic reasons, maybe the result of a particular burst of creativity. Or maybe a certain shape "called" to the toolmaker and she became a stone-age version of Michelangelo.

For example, at a site called Boxgrove in England, Pope and colleagues provide evidence that tools were made in relatively consistent ways and that these regional patterns spread across wide areas and were preserved across a good stretch of time. The tools were found clustered across the landscapes, often in numbers that are pretty high and with many unused tools found in multiple locations. It's possible that these clusters of tools, and the tools themselves, meant more to those making them than just utensils or items for use in butchering animals and shaping other tools. Maybe these tools and their presence on the landscape were a way to enable the groups of *Homo* living there to create a kind of meaning in that landscape that they then developed, manipulated, and moved. The stone tools and their manufacture became a way for groups

to develop their sense of identity and do what anthropologists call changing "space" to "place" in making the landscape their own.

This making of "place" is wonderfully demonstrated deep in the
Bruniquel Cave in southwestern France. Nearly 200,000 years ago,
groups of Neanderthals moved deep into this cave (more than 1,000 feet
in from the entrance) and built rings of stone. They took stalagmites rising from the floor of the cave, broke them off, and used them to build
small circular walls. These low-walled circles were six to fifteen feet in
diameter, and there is evidence of smaller such mounds with fires on
them inside these larger circles. The Neanderthals of Bruniquel moved
deep into the cave, built small circles of stone, and illuminated them
with fire. Stones were used to build a Neanderthal place.

Stones did more than make a physical "place." There is evidence in the
archeological record of tools that appear to be made with great effort but
not used. A perfect example is the beautiful single rare stone tool (called
"Excalibur" by the team who found it) found among the bodies at Sima
de los Huesos in Atapuerca, Spain, in what might be one of the earliest
burials. Why did the group of *Homo* there go to so much trouble to get
a stone from thirty miles or so away, meticulously shape it, and then
discard it into the pit where they'd dumped a bunch of bodies? And why
just this one tool, no others? It's not clear; maybe it was the fact that the
tool was aesthetically pleasing, even beautiful; maybe it was wholly art
and never meant to be used as a cutting or chopping implement.

The next stage in the evolution of human art takes us to another level,
the creation and use of color.

Ochre is an earthen pigment that draws its coloration from varying
levels of iron oxide in it. Some ochres are yellow, others brown, orangish,
and red. They come in the form of clumps, sort of like relatively soft
stones. There is evidence of some groups of *Homo* using ochre by at least
280,000 years ago, and maybe as many as 500,000 years ago. There are at
least two main uses we see in the archeological record and a third that we
can infer. Ochre is marked and engraved on, and it is ground up and used
as a binding agent in the glue-like mixture in the hafting of stone or bone
to wood (stone-tipped tools). The inferred use is that the ochre was
ground (and possibly mixed with liquid) to produce a pigment that could

be applied to bodies, tools, or other locations. For example, the archeologist Wil Roebroeks and colleagues report on a site in Europe that is about 200,000 to 250,000 years old, contains a wide array of tools and other evidence of occupation, and, most interestingly, is covered with small dried spots of red pigment that was originally in liquid form. The members of the genus *Homo* at the site were using a red ochre by mashing it and adding liquid, then doing something with that pigment that caused them to spill drops of it frequently. There is no evidence of painting or of the ochre being applied significantly to tools. Were they putting it on their bodies or faces, or both? Whatever they were doing, they had intentionally sought out and transported the ochre from a location dozens of miles away, made it into liquid form, and used it on something that was not their tools or the immediate fixed surroundings. If they were painting themselves, that is a clear indication of the use of aesthetics in a more complex way, making their imaginations real. By 40,000 to 70,000 years ago or so, we find many sites with ochre being used for a range of purposes, along with other pigment colors, including black pigments. This was art.

While humans were using colors to change the way they, and the world, looked, they were also decorating themselves with things aside from pigments.

Beads are items that are perforated, and those perforations are used to somehow display the beads. This is most often done by running a simple cord (of sinew or plant material) through the holes in the beads and stringing many of them together as a necklace or wristlet or the like. This way of creating art is common in many societies across the planet today and has deep roots in our past. Even today, however, there is seldom one uniform meaning for the wearing of beads, what it might represent or why particular things (stones, shells, bones) are used to make the beads.

In a study of one modern foraging group in South Africa, the anthropologist Polly Wiessner demonstrated that even in one group of people, aspects of style, taste, and interpretation can vary widely when it comes to aesthetics and communication in the use of beads. In Wiessner's study of beaded headbands, she found that although there was a set of fairly consistent patterns for designs and that beaded headbands were shared aspects of the culture, individuals placed varying degrees of emphasis on what was most important about them (group identity, individual taste, particulars of aesthetic design and skill, value as a trade object, etc.). When we look into the past and identify things like beads we can know two things for sure: They were made and used intentionally (most likely for individuals to wear or use and for others to see them), and the beads probably did not always convey the same messages to all wearers and viewers. While these two features make deciding on the "purpose" of the beads difficult, they do not detract from the fact that they are an artistic endeavor deep in our past.

The earliest reports for beads are from a site in Germany that dates to about 300,000 years ago, but the dating is a bit contentious. By about 70,000 to 135,000 years ago, we start to see beads more regularly, especially in coastal areas along the southern and southeastern coasts of the Mediterranean and in South Africa. These beads are most often shells, and surprisingly they are frequently from one type of mollusk: the genus *Nassarius*. While some other types of mollusk shells were used as beads, the vast majority of early shell beads found in both the Mediterranean region and South Africa are from just two species in the genus *Nassarius*. *Nassarius* are a kind of sea snail that is very common around the planet and have a whorled shell that spirals back into a point. They are usually light brown and white, with a range of color variations: They look pretty cool. *Nassarius* often get infested with a kind of parasite that bores holes in their shell. There is good evidence that humans collected these shells with the natural holes and expanded the holes or just used them as they found them and strung them together on a cord (we can see wear marks from where the cord rubbed against the edges of the holes). There are also many cases where holes were made by people, maybe taking a clue from the natural context and manipulating the shells further, enabling these early jewelers to string more *Nassarius* together. Why? That is more difficult to interpret, but we can expect that the peoples doing this found the beads aesthetically pleasing when strung together and that the collecting, perforating, and stringing were intentional. Obviously the beads were meant as an artistic statement, but what the message was and how many messages there were are locked in the past.

By the time we find beads in the archeological record, some groups were already using ochre, likely on their bodies or faces, so the addition of another way (beads) to make statements about image, identity, or group unity is not very far-fetched. There is even evidence that beads were not the only artistic jewelry in play at this time. Recently a group of researchers went back through the large collection of artifacts from the famous Neanderthal site of Krapina dating to about 130,000 years ago in what is now Croatia. They found eight white-tailed eagle talons in the vast collection that no one had closely examined before. Four of the talons had multiple cut marks, and all eight had parts near their bases that had been "polished" (smoothed down via wear against something). These talons were taken from an eagle (that the Neanderthals most likely ate) and strung together as a piece of art, most likely worn. There is also evidence from cave sites in Gibraltar and other locations that other groups of *Homo* removed the feathers from birds and wore them in some fashion. The use of feathers and bird parts for ornamentation is found across the planet today. It has long been assumed that there are aesthetic reasons for this: Birds are often colorful and their songs are often aesthetically appealing. But birds also fly, and flight has long interested humans, maybe even deep in our past.

The presence of ochres, the presence of beads made from snail shells, and the use of talons and feathers tell us that by at least 130,000 years ago humans were seeing objects that created aesthetic pleasure, or at least caught their eye in the world, and they were taking these items, modifying them, and wearing them. Our ancestors were changing their bodies intentionally by altering material items and making them distinctively new, connecting them with the human body and infusing them with meaning.

There was also doodling. Humans began to engrave, and carve, lines into other things—things that were not worn but might have been carried, traded, or just admired.

Just over 300,000 years ago in what is today the island of Java in

Indonesia, an early member of the genus *Homo* picked up a clamshell and a sharp implement (maybe a shark's tooth) and engraved a zigzag pattern on the inside of the shell. Why the clamshell and why a shark's tooth? Why the zigzag pattern? Was this art? Was it doodling? Is there really a difference between the two? Unfortunately, we cannot answer the first four questions. But the last one, doodling versus art, is possible. The two are connected; the capacity to doodle is a necessary precursor to the capacity to draw, engrave, and create imagery. Just as imagination and ritualistic activity were needed to be able to develop religious practice and belief, to draw and to create lifelike or representational imagery, one first has to be able to connect the use of one item to modify another item intentionally via changing the surface of that item. We already know that many animals can do this (many primates and birds use simple tools). We also know that since the earliest members of our own genus we have been able to make stone tools (a step up in complexity from all other animals). On the other hand, doodling is different. It is not functional in the way that making a tool or using a tool is. The doodle, the active engraving of lines or shapes into an object, is pleasing aesthetically for whatever reason and is done to occupy the imagination, not to get food or get some job done. The capacity for idle daydreaming and doodling are connected and might be a critical ability that the lineage *Homo* developed and cultivated over the last 300,000 years.

We do not find many instances of doodling in the early human record, but then again no one has been looking for them. We do, however, have possible evidence of engraved bones in what is today Germany at around 300,000 years ago, and by between about 100,000 and 150,000 years ago we start to see clear evidence of engraved artifacts showing up in multiple locations around the world. What is particularly fascinating is that by the time engravings become more common, they are remarkably similar, regardless of the item being engraved (we find engraved ochre, ostrich eggshells, bones, etc.). The engravings are usually series of lines, crossing one another, as hash marks, or clusters of straight and curved lines. Basically they look like advanced doodling. Maybe there is a particular aesthetic sense for humans in the creation of lines and where they lead us to think and imagine.

OCHRE ENGRAVINGS

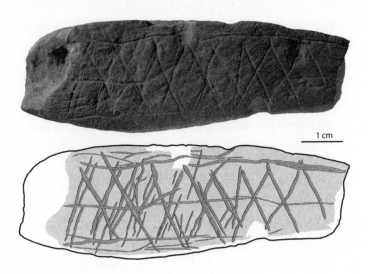

1 cm

The transition from doodling to lines to creating objects that are shaped to look like people and animals took a bit longer. There are two possible very early figurines. The first is called the Tan-Tan figurine from a site in Morocco that dates to around 500,000 years ago. It is a naturally formed quartzite rock that looks a lot like a human body, and there is some evidence the features were then modified by a stone tool to look more humanlike. The second is a stone from the site of Berekhat Ram in Israel (about 300,000 years old) that also has a naturally human-looking form. Some researchers argue there is evidence that it was further modified to look even more human (female). But both of these claims are fiercely debated. Surprisingly, given the early appearances of beads and engravings, undeniable human-made figurines show up much later in the human story (about 35,000 to 40,000 years ago).

The earliest universally agreed-upon figurines are those of animals and hybrid human-animal beings, with the oldest being what looks like a half-lion, half-human figure dating to about 40,000 years ago. There are also figurines of lions, mammoths, and rhinoceroses in the earliest clusters. Associated with the figurines are lots of beads and other types of body ornaments. It is hard to know what these small, portable animal images meant to the people who made them. Most researchers have assumed that they were some kind of hunting good-luck charms or maybe ways of telling stories about hunting. Others have suggested that these were clues as to what was important in the lives and worldview of the peoples who made them (the earliest ones are found in western Europe). It is possible that the figurines of the animals reflected a kind of emerging animism, where these people used their imaginative capacities to create art that reflected the living and dynamic things around them, and that this was tied to the development of a kind of ritual practice or even belief system centered on the humans' relationships with other animals. Then again, maybe these were created just for aesthetic reasons. Human-shaped figurines show up later than the earliest animal ones.

Probably the best-known human-shaped figurine is the Venus of Willendorf, a four-inch-tall carving of a female found at a site in Austria and dating to around 27,000 years ago. She is a large-bodied woman with what looks like a woven cap or hat covering her head. During the time period between about 20,000 and 27,000 years ago, small carvings of the female form are quite common in sites across Western Europe (more than 200 have been found), with many of them having similar-looking headgear and some covered with red ochre. Why female forms and why the woven hats? The second question has recently been answered with some evidence of rope and other types of woven material dating back to about 22,000 to 25,000 years ago. People were likely wearing woven caps and clothing by that point—either that or they had pretty complex hairdos.

The first question (why females?) has usually been answered by the old "it must be religious" line. Earlier scholars looked at the figurines and their often exaggerated representations of the breasts, buttocks, vulva, and stomachs of the female form and suggested that these figurines were "fertility goddesses" or other types of fertility icons used in some form of ceremony or ritual. However, in the past few decades researchers have revisited these ideas and offered alternatives. One idea is that female artists were making the figurines and the disproportionality of certain body parts came from the perspective one gets when looking at one's own body. Others disagree about the auto-artistic pattern and suggest that the varying emphases on different body parts are most likely due to specific cultural traditions and artistic tastes involving particular emphasis on female forms. Some even suggest that we are mistaken to think only about the visual here and that these figurines (as small as they were) were meant to be held and thus the exaggerated body parts were an element of the sensory aspects of holding the figures.

If you look at the whole range of small figurines from the earliest human figurines at about 30,000 years ago to more recent ones even 10,000 years ago, you see a lot of variation. Most are females; some are males; many are also animals or hybrid human-animal mixes. They range in body shape and relative emphasis on different body parts. Rarely do they have details of all body parts clearly present. This diversity suggests a range of visual and tactile meanings from the purely aesthetic to the ritual and even the religious. The meanings behind these figurines probably depended a lot on the specific group that made them, and thus there were likely many reasons for the figurines.

One of the most interesting things about figurines is that they show up around the same time, or just after, paintings on cave walls. We already discussed the earliest likely paint-like substance: ochre mixed with some liquid (dating to around 200,000 to 250,000 years ago or even earlier). But this simple ochre blend would not have had the fluidity, density, and adhesiveness needed for more detailed painting on cave walls or other objects. One could smear or rub it on items, but creating strokes, curved lines, and detailed depictions on larger surfaces and having it dry in that same form was unlikely.

The earliest evidence of a true paint-like substance comes from ochre blended with fat from the marrow of an animal found in abalone shells in South Africa dating to about 100,000 years ago. But no evidence of painting is found in association with it. Another tantalizing find from a South African site called Sibudu, dating to about 49,000 years ago, provides evidence for a blend of ochre and milk from a wild bovid (cowlike animal). This find shows us that the humans living there had to have hunted a wild bovid that was lactating and that they took the milk for making pigments and possibly other uses. But, unfortunately, this site also does not have any evidence of how the pigment was used.

The first evidence of actual paintings comes from sites in Southeast Asia and Southern Europe. In Sulawesi, Indonesia, at a site called Leang Timpuseng, on a cave wall, is a clear image of the outline of a human hand dated to about 40,000 years ago, and a running babirusa (a kind of wild pig) dated to about 36,000 years ago. Nearby at Leang Jarie there is another hand stencil dated to at least 39,000 to 40,000 years ago. At a site called El Castillo in Spain there is a red disk dated to about 40,000 years ago and hand stencils dated to about 37,000 years ago. From these points on we find cave paintings increasingly at different locations around the world.

Among the most common images on cave walls are those of hand stencils (remember from the chapter on sex and gender that most were made by females and children). These are followed by images of animals such as horses, large buffalo, pigs, and deer. There are frequently scenes with multiple animals of different types in them, and often new paintings were done directly over older ones, sometimes thousands of years apart. Humanlike figures are rare in the early paintings but start to show up more frequently in the last 15,000 to 25,000 years.

Looking back from our twenty-first-century world with museums, books, movies, television, scanners, and the Internet, it is hard to understand how significant these cave paintings were for those who made and experienced them at the time they were painted. These cave paintings reflect a truly human and really distinctive imaginative, and collaborative, investment. For example, the first paintings in the caves at Altamira, Spain, a World Heritage site, were painted earlier than 22,000 years ago, and the most recent ones were finished about 13,000 years ago. This cave system was used by humans for more than 9,000 years as a place for the creation of images, stories, and wonder. To put this in context, it has been only about 4,600 years since the great pyramids at Giza, Egypt, were built, and only about 230 years since the United States was founded. For more than 9,000 years people walked into the dark of the caves at Altamira with flickering lamps that illuminated the caverns, passageways, and walls, and they painted. They translated their imaginations to reality, and it remains there today. On those walls images of deer, bison, and horses spring to life, some of them almost six feet in length, appearing to bolt across the caverns in vibrant reds, yellows, and blacks. The natural curves, bumps, and bulges in the rock are covered with outlines and images, giving the sensation that they are beings, alive, and are following the spectator. Altamira, like so many of the caves strewn with human painting, is a massive sign of humanity's intense relationship with the visual arts and our distinctive capacity to make meaning by imagining, collaborating, and creating.

As impressive as the cave art and figurines are, there is one curious subject missing from nearly all of them before around 8,000 to 10,000 years ago: detailed human faces. There are human forms, and some have faces, but any detail in the faces is uncommon. Rarely do the faces have any characteristics aside from a dot or indention for eyes, a protuberance for a nose, and maybe a line for a mouth. But from about 10,000 years ago onward, detailed faces become more common in art in many places across the planet. The archeologist Ian Kuijt and others argue that it is not until about 10,000 years ago or so, with the advent of villages and agriculture and the concomitant increasing commitment to senses of property, identity, and place, that the role of the human face in art starts to take shape. It's in art related to mortuary practices that these faces become most common, at least in areas of the Middle East where this is well studied. This shift, to sedentism and the issues of creating identities associated with agriculture and animal domestication, is a shift from the small-scale groups to larger and more sedentary communities and appears to have brought with it a reconceptualization of identity and social relationships. The appearance of detailed faces in the archeological record is just another in the long line of creative innovations in our more than 300,000-year-old fascination with visual arts. This makes the material remains of visual arts, the hard evidence of the human imagination, one of the most important tools we have to see the shifting ways in which humans are perceiving and making meaning in the world.

But not all art is visual or leaves behind durable material remains. Three of the most important forms of human meaning-making have to do with the ephemeral entities of sound and movement that leave little or no material record: These forms are song, dance, and storytelling.

Many anthropologists and archeologists will declare that of course song, music, and dance were as central to humans in the past as they are to humans in the present. Off the record some might even suggest that this immersion in sound and movement might go back very far into our lineage's history. They do this off the record because there is little we can find in the way of evidence for such endeavors. But that does not stop all the researchers from going out on a limb and singing the praises of the possibility that sound and movement constitute some of the earliest and most important aspects of human creativity.

The archeologist Steven Mithen argues that musicality is a fundamental part of being human. He suggests that the capacity to create melody with our voices and with material items and to use this melodic process to tell stories, to bind groups together, and to express our imaginations is deep in our evolutionary roots. He makes the case that language itself evolved out of a protolanguage of musical and emotional expression. Mithen asserts that earlier human ancestors developed a system of communication he calls "Hmmmm" that was a mixture of gesture and melody and was the precursor to language. He sees our ancestors as making "extensive use of variation in pitch, rhythm and melody to communicate information, express emotion and induce emotion in other individuals."

Basically his argument is that the other primates use vocalizations, gestures, and body postures for communication, thus our ancestors shared those deep primate capacities. Many nonhuman primates also use vocalizations, often melodic ones, to communicate with one another about emotion states and dangers and even as part of the creation and maintenance of tight social bonds. All the apes use such vocal behavior, and one set of apes, the gibbons, uses highly melodic calls (primatologists call them "songs") as their main mode of communication. Mithen goes further and asserts that there is an inherent musicality to primate vocalizations, and thus our ancestors had, and used, this capacity even before the appearance of our own genus, *Homo*. As the members of the genus *Homo* developed more complex cognitive and behavioral patterns over the first 1.5 million years or so of their evolution, we know they must have developed more complex ways of communication; the tools, power scavenging, and complex child rearing and teaching would not have been possible without it.

Mithen suggests that part of this new system of communication was the increased use of "sound synesthesia," in which vocalizations are used to represent the size of things, their movement, or both. Think about the whistling sound we often make when describing something falling to the ground (*pheeeeeeeeooowww, boom!*) or the sounds we use to describe the galloping of a horse (*gaalump, gaalump, gaalump*). Mithen argues that with the emergence of more complex types of material expression (art), hunting, fire, and increasingly complex social lives, the direct ancestors of modern humans took this protolanguage Hmmmm system and modified it into more complex melodic aspects (music and song) and at the same time to more particulate vocal aspects (more sounds that had discrete meanings), leading eventually to language. In this scenario, music and language go hand in hand, and there is some good neurobiological evidence that the two are tightly interconnected.

Not everyone agrees with this scenario. There is a range of issues, from what anatomical evidence we might find, to a lack of material evidence of these shifts, to the argument that much language today is structurally not like music or melody such that the two are not really that entangled. Also, Mithen probably underestimates the capacity for information-dense vocal communication in other animals (birds, for example) and the depth of gestural communication even in the other primates. Finally, it's not clear how we would test when such a capacity went from Hmmmm to early music and then on to language. Maybe the changes in the visual arts from early ochre use and engravings to beads and figurines reflect changes in the cognition and behavior of *Homo,* representing a move from general sound synesthesia and Hmmmm-style communication to more elaborate sequences of sounds and meaning (songs). This was then followed by more particulate use of sounds for specific meanings (early language) as we see the details of visual arts increase in complexity. Nice story, but without a trusty time machine it is presumably impossible to verify.

A related argument is put forward by the philosopher Maxine Sheets-Johnstone, who argues that dance and movement are central to both our cognitive development and the ways in which humans have created complex emotional, behavioral, and communication systems. In line with

Mithen's assertions about melody and music, and those of the philoso-pher Merlin Donald, who argues for mimesis (in which humans began to rehearse and refine movements in controlled and systematic ways, with this ability enabling them to reproduce the movements on com-mand and imbue them with more and more complex meaning), Sheets-Johnstone places an emphasis on dance and the use and coordination of movement to convey empathy, meaning, and content. Sheets-Johnstone argues that humanity danced itself into our current form.

The focus on melodic sounds and movement is likely very important, and these arguments do sound attractive. But the evidence in support of them comes mostly from modern human behavior, comparison with liv-ing primates and other animals, and a small bit of data from the archeo-logical record. Bone flutes are the earliest clearly musical instruments identified, and they date only to about 43,000 years ago, found at a few sites in what is today Germany. When played they do indeed sound like notes we recognize (a clay replica of a 33,000-year-old bone flute was made and played). It is only in the last 14,000 years or so that we start to find broader evidence of musical instruments. Paintings or art that clearly depict music or dance are also very recent. However, that does not mean that melodic sounds, especially percussion sounds (drumming), and dancing did not show up much earlier. Many human cultures use some form of drumming and some form of repetitive vocal chanting and melodic movement as part of their ways of expression. It is not a stretch to assume that early members of the genus *Homo* developed a knack for sound early on. In the process of making stone tools there is a lot of sound, and much potential to develop that sound into melody. Chim-panzees sometimes drum on fallen trees to draw attention to themselves, and many birds (like woodpeckers) make highly sequential melodic pounding sounds. Our ancestors could have followed suit and slowly, over great amounts of time, incorporated some sounds and the structures of those sounds into more than just a sense of pleasure from making melodic noise or the direct function of pounding or drumming rocks together.

The jury is still out on the role of sound, melody, and dance in human evolution, but I'm willing to make a substantial bet that the sensations one feels, and the meanings one infers, on hearing the "Dance of the Sugar Plum Fairy" from Tchaikovsky's *The Nutcracker* or Charlie Parker's "Summertime" or the Rolling Stones' "You Can't Always Get What You Want" have very deep roots.

Verbal and gestural storytelling is the final type of art that does not truly fossilize. In truth, all art is about storytelling of a sort. Art has meaning to those who made it, and the conveying of that meaning is the basis of what we call a story. But the human capacity to gather a group together and, via sounds, gestures, and possibly visual aids, to relate a set of ideas, events, hopes, and dreams is more than just distinctively human; it is probably the key outcome of our evolution as a creative species. Storytelling is how we humans navigate the world. On a daily basis we relate to others events, ideas, and experiences that are separate from the moment in time and the physical place in which we are relating them. From mundane explanations at work, to recapping the day's events to family and friends, to daydreaming (telling ourselves stories about possible futures), storytelling is something we practice every day.

The way I've just laid out the use of storytelling necessitates language. But one can also see that whatever the forms of protolanguage in our ancestors, they would have had to have been used and experimented with in order to further develop a storytelling capacity. The urge and drive to communicate increasingly complex and imaginative thoughts and the need to collaborate with others in intensive ways to make that happen are likely at the base of everything we've discussed in this chapter so far. The creation of art is the story of storytelling. Nearly 2 million years ago the earliest members of the genus *Homo* developed and shared the capacities to make Oldowan stone tools; then they coordinated power scavenging, the exploitation of new foods, and the development of new tool types. They moved on to hunting and fire and the use of ochre, the creation of engravings and figurines, the advent of domestication and agriculture, and the development of the visual arts. All the while our ancestors were moving, gesticulating, humming, grunting, dancing, singing, and eventually talking their way into the world we now live in. What's more, there is no evidence at all that we have slowed down. The creative species is on a roll.

Religion, Art, and . . .

Humans form and are formed by a meaning-laden world. Our ancestors' creative ability to shape stone, wood, bone, and so many other items, and imbue them with meaning, has generated the opportunity for the explosion of art as a major aspect of what humans do and has reshaped how we see the world. The creative spark is in every one of us. It flourishes in individual efforts and develops and expands through our deep capacities, and propensity, for collaboration. Creating items of art reshaped the human experience and became central in telling stories and expanding the transcendental and imaginative aspects of being human. This opened the door for the use of art to push ideologies, especially those related to inferences about the supernatural. Religious ideas are often symbolic, represented and revealed through art. Some even argue that art and religion are one and the same. But the evidence of artistic creativity predates, by far, the origins of any structured religious practices and rituals. One can effectively argue that the creative capacities facilitating art were also crucial in the human ability to develop meaningful systems of belief that were rooted in more than the material here and now of daily life (what we currently call religion). Across human history, and today, most art is not associated with any particular religion or religious practice. Religion uses art, but art is not necessarily religious.

While these two areas of human creativity (art and religious belief) can overlap, they are not the same. Nor are they alone in arising from our creative spark. Human creativity also gave rise to another core process, one that is often set in opposition to religion and one that certainly has become a driving force in explaining why humans have come to manipulate the planet like no other species. Our creative spark is also at the root of science.

SCIENTIFIC ARCHITECTURE

Opening a tin can is easy, if one has a can opener. Stepping on the gas of a car propels us forward because the engine hosts a series of controlled explosions, forcing pistons up and down and turning the crankshaft. The thousand-ton plane lifts off the ground at 165 miles per hour because of the aerodynamic design of the wings. Taking an aspirin lessens the dull ache in our heads because it inhibits a particular enzyme that tells the brain about pain. The can opener, internal combustion engine, airplane wing, and aspirin all have one thing in common: They exist thanks to science. All of these solutions are here in our lives because communities of humans set about to tackle a problem, answer a question, or solve a riddle by creating new ideas, new apparatuses, and new perspectives.

The modern toothbrush was invented nearly a century and a half ago, toothpaste a few decades later. Both were developed to assist in the cleaning of teeth to avoid the cavities and dental damage that have been with us since the advent of domestication. Toothbrushes and toothpaste have improved dramatically in the past fifty years in concert with the heightened challenge to our teeth brought on by our knack for consuming sugary, high-carbohydrate foods. More Americans rated the toothbrush as the invention "they could not live without" than any other item in their households, and that was back in 2003. The 2003 toothbrush worked fine, but that did not stop us. We can't seem to leave things alone—we keep tweaking, improving, and modifying them, and in the case of the toothbrush producing the humming, twirling, vibrating, plaque-destroying apparatuses of today. Humans rarely stop at one answer or one solution to a problem. Any solution can be tweaked, fiddled with, manipulated, and improved.

No one questions that the products of science have forever changed the way humans interact with the world and one another. But science is not just about producing technology; it's a love of understanding that can reveal worlds beyond any we have previously experienced. It's an awesome blend of curiosity, perseverance, cooperation, innovation, luck, and creativity. Like art and religion, science reflects a coming together of some the best facets of what makes us human.

Most people think that science started in the last 400 years with people like Galileo Galilei, Francis Bacon, René Descartes, and Isaac Newton, who assembled the core of what we now consider the scientific method. Others put its origin at around 2,600 years ago with the Greek philosopher Thales of Miletus, who inspired Aristotle. Thales sought to develop a natural philosophy that asked questions about the origins of matter, the functioning of the earth, and all things on it. He also sought to apply similar concepts to the study of astronomy and attempted to develop explanations that were rooted in material processes, not supernatural ones. Others see the works of the early Egyptians and the Babylonians as scientific and the Tang dynasty of 1,100 to 1,400 years ago in China (where the compass, gunpowder, papermaking, and printing were invented) as the true seat of scientific innovation. These are all decent places and people on which to hang the origins of science, but they are all a little off.

If we are referring to one specific aspect of modern science, like the scientific method, or the history of Western natural philosophy, or if we identify science as that which leads to the production of modern technology, these explanations work well. But what if we think of science as a distinctively human way to understand the world, one that goes very deep back into our history? Then we discover that the human capacity for science is rooted in our creativity.

Is It Just a Mechanism?

Most people who care about science see it as simply the process of using the *scientific method*. This method includes the observation of phenomena, the construction of a testable hypothesis to explain the phenomena, and the testing of that hypothesis. If the original hypothesis is tested and shown to be incorrect, then it is back to the drawing board, and a new hypothesis must be developed. If the original hypothesis is supported, then it needs to be tested again and verified. If the hypothesis survives many tests without being refuted (shown to be wrong), then we can say it's strongly supported and is the best current explanation for the observed phenomena. We can subsequently use this and other supported hypotheses to develop a broader theory for the patterns and process we are looking at. For example:

- The observation of phenomena: If you throw something up into the air it falls back to the ground.
- The construction of a hypothesis to explain that phenomena: Planets like ours have a gravitational field whose strength is proportional to the planet's mass and inversely proportional to the square of the distance from the center of the planet. This field causes things to be drawn toward the center of the planet at a fixed rate of acceleration (to "fall").
- The testing of that hypothesis to see if it is supported or refuted: Testing this hypothesis is done by dropping various things from various heights in various conditions, mapping and monitoring movements of objects in our galaxy and beyond, and conducting a series of mathematical analyses. In the case of gravity, we discover that the maximum rate of acceleration that things fall (on earth) is 9.8 meters per second^2 (which is 32.17405 feet per second^2 and varies a little depending on your distance to the equator, location in mountains, etc.), and this answer gives us verification that there is a reasonably uniform field of gravity around our planet. With the science of physics we can demonstrate that a gravitational field is why items fall.

Gravity is now part of a much larger body of hypotheses and resulting theory, including relativity and quantum mechanics, that explains how the four forces that rule the entire universe act (the weak nuclear force, the strong nuclear force, electromagnetism, and gravity). But again, gravity is the best measurable and testable explanation of particular phenomena, not the ultimate and one true complete and unerring answer. Scientists are devoted to continuing to test and tweak our understandings. In 1915 Albert Einstein hypothesized that gravity waves exist (as part of his larger proposal about relativity). For a hundred years researchers failed to find those waves via scientific experiments. But in 2016—after a century of failure—an ingenious technology that can "hear" outer space as well as see it enabled their discovery. Science is ongoing and malleable.

The scientific method is distinct from other methods of asking and answering questions about the world in that it relies on a process that seeks to refute assertions or support them via replicable testing and verifiable measures. The scientific method can never "prove" something right. It can prove things absolutely wrong and it can demonstrate how something is accurate as far as our tests allow us to assess (supporting a hypothesis and developing theory). Gravity is a correct assumption as far as we can test. As we are more able to test smaller and smaller details about the forces of the universe, our understandings about gravity (for example, that it comes in waves or that quantum gravity exists) are modified and improved. Scientific inquiry does not end when we have a reliably tested answer, as current answers are rarely the best ones we'll ever have. This is very different from other approaches that rely on philosophical, theological, or logical rhetorical arguments. The scientific method can tell us which explanations are not measurably correct, it can show us which explanations are likely correct via measurable verification, but it cannot tell us that those that appear correct now are the absolute best answers possible.

Take the big bang. This is a hypothesis about the origin of the universe, basically stating that it began as a superdense, superheated mass that began to expand and cool a very long time ago and that continues to expand today. There are a series of calculations and observations that support this; galaxies are moving away from one another with a velocity proportional to their distance (called "Hubble's law"), demonstrating that the universe is expanding. The presence and structure of cosmic microwave background also shows this expansion, and the overabundance of hydrogen and helium, (they are among the earliest elements produced) gives us an indication of the history of cooling and element formation in the universe. These are all measurable factors and enable us (or, rather, astronomers and physicists) to calculate the age of the universe. It is about 13.77 billion years old. But this figure is not an end to the inquiry. It is the best possible answer given our current ability to test the processes in the universe. Explanations for the universe will be refined again and again as our abilities to test and to model astronomical features continue to get better.

Equating science with the scientific method is useful for some trains of thought and argument. But it's also reasonable to acknowledge that this kind of science is merely a methodology, one that was formalized only in the last 300 to 400 years or so.

The Science Council of the United Kingdom defines science as "the pursuit and application of knowledge and understanding of the natural and social world following a systematic methodology based on evidence"; sounds pretty reasonable. The science fiction author Isaac Asimov tells us that "science doesn't purvey absolute truth. Science is a mechanism. It's a way of trying to improve your knowledge of nature. It's a system for testing your thoughts against the universe and seeing whether they match." Meanwhile, the famous anthropologist Claude Lévi-Strauss tells us that "the scientist is not a person who gives the right answers, he's one who asks the right questions." Taking these three definitions of, or musings on, science, we can establish a baseline for assessing science in the human past:

- Science is about trying to figure out how the world works and seeking the answers in material explanations.
- Science involves some kind of testing of explanations or ideas in order to see if they "fit" with expected material outcomes (for example, things fall when you drop them; that is a material outcome, and gravity is our current, well-tested, scientific explanation for that).
- The goal of science is to develop the best questions and improve our understandings, not to know all the answers.

If these three basic points are valid, science is potentially a highly imaginative endeavor with lots of room for failure (good science has a lot of failure—it took a century to find gravity waves, even though physicists were pretty certain they should be there). Good science also requires acceptance that we do not know all possible outcomes for any given question. It embraces the assumption that no matter how much we know at any given moment, there remain bits of relevant information we do not yet have. Accepting these caveats is a lot to expect of humans. But we do it all the time. And we do it because we are very curious and very creative.

We have ample evidence of deep creativity in the human lineage, but in order to tap into that creativity for the kind of inquiry that fits into what we call science, we need a particular tenacity and wherewithal to commit to solving problems. Undertaking science requires curiosity beyond just the drive to satiate hunger, thirst, or the need for sleep, sex, and safety. Engaging in science requires a deep desire to know how and why, and the persistence to try to figure out the answers to those questions, regardless of the frustration and failure we encounter. Doing science relies deeply on a driving curiosity and a capacity to imagine, to innovate, to experiment, and to create. Our creative evolutionary history, driven solely by neither competition nor sex nor violence, predisposed us to it.

Curiosity

Other animals are good problem solvers. Nature gives us countless examples of amazingly complicated solutions to environmental challenges. Think about termite mounds, bird nests, squirrels hiding nuts for the winter, or dolphin groups blowing bubble nets to herd fish into tight clusters and eat them. Some animals are innovators in taking the world around them and manipulating it through the use and development of tools. New Caledonian crows use tools that they select, modify, and use to get food. These crows modify the leaves of the pandanus tree (a palm-like plant) by stripping off threads and using these threads in the collection of insects. The process the crows use can be cumulative: They sometimes make a set of sequential modifications to the same tool to hone it for better use. We see this type of tool innovation and experimentation in many primates: macaques, chimpanzees, *Cebus* monkeys, and orangutans all use wood and unmodified stone tools to enhance their abilities to get particular types of food. These primates learn how to make and use these tools by watching others and experimenting, via a sort of socially facilitated trial and error.

Many primates innovate when challenged by the environment outside of just food acquisition. Orangutans take large leaves and hold them over their heads when it rains; chimpanzees eat certain bad-tasting leaves covered with teeny bristles when they have intestinal worms, and the leaves help clean out their systems. Many other animals rise to ecological challenges via taking items in the world around them and using them for novel purposes. While such behavior must include some curiosity—some wondering of "What happens when I do this?"—nearly all of these innovations are driven by functional goals: hunger, thirst, illness, comfort, and so on. The process of evolution has honed many species' responses to the challenges of the world into amazing and innovative capacities. Their solutions are usually obtained by some degree of learning, observing others, and a lot of trial-and-error experimentation. But remember, it takes a young chimpanzee many months, if not years, to learn how to effectively use a rock to crack open nuts, whereas the same skill can be taught to a young human in a day.

Give a monkey a box with some food in it and she will do her darnedest to figure out how to get at the food inside. Put a new squeak toy in front of most dogs and they will spend hours, if not days, playing with it, investigating where and how to bite it to produce the squeak sound, and maybe taking it apart, pulling the squeaker out, and possibly losing interest once the toy no longer squeaks, no longer sparks their curiosity. Some apes show great curiosity about new objects that appear in their environment, investigating them for hours on end. There is no doubt that novelty and strangeness can inspire interest and curiosity in other animals.

Humans do a lot of similar functional experimentation and have enormous curiosity tied to solving problems associated with life's challenges. They do more than observe others and learn through trial and error. Humans investigate and experiment far more than is necessary for function and survival. And then they teach one another about it. Humans want to know why and how, and we collaborate to build on previous information to develop more questions and ever more comprehensive, effective, and novel answers. This is the core of science.

Beyond Hit or Miss

Science emerges from an especially creative problem-solving system that can lead to the augmentation of existing solutions—humans build on previous knowledge to develop more complex and multilevel explanations and understandings. The human desire to tweak things leads to an ability to improve them. This produces some important differences with other animals.

A young chimpanzee regularly gets to see his mom and other adult chimpanzees cracking nuts and eating the insides. He might get some of the scraps and recognize that they are tasty. He puts the basics together. There is the nut that has food inside it and some stuff one can use to get at that food. He sees that the adults grab items and hit the nut with the items and after a few hits the nut opens and the food is accessible. So, he starts trying to open the nuts using what he finds at hand—small sticks, rocks, branches, clumps of dirt. He learns that some items work better than others and, maybe in concert with more watching of the adults, he begins to focus on using harder and larger items to hit the nut. He cracks open a nut, every now and then, and gets the goodies. After a long while he develops an understanding of the qualities of a hammer that make it more likely to be effective at opening the nut, but only after considerable trial and error with different possible "hammers." Eventually, he might become expert at nut cracking and be one of the adults that the young watch, rapt, trying to figure out how to get at the goodies in the hard shell. But the process of becoming expert can take months or years. And not all chimpanzee groups with access to nuts and stones to crack them do so.

Now, not all human groups use all available foods in their environment either, but most do use the ones highest in nutritional value (like nuts). And even if they don't use a specific food, the technologies (tools) to exploit and process foods (hammers, knives, etc.) are usually present even if not focused on one particular food type. The chimpanzees that do not crack nuts do not use hammer stones for other purposes. This is not to say that chimpanzees are not innovative relative to other animals and other primates (they are); it is just that in comparison to humans, chimpanzees use tools and innovate with tools much less.

There are a few reasons for this difference. First, humans ask "Why?" and "How?" more frequently and often do so collaborating in groups. Each individual's capacity for creativity melds with our knack for cooperation and group coordination and becomes a central force in discovery. Humans have a dense kind of shared intentionality (the capacity to consciously agree on the same cognitive interpretation and goals); this enables us to focus together on challenges and solutions. Our ability to convey information, ideas, and innovations is more substantial than that of other animals, even early on in the history of our genus. Humans have a great capacity to ratchet up, or scaffold, information.

Early humans could take rocks and crack open nuts, just like chimpanzees. Early *Homo* could also differentiate between stones to select better hammers, like chimpanzees (chimp adults, at least). So, early *Homo* had the information: Stones crack nuts; certain stones are better than others for this. But they had the capacity to work together on the nut-cracking issue, to transfer information about it and to investigate. Say a few times they cracked nuts with the sharp edge of a stone . . . and it worked better than other hammers. Or they used a slightly larger flat stone and ended up cracking two nuts at once. In both of these cases they could get together, combining individual discovery and group collaboration, to realize that there are specific size and shape variables that might enable better success or productivity in nut cracking. They could then take this information, share it, and further refine the tools they use, to increase production (multiple nuts at once) or to go in some other direction with the information. This process is *ratcheting* in its most basic form and is the connection of individual experience and group collaboration necessary for moving toward a capacity for scientific investigation.

A hook and some string allow us to hunt for food in the water, where we cannot see or breathe. Putting some food on the hook and using the tension in the string to tell us when there is a fish biting on the other end is all there is to it. But humans don't leave it at that. Once we have the hook, someone will fiddle with it to improve its function: add barbs to make it harder for the fish to disentangle itself; add color or additional aspects to make the hook look like a prey item; or forget the food and just dress the hook up to look like a small fish or insect (a lure). Humans have the capacity to invent, but they also have the desire to take the invention and the information that comes from using the invention and revisit basic concepts and design.

Other animals do some ratcheting and scaffolding, but they lack the human combination of discovery, innovation, cooperation, and information transfer. Human cognitive capacities and manual dexterity (our brains and hands) and our hypercooperation give us a broader range of ways to manipulate the world relative to other species. If dolphins or orcas had hands and spent time on land, this story might be different, but they don't.

Humans ask "Why?" and try to use the answers we come up with to create better solutions (or at least to ask better questions). While we didn't always succeed at this process with the level of refinement and accomplishment we do now, it is clear that iPhones, airplanes, electrical grids, research institutes, and medical technologies have their roots in the curiosity, experimentation, innovation, and creativity our ancestors applied to stones and wood in the deep past.

The Trajectory of a Spear

The earliest evidence for something like science takes us back to the start of our genus and the early stone tools. Take the context for Oldowan tool creation, for example. Early members of the genus *Homo* grew up in a group that had some very simple stone tools, and they knew the basic strategy of using one stone to alter the shape of another one such that it took on new capacities for use. The simplest stone tools predate the appearance of our own genus. Early *Homo* inherited a world where stone toolmaking was already present—and they improved on it. Somehow, possibly through trial and error, they began to realize that there was significant variation in the quality of different stones. This variation in quality meant some made better or more effective tools, lasted longer, and had sharper edges. Alas, the better rocks were not available everywhere. Working together, groups of early *Homo* learned to search across their landscape to find the better rocks. This worked pretty well. We see this pattern (the creation of basic Oldowan tools) across a long time period (about half a million years) without too much structural change. When something works well, there is not much pressure to change it. Eventually, however, a bit of curiosity leads to ratcheting, probably only in some groups at any given time. We see variation in which stones are used and in the styles of the subsequent tools. The curiosity–experimentation–innovation cycle, once it got going, started to change the ways in which our early ancestors' brains worked and the ways in which they communicated with one another.

By today's standards the process of developing ways to make slightly better sharp-edged stones or creating more types of stones to crush or scrape things with is not all that impressive. But when we consider that these methods were undertaken by organisms with no language, much smaller and less complex brains than ours, and only the rudiments of our cognitive capacities, the achievement is not too shabby. While it took a very long time to flourish into the kinds of investigation, experimentation, and discovery that we associate with science today, we can identify a few instances of this innovation as particularly important in our history in regard to the refinement of human creativity and curiosity into science. These are the skills to make and use tools to hunt, the ability to control and create fire, the development of pigments and adhesives, and the initial forays into domestication. We've touched on these details previously, so here I'll just highlight how they set us up for the eventual capacity to fly in airplanes, generate electrical power, maintain dental hygiene, open cans, and grow food for millions of people.

Reshaping a simple stone tool by knocking flakes off both sides is impressive (no other animal on the planet has ever done it) but not a giant leap in the progress toward scientific research. The changes in early *Homo* technology that take precedence are a bit more recent, mostly in the last

300,000 to 400,000 years. One of the most striking changes in tools is the development of thrown spears, enabling us to hunt at a distance.

The earliest solid evidence of throwing spears, or javelins, comes from the 300,000-year-old site of Schöningen in what's now Northern Germany. Throwing spears are wooden tools sharpened at one end, of moderate length (four to six feet or so), and thin and balanced. Schöningen is a horse-butchery site (more than twenty horses were butchered there) with a massive array of stone, bone, and wood tools. The site was flooded and waterlogged, enabling the preservation of much of the organic materials (wood). Making a throwing spear is no small feat. We have evidence of thrusting spears (heavier and thicker wooden sticks sharpened at one end) at this site and at a few earlier ones, so we know that by 300,000 years ago (and likely much earlier), members of the genus *Homo* had put together the concepts of sharp stick + stabbing action + animal = food, a basic equation that set the stage for thrown spears.

When *Homo* of 300,000 years ago were hunting and found a horse, they'd collaborate on a plan. A few of them would sneak up behind the prey as others chased it into a small open area between two thick groves of trees. Those behind would block the animal's options for exit, and others would rush out from the trees to stab or club the animal. But horses are both fast and large. Often the horse crashed through the two or three members of the group stabbing at it with the sharpened sticks. Sometimes they caught it head-on, driving the spear deep into the horse's chest. Other times they were knocked aside or trampled, spears missing the mark in the heat and frenzy of the moment. As the horse ran past, some might heave the spear or toss a club or rock at it, usually in vain. But every now and then a thought might occur, and an idea might start simmering.

Homo of 300,000 years ago had probably thrown rocks at rabbits and other small prey, with occasional success. And maybe playing around a bit, members of the group tossed the heavy spears at one another or hurled them into the ground in frustration when the prey got away. The spears sometimes stuck. Someone, likely more than one, noticed this. As a group they might have started experimenting with throwing the spears, but the heavy and unbalanced versions rarely hit a mark, or when they did, they as often as not connected at an off angle instead of head-on. This is where working together and innovating come into play. What if one or two of the thrusting spears happened to be a little lighter or a bit better balanced, maybe made by one of the younger members or a small woman who really liked to hunt. Maybe one time as the horse ran past she flung the spear at its haunch and it stuck. It pierced the flesh and hung there for a few moments, eventually dropping out as the horse ran off. But the seed was planted; they'd seen this and the gears of their minds started turning.

A new calculus emerged: sharp stick + small circumference + light weight + throwing + animal = food. Now they could experiment, even calculate. In most cases nothing new came of it, but sometimes members of the group experimented with weight and balance, with throwing different sizes and shapes of sharpened sticks. This set the stage for new types of hunting tools, new types of technology and understandings of the world. Physics, anyone?

There is a very simple example that is used in introductory physics classes to illustrate how human minds began to incorporate math into their hunting. The model is called "the monkey and the hunter."

A hypothetical hunter is walking through the forest when she sees a monkey hanging under an exposed branch in the tree. If she has encountered this before, she knows that when she throws her sharp stick at it, the monkey will likely drop down to avoid being hit. So a quandary emerges: Where does she aim the spear? At where the monkey is now or at where she knows it will be shortly after she releases the spear? This is where humans' implicit recognition of gravity, trajectory, mass, and even basic math melds. You might think the answer is to aim the spear just below the monkey. And you'd be wrong. You aim at the monkey. This is because gravity works equally on the spear and the monkey, so both fall (are pulled by gravity) at approximately the same rate. The spear is traveling in two directions, so it has what we call a trajectory: It's moving toward the monkey due to the force applied by the hunter and it's moving toward the ground due to the force of gravity. Its trajectory is a parabola, not a straight line. So the vertical component of velocity of the spear (let's call it vy) has an initial value vyo but decreases due to gravity and the time it is moving toward the monkey (gt): $vy = vyo - gt$. As time elapses between the release and the potential strike of the monkey, there is also the feature of time in the equation, so the change in the height of the spear is affected by its velocity, gravity, the time from the moment it is thrown, and of course the initial level it is aimed at. This gives us the equation $y = yo + vyot - 1/2\,gt^2$ (where t is time) to explain the vertical position of the spear in its trajectory. Our ancestors did not envision the math as a literal equation. The formalization of algebra and calculus came much, much later. But they did begin to figure out the relationships described by the equation and use them as a basis for not just spears, but a whole array of other thrown items.

Throwing spears emerged, as did a whole new way of hunting. Our ancestors did not have language like we do, but they obviously had the capacity to communicate to one another, show one another ideas, and work and think together to solve this problem, and this often resulted in the creation of a new technology and new ways to hunt. Being able to connect with prey without being close enough to touch (or be bitten, kicked, etc.) radically changed the shape of hunting, and of humans. By 200,000 to 300,000 years ago, humans became hunters at a distance, and the concept of projectile weapons, of shooting, became part of the human equation. This series of hunting experiments starting 300,000 years ago set the stage for humans to create high-powered sniper rifles, surface-to-air missiles, and space exploration. This same basic equation concept, with a whole lot of added variables and complexities, is what we calculate in order to launch a rocket to fly humans to the moon and to launch spacecraft to the outer reaches of our solar system and beyond, and it is what will soon put humans on Mars.

Throwing weapons was only one way to extend the capacities of human bodies. Hafting was another. Hafting is the creation of a composite tool: the combination of two tool types, stone and wood or bone and wood, via tying them and/or gluing them together. This enhances a tool's capabilities. Take a hammer, for example. Hammers are two units bound together, the head and arm. Anyone can drive a nail into wood by hitting it with a hard object held in the hand, and it takes a lot of energy. The force at contact with the nail is proportional to the energy invested in the swinging of your arm. By using a hammer, we take advantage of physics (the lever action of the handle): We reduce the energy we put into the swing (compared to using a hard object in the palm of our hand) and get a higher force at impact. Consider also the improvement of a wooden spear with a stone point attached to it. Wood can be sharpened, but it cannot be as sharp as the thin edge of a stone, nor can it be as hard as the stone. Fixing a sharp flake to the end of the spear radically improves the effectiveness of that spear in piercing skin and flesh. Compound tools are better than simple tools, but they are harder to make.

To assemble a compound tool you need to (1) imagine the combination of two tools, (2) assemble the compound tool by modifying each of the parts to fit together, and (3) make sure that the two parts stay together when you use the tool. Part 1 is not too hard, but parts 2 and 3 are. Part 2 entails modifying tools not just for their use but also to fit into, or with, each other. And part 3 requires rope or twine and some kind of adhesive, a glue. The composite tool is not one invention; it is at least three wrapped in one, and its presence is the sign of a complex investigative mind.

Part 1 probably occurred many times starting about 300,000 years ago or so, but in most cases the individuals, and their group, could not figure out how to get from part 1 to parts 2 and 3. There are probably a lot of failed attempts that we'll never see in the archeological record. But we do see the successes. True hafted tools show up at least 125,000 years ago and more widely by 70,000 to 80,000 years ago. We can imagine a lot of toolmaking and complex behavior going on without direct instruction and language, but composite tools are different—humans had to invent glue.

Some of the earliest adhesives were probably made using ochre, the pigment that shows up at some *Homo* sites as much as 200,000 to 300,000 years ago. But the earliest ochre sites don't have composite tools, nor do we know how the ochre was used. We have no direct evidence of adhesives until about 200,000 years ago, and little evidence of regular usage until about 80,000 to 125,000 years ago. The archeologist Lyn Wadley and colleagues demonstrate just how difficult, and inspired, the development of adhesives was by going back to the site of Sibudu in South Africa. This site is more than 70,000 years old and is rich in evidence of the roots of science.

At Sibudu researchers have found long and sharp flakes that were shaped to be hafted to a wooden handle or spear. In the places where they are shaped to connect with the wood, there is evidence of adhesives: mixtures of ochre and plant gums (like tree sap). Sibudu provides evidence that earlier humans recognized that the sticky sap oozing out of trees could help them. It is possible that while foraging for fruits in certain trees or bushes, the group would get covered with the sap, and grass, sticks, and other small items would stick to their hands. The sap got on their tools and every now and then stuck a few stone flakes together. When the Sibudu people got back to camp, one found that the sap had dried and hardened and the flakes were stuck together. Maybe she showed the fused flakes to the others, one of whom had been fiddling with the idea of connecting wood and stone (maybe he was even made fun of for his attempts and failures). In that instant a realization struck both the failed toolmaker and the holder of the fused flakes: Sap can stick things together. Why not use it to make new tools? It probably took a long time to explain this to the group and even longer to demonstrate how it might work. But perseverance pays off. The group experimented with types of tools and amount of sap, eventually figuring out how to shape the flakes and the wood to create grooves and flat edges to maximize surface area of contact and even spread of the sap. Composite tools were created. But they weren't very good.

Sap is fickle. It can dry and act as an effective adhesive, but it becomes brittle and breaks on contact. Or if it gets damp it loses a degree of its stickiness and the tools can fall apart. This is where the ochre comes in. When one mixes ochre with plant gums, the resulting adhesive is firmer and more reliant and does not loosen when damp. The iron oxides in the ochre interact with the chemical structure of the plant gums to create this property. However, to achieve this effect one has to mix the two together in the right proportions, and to dry the mixture thoroughly it must be exposed to heat from a fire. This is exactly what Wadley and colleagues found in the tools from Sibudu. The groups of humans residing there discovered that the equation of ochre + sap + heat from fire = strong adhesive. This process fixed their composite tools and made them stronger and more effective than anything they'd had before. The people of Sibudu thought about, and experimented with, the adhesive qualities of the gums and the chemical properties of the ochres without any formal knowledge of chemistry and physics. They were doing science in its earliest form.

Like so many discoveries in chemistry, happenstance played a major role in the outcome. The people at Sibudu were already using ochre as a pigment, maybe even coloring their tools. The ochre would have occasionally mixed with the gum in these new composite tools and, when left by the fire, dried and hardened in a resilient manner. The group probably recognized this variation in their tools and tried to replicate it, mostly failing, for months or even years. But eventually, after enormous investigation and perseverance, they developed the recipe for creating a good adhesive, and the idea spread to other groups in the area. This pattern was not unique to the groups at Sibudu. We see evidence of the same process arising at sites around Africa and Eurasia around the same time, and it spread in those areas as well. Imagination of possible relationships between things, experimentation with the material world resulting in the discovery of new relationships between things, a new understanding of how things work, and the sharing of these discoveries became common. The roots of modern science are evident in the creation of glue more than 70,000 years ago.

Glue is an extremely handy invention. It and hafted tools, new weapons, increased use of rope and twine, the development of wet pigments and painting, and many other innovations start to flood the archeological record between 125,000 and 10,000 years ago. But the domestication of plants and animals is the next truly giant leap in the human proclivity toward science. The transition to growing crops and shaping animals sets the stage for the massive experimentation on, manipulation of, and understanding of the natural world that characterize humans (and science) of today.

We know that early domestication and sedentism (staying in the same place) didn't always work out so well. Health issues, conflicts with neighboring groups, and a lot more work characterized these early farming communities. But most stuck with it. Curiosity, imagination, and investigation drove them to it.

The process by which groups of people in the Pearl River valley of China selected and protected those rice stalks that had the shatterproof, less brittle genetic mutation fits almost perfectly into the terms of the scientific method. The people of the Pearl River valley collected the wild rice for food. It was a long and labor-intensive process to pick all the stalks and get all the ripe grains (protorice) before they fell off and/or birds and other animals got to them. But some must have noticed that there was variation in the ease with which grains fell off the stalks and shared this information with the others. The group could then work a bit to determine if there were ways to tell the difference between the easy-drop-off and the shatterproof varieties. They did not know they were using the phenotype (outer characteristics) to assess the genotype (underlying genetic patterns), but the result was the same: basic genetic experimentation. The first logical response was to then exploit the easy-drop-off grains early, as soon as they ripened, and save the shatterproof ones until later. Those tougher grains stuck to the stalk longer and were less likely to be eaten (and more likely to have the genetic mutation $sh4$). And this produced the first experimental success, even if half of it was not intentional. Taking the easily obtained ones first and saving the others until later, the people reduced the rate of reproduction of the easy-fall-off variety (more seeds of this kind eaten, thus fewer seeds germinating) and gave an upper hand in reproduction to those with the shatterproof genetic mutation—inadvertent genetic manipulation of plants, the start of farming and old-school creation of genetically modified organisms.

This selective process tilted the population of early rice toward the shatterproof variant, which led to the first "hypothesis." The Pearl River folks soon realized that more and more of the rice was shatterproof, and thus it took more work to get the seeds from the stalks. However, if they controlled access to the stalks, they secured all the grains. They put two and two together and hypothesized that they could control the life cycle, or at least the variation of types, in the early rice and make it give them more sustenance. Then they got creative with the second experiment (although it took many generations and a few centuries). They cleared areas around the rice of other plants and possibly put some guards, maybe children or young adults, in the patches of rice when it began to ripen to keep away birds and rodents. Then they'd organize the group (a community at this point) to collect all the ripe rice at the same time and take it back to the village or the seasonal camp. They didn't worry about losing too many grains (they were mostly shatterproof at this point). This was a harvest. After, they'd process the rice to extract the grains (threshing) and have more than enough food for all. Thus they'd have to create expanded storage techniques (pottery and other types of storage). They also had to assign people to guard the storage and manage it. You can probably see where this experiment is headed.

The same type of thing happened with different animals across the globe. In the Russian fox experiment, researchers demonstrated that one could select the friendliest pups and after forty generations have what looked and acted a lot like a domestic dog. The human + wolf + shared space + time = dog equation was a clear manipulation of dog genetics and development worked out by humans in many places around the planet. It was more of a mutual experiment, as the wolves experimented on us and we experimented on them—though our experiments were deeper and more creative (so they became our sidekicks; we did not become theirs). For animals that humans were preying on, like early goats and sheep, the direction and intent of the experimentation were more akin to those used on plants. Humans experimented with their food, changing the genetics—the development of muscles, bones, and fur—and reshaped the behavior.

Selective hunting of males and shaping of wild herds by management of hunting is evident in the archeological record pretty far back. In the last 10,000 years, that management ratcheted up to more than hunting experiments. Capturing and raising young animals led to a whole suite of new possible hypotheses and experiments. One challenge was to be able to raise the captured young. A key complication was the feeding of infant wild goats, sheep, or other mammals. They needed milk and a lot of nutrition on a daily basis. Today we know that many human groups, from herding societies in Mongolia to Amazonian foraging societies, will spend great time and effort to raise young animals, even to the point of feeding them with human milk from lactating mothers. This is also very likely one of the experiments tried many times by past groups, early in the domestication process. It worked, but it proved costly in terms of nutrition and time. Plus, setting up competition between one's infants and the animal infants that you are growing for food isn't the best strategy. A bit of imagination and creativity led to the solution we practice even today.

Most groups of humans who hunted animals had made a series of observations by this point: (1) There are two types of animals in each kind (species), and one type gives birth (females), and (2) in most kinds of animals, females nurse and do most of the caretaking of the young. An initial experiment was to capture females, corral them in some way, and wait for them to give birth and raise the young. One could have the animals themselves producing food for the group—much better than having to hunt them all the time. People soon discovered they'd not quite got the whole equation down. Females by themselves might give birth to one young, but not any after that. Something was missing. The females would not get pregnant again. It might have taken some time, and maybe not everyone put the pieces together, but most did. Around the planet, humans who were experimenting with capturing and raising animals to keep the meat close at hand began to figure out the solution. Male animals were good for something beyond eating. The whole equation was females + male(s) + captivity + time = offspring, a kind of biocalculus. Once this was discovered, humans gained two important bits of data, true scientific insights: (1) Reproduction requires males and females (it takes two to tango), and (2) the offspring had properties similar to those of the parents. Thousands of years before Gregor Mendel and Charles Darwin elaborated on these processes, the floodgates were opened, and selective breeding—human genetic manipulation of other species—had begun. Today we see this played out in nearly all of the animals we are familiar with, and well beyond breeding: This was the start of experimentation on other animals to manipulate them and to reshape their bodies and our uses of their bodies. The benefits to us have been high; the costs to, and impact on, other animals have been massive; and the benefits to them have been increasingly few.

Once people realized they could control the breeding and the shape and behavior of other organisms (plants or animals), knowledge, imagination, creativity, and experimentation fused into a system that integrated math, biology, and experience as well. Such a system, in which humans assume they can figure things out, manipulate them, and reshape them to their own ends, heralds the emergence of applied science as a human endeavor. From that point on, the connection between scientific inquiry (curiosity about how the world works) and technological development (how we create solutions to make the world work better for us) starts to ratchet up at a pace never before seen on this planet, thus initiating the Anthropocene, the age of the humans, and currently putting us, and the planet, on the brink of serious catastrophe.

Over the last 10,000 years, our knowledge base and technological developments have continued to accelerate. The more we know, the more technologies we have, and the faster and more dramatic our scientific endeavors and outcomes become. Knowledge, curiosity, imagination, creativity, technological improvements, and our intense capacity for cooperation and coordination, combined with the increasing density of humans, the needs of growing populations, language, economies, and so many other factors, set us up for the modern scientific explosion in engineering. Towns, cities, nations, roads, water systems, electrical grids, global transportation systems, and the Internet all emerged from the same underlying processes our ancestors utilized. But the playing field has changed. Rather than taking millennia or centuries or even generations to make substantive changes to our knowledge, our practices, and the world at large, the last few thousand years represent a whole new pace of scientific innovation and invention. Change is happening so fast today that it makes the whole preceding 2 million years of our story look like it was in snail-paced slow motion. When I was born, in 1966, there were no cell phones and no home computers, the Internet was barely a dream, NASA was preparing to send men to the moon, and the first large superlong-range passenger plane, the 747, was three years away from its maiden flight. At that time there were about 3 billion people on the planet. Today, just over half a century later, there are nearly 7.5 billion people on the planet. My iPhone has more computing power than NASA did when it launched its first spaceflights, I can video chat with anyone around the globe, and the 747 is antiquated.

Scientific Inquiry Turned Inward

The global changes initiated by our penchant for manipulating the world are likely to determine how long we last as a species—after all, most species eventually go extinct. But there is another, equally powerful and important, outcome of our capacity to do science: a distinctive capacity to look within. We are the only species that has a scientific curiosity, and we have turned it on ourselves, producing both practical and existential challenges. In addition to seeking supernatural explanations for why we are here, we've recently begun to ask the questions, "Who are we?" and "What are we doing here?" through a scientific lens. This leads to some interesting, and often contentious, results.

Humans have long investigated our bodies. Early philosophers of many societies dissected humans' and other animals' corpses and noticed similarities and differences. Roman physicians, Tibetan doctors, and Aztec priests all developed robust understandings of the human body and its functions. All noticed the similarities between humans and other animals.

The local people in part of southern Kalimantan (the Indonesian portion of the island Borneo) have an origin story about humans and orangutans. They tell of two brothers who lived in the forest. After many years one of the brothers tired of hanging out in the trees all day and decided to make himself productive. He set to work clearing an area of the forest, building a house for his family, and starting to grow fruits and planting a garden. Meanwhile the other brother lounged in the trees, eating ripe fruit and teasing his industrious brother for working so hard. The hardworking brother became the ancestor of humans and the loafer in the trees gave rise to the orangutans. This story is not just something to pass the time. It contains scientific reflection. Why the orangutan as humanity's brother? Why not a snake, a pig, or a bear? Because when humans live around the primates, especially apes, their incipient scientific capacity kicks in—they see the similarities. When placed side by side with apes, there is no doubt, we are very close to them indeed.

This pattern happens in places where there are no other primates. The human groups in such areas choose animals that are socially complex or have specific behavioral traits that remind them of humans—wolves, coyotes, killer whales (orcas), ravens, and so on. Humans notice similarities between themselves and other living forms and use these observations to derive understandings about relationships in the natural world. This contemplation reflects our scientific curiosity, and in the last few centuries it has exploded into a whole new way of thinking about who we are, where we come from, and what that means.

Charles Darwin published *The Descent of Man, and Selection in Relation to Sex* in 1871, twelve years after releasing his opus *On the Origin of Species,* forever changing our understanding of evolution and biology. That second book, *Descent,* was more shocking than the first; it argued that humans, just like all other life on the planet, had evolved from earlier forms. Darwin was not the first to assert this notion; others, including his grandfather Erasmus Darwin, flirted with formal ideas in the same vein. But Darwin was the first to provide a coherent, and eloquent, scientific account: a testable proposal for the material evolution of our species. His arguments laid out a series of hypotheses that we could assess, confirm, or refute. That humans were biologically related to (or even in) the mammalian order Primates was a well-known fact: Countless societies noticed it and the father of taxonomy, Linnaeus, placed it into the modern scientific canon more than a century before Darwin published his books. But the hypothesis that we had evolved over time from nonhuman ancestors into human beings was revolutionary and terrifying for many. It was also science. There would have to be ancestral forms discovered, there would have to be continuities in form and function across closely related primates, and all humans would have to be closely related to one another and derived from the same stock. All of these hypotheses have been tested; we reviewed the evidence in the first few chapters of this book. Darwin was right: We evolved, and we are still evolving.

Many of the processes for specific patterns of human evolution that Darwin proposed turned out to be not quite right, and his assertions about different human groups being more or less "evolved" were totally wrong. Unfortunately, the nineteenth and twentieth centuries were full of people who misrepresented and mangled evolutionary theory to promote racist and sexist ideas, in some cases leading to horrific policies, oppression, and atrocities. Today in the twenty-first century there are still some who do the same, but their number is dwindling as many scientists fight against the misuse and misrepresentation of evolutionary science.

Darwin started a trend, a branch of scientific inquiry that is still flourishing. Centuries of medical scientific investigation have created a powerful suite of technologies for humans to fight disease and damage to the body. But the addition of evolutionary theory, the expansion and fuller development of the ideas of Darwin and many others over the last century and a half, has revolutionized medicine. We can meld our studies of viruses, neurobiology, bacteria, and public health into complex understandings of the dynamic processes that make up the human body.

Some of our most recent scientific innovations have enabled us to excavate our past and to interpret what we find in the light of evolutionary processes. Over the last ten chapters this quest has provided us with insight into the grand narrative of human existence. But there remain many, many questions for our future . . . and answering them requires more than just a focus on the testable, material facets of our existence.

Science requires imagination, but the human imagination goes well beyond informing science. Albert Einstein told us that "the most beautiful experience we can have is the mysterious—the fundamental emotion which stands at the cradle of true art and true science." It is the allure of the mysterious, and our desire to clarify it, that drives so much of human existence. The actor/producer Bill O'Brien tells us that "at their core, artists and scientists are not so different from one another. Both endeavor to solve humankind's greatest mysteries through the power of imagination." The human capacity for science goes hand in hand with our capacity for wonder and imagination: We are the creative species and our future depends on it.

The best answers to where we are (or can be) going will be generated in conversation with the evolutionary sciences but cannot come from science alone. Knowing about the past few million years of our evolution is critical, but not sufficient, to clarifying what the rest of this current century will bring. If this story of our past tells us anything, it is that we need to be truly imaginative and creative to best move forward as individuals, as communities, and as a species. It's not that we won't encounter, even generate, conflict and cruelty and make many mistakes, but our past demonstrates that it is in precisely those situations when things are most challenging that working and thinking together create the best solutions.

CODA

THE BEAT OF YOUR CREATIVE LIFE

As I mentioned in the "Overture," the anthropologist Ashley Montagu told us that the human niche, the way we live in the world, is created through our ability to use symbols, abstractions, ideas—to think big, to dream: "The symbols, the ideas, are created in the mind . . . but the human animal learns not only to create them, but to project them onto the external world, and there transform them into reality." Our ability to dream things up and to make them happen is what makes us distinctive.

More than half a century ago Rev. Martin Luther King Jr. shared his dream.

> I have a dream that my four little children will one day live in a nation where they will not be judged by the color of their skin but by the content of their character.

Martin Luther King's impassioned vision strikes a chord not just because it argues powerfully against injustice and for equality, but because it draws on our shared capacities to imagine and create a better world. When Dr. King talks about his "dream," he is really talking about our capacity to imagine and create change. Our lineage developed the capacity to dream, using it to change the world over the last 2 million years. It makes us the creative species. It also makes our lives really complicated.

Becoming and being human is messy, long, and difficult. From the start of our lives we are social, reliant on others, confused, and curious. We can't walk or talk for the first few years. It takes us at least a few decades (if not more) to get good at being human. What members of our community think, see, eat, feel, do, hope, and dream shapes who we are and how we do each of those activities. But we each put our own individual spin on the process. We are distinctive not only as a species, but also as individuals in that species. Being so creative and having such a long development means that every one of us is unique. This creates a diversity of voices and capacities inside the overall unity of our species, a diversity that creates many challenges but offers even more opportunities.

Creativity is both an individual and a group activity. The ability to effectively meld these two facets is what makes humans successful. As we each seek to fulfill our respective potentials, we must recognize the need to cooperate with others, loudly or quietly, regularly or sporadically, soberly or passionately. Cooperation among members of a community across ages and genders from the very first day of life is our pattern. This pattern comprises innovation, sharing and teaching, conflict and challenges, communication and complexity, even failure. Living as a member of the creative species is no small feat, especially today.

This final chapter is a reflection on how our evolutionary story can act as a guide, a set of suggestions, ideas, and tools that can help us embrace our creative lives. The whole premise of niche construction, the process of evolution that humans do so well, is that through both individual and group actions we can reshape the landscape for the generations that come after us. The next centuries and millennia of humans are the inheritors of our evolutionary legacy, just as we inherited from our ancestors of 1,000, 10,000, 100,000, 1 million, and even 2 million years ago.

Over the last 10,000 years (what we call the Holocene) the pace of change increased, as did the challenges. Settling down, farming and raising animals, building cities and nations, created new options for creativity and expanded the ecological and social challenges we face. But today we are in the Anthropocene (where human action is now a, or *the*, major force in climate and landscape change), the pace of change and the intensity of challenges make the Holocene look like it was in slow motion. The stakes are higher than ever before. It's up to us not to screw it up.

Our lineage has overcome enormous challenges. When the cards are against us we dream big and then we act. If we succeed and make the twenty-first century a beneficially creative era, the stories our descendants tell about us will emphasize our creativity and collaboration, not our blunders and disunity. That's the kind of legacy we hope and dream for. It's also one we must work for.

First Steps in the Human Dance

Once we recognize and value our ability to imagine solutions and realize them through collaborative effort, the greatest challenge we face is managing the inevitable failures.

Diversity, challenge, and conflict help us maintain our imagination. Most people assume that conflict is bad and that being in one's "comfort zone" is good. That is not exactly true. Of course, we don't want a giant saber-toothed cat bearing down on us, nor do we want to find ourselves without a job or medical insurance or in a fight with our partner, family, boss, or co-workers. One bad experience with a saber-toothed cat, or a similarly intense crisis, can be sufficient to last us a lifetime. But small disagreements with family and friends, trouble with technology or finances, or challenges at work and at home can help us think through our own capabilities. Problems that need solutions force us to use our brains and one another in order to develop creative answers. Navigating landscapes that are varied, that offer trials and occasional conflicts, is more conducive to creativity than hanging out in landscapes that pose no challenge to our senses and our minds. Our 2-million-year history is packed with challenges and conflicts.

In the deep past, when we lived in small foraging groups, each member of the group had much in common with everyone else. That homogeneity fostered the understanding, communication, and collaboration that triggered our creative processes. But as humans began to expand and develop, the groups got bigger, communities merged, roles differentiated, and the social and ecological challenges diversified. Having variation in experiences, opinions, and perspectives within communities became necessary fuel for the creative fire. Eventually expanding beyond individual groups, mixing and re-creating ideas, processes, and traditions became the way in which humans innovated more effectively. The human pool of creative options is now rooted in access to some degree of diversity. If we lose diversity, variation in thinking and seeing, we all have less to draw on when challenges arise.

Author David Giffels offers a telling example of a twenty-first-century challenge to diversity. The big-box store and strip-mallification of the United States are killing our imagination. He points out that local businesses, small shops, and a diversity of buildings housing them are being replaced with big-box stores, clone chain restaurants, and uniform strip-mall constructions. Over the past thirty to forty years this has created a homogeneity that suppresses the American imagination. If everything is the same no matter where you are as you grow up, your mind will be shaped by that sameness.

This imposed homogeneity is not the same as an individual choosing to have the same thing for breakfast every morning or preferring to take the same evening walk, wearing the same clothes, or even seeking out the same cup of coffee every day. These are choices for continuity or familiarity that can offer comfort, even help folks into the space where they can be the most creative. But such choices come from us; they are part of our creative lives, not imposed on us. Choices are not possible in a homogenous landscape. Back to Giffels's example; a landscape with multiple kinds of stores, each selling different items, exposes one to different locations and to interactions with different people. It provides a different kind of experience, and fodder, for imagination and creativity. Even if we go back again and again to the same store, the others are there shaping the landscape and offering sustenance for our creative imaginations. The homogenization of the retail landscape in the United States has diminished the diversity of our experiences. One can walk into a Starbucks anywhere in the United States (and much of the rest of the world), and it looks the same, has the same colors, menu items, uniforms, standard greetings, and exchanges between customer and server, even the same drinks. While this might be a good business model and offer some advantages to consumers (like access to espresso where there used to be none), there are also trade-offs. Our brains develop slowly, with lots of space for input and experience. A lack of variation, even in our experience of getting a coffee, can dampen our creative capacities.

So, embrace diversity. Accept the challenges it presents. That is the first simple guideline.

What's next? Failure as part of the creative process.

It took the swimmer Diana Nyad five tries to swim from Cuba to Florida. Alfred Nobel blew up his laboratory (and his brother) in his eventually successful quest to develop dynamite (and went on to fund the Nobel Prize). The majority of scientists are wrong most of the time, and nearly all athletes fail most times they attempt a goal, a hit, or a basket. Gather any group of exceptional scientists, athletes, or artists and ask them whether they've experienced more success or more failure, and it will be failure every time. They will tell you that in each case, no matter how depressing or frustrating the events were, the failures taught them a lesson, enabled forward movement, even if on a different path. Being human, seeking to be creative, requires failing often.

Our ancestors tell us a lot about dealing with failure. It was the ability to deal with failure in novel ways that enabled early *Homo* to navigate around and out of Africa hundreds of thousands of years ago. Imagine how many times small groups of human ancestors must have tried to make a functional stone tool or a wooden spear or communicate about power scavenging, better stone sources, or a way to avoid predators—and failed again and again. It took our ancestors a million years of effort to learn to control fire and to hunt large game; it took another half million to figure out how to paint their stories on cave walls. Human history is built from far more failures than successes.

The journalist Hannah Bloch writes, "without the sting of failure to spur us to reassess and rethink, progress would be impossible." Failing at an endeavor acts to demonstrate limitations, to force us to rethink or reevaluate how we do things, and to learn how to do them better. Unfortunately, all too often in today's society, trying and failing is seen as a flaw; it's considered a failure of character.

In science the most common outcome from any experiment is failure. Most successful science is generated by refuting hypotheses—by demonstrating what is wrong, not what is right. It is the examination of the details of the failures, the reconstituting of approaches, that gets researchers closer to success. Consider the development of electric lights, antibiotics, the Internet... all creative successes whose antecedents were rife with failures.

Not all failures can be shrugged off. Most groups on the human lineage went extinct, leaving little or nothing behind. And yet here we are. So when we fail we have to remember that we are in excellent company—2 million years of it, give or take.

So that's the two-step signature of a creative human life:

- Embrace diversity.
- See failure as part of the journey.

Sure, but Can You Be More Specific?

Examining the human story can offer key themes, and specific bullet points, for our creative lives. While I don't pretend to be a nutritionist, sex adviser, therapist, or art critic, there are ways we can help ourselves and our communities flourish by acting creatively, with evolutionary consequences, on issues concerning food, sex, relationships, violence, faith, art, and science.

Food

We are not only what we eat, but how and when we eat too. Humans are especially creative omnivores and social eaters. Our bodies are well structured to consume and digest an array of plant and animal parts as we seek to get the right balance of macro- and micronutrients and water. What and how we eat have played major roles in how we evolved. The uptick in protein and nutritionally dense foods alongside our increasingly cooperative social lives enabled us to slow down and elongate the growing pattern, increase the success of raising children, and learn together in ways that caused us to get more and more creative. There are a few evolutionary insights about human diets that can help us in today's dietary landscape.

First, humans need a range of dietary items to acquire the correct balance of nutrients to keep us healthy. This is especially important for young humans. Between the time of birth and the time we stop growing (between seventeen and twenty-two years of age or so) the failure to sustain a good balance of nutrients can derail brain growth and development and muscle growth and cause cognitive and other behavioral delays. It can also open us up to a whole range of negative health issues. This pattern of harm to our development and potential is especially evident in the "food deserts" in many poor urban areas. Developmental missteps can be corrected, and the solution always includes sufficient good food.

Some people intentionally avoid certain foods. Vegetarian or vegan lifestyles seem healthy, but our ancestors sought animal protein for a reason: It has some of the most accessible and densely packed nutrients available—especially the kind needed for brain and muscle growth during childhood. Humans have steadily modified the plants we use over the last 10,000 years to up their nutrient potential, so today we have many options for getting important proteins that are not from animals. Adults in many parts of the world can achieve a good nutrient balance without consuming animal protein, but it takes work and careful planning. The same cannot always be said for children. It's very difficult to provide all the appropriate nutrition to growing human children without some animal protein. Humans start with an all-animal-protein diet via mother's milk. This sets the stage for the nutrient balance needed for growth. So while a non-animal-product diet can work for adults, it's much more difficult to be safely vegetarian, especially vegan, as a child. Children don't need much meat or fish, but they do need some.

The so-called raw diet and the Paleo diet concepts are not balanced. Our ancestors worked for more than a million years to master fire and cooking. Cooking improves our capacity to extract nutrients from many foods, and it enables us to develop cuisines—two major innovations in human history. Many food items are fine raw but nutritionally far better when lightly cooked. A true Paleo diet makes no sense. Our ancestors ate what they did (lots of protein, low amounts of carbs, no grains or processed foods) because they did not have the option of growing their own food; popping into a supermarket and getting some organic beets, carrots, a sweet potato, whole-grain bread, and some sustainably farmed trout; or stopping at a Chinese takeout joint and getting a plate of kung pao chicken. We have developed some amazing foods that are healthy, packed with particular nutrients, and very tasty. Our ancestors, given the option, would have preferred to eat like us. Restricting ourselves to the kinds of foods humans had access to 20,000 years ago is neither preferable nor possible in the twenty-first century. The evolutionary fact is that our bodies and minds develop in concert with the foods we eat, so eating healthy as best as one can is important. But we should also enjoy our creativity. Humans have developed some options that are not so nutritious but that are fabulously creative (e.g., chocolate lava cake)—and healthy enough in moderation. A million years of creative effort to cook food and craft cuisine should be respected.

Water does not get enough respect when we think of food. Dehydration can hinder our cognitive functioning and cause serious health issues. Diarrhea due to dehydration is the second leading cause of death for children under five. Access to safe drinking water is a global crisis, and those who lack it suffer horribly. Even in wealthier regions, places where safe drinking water is abundant, the consumption of high-calorie drinks, such as sodas, can create serious hydration problems.

If we put our minds to it, we can come up with good diets based on what is available, in most places. Keeping some animal (especially fish) protein in the mix is advisable, but we don't need too much. Having a degree of fibrous and other plant materials is important, and balancing it out with access to some carbohydrates from starchy roots and juicy fruits rounds out a good diet. As the journalist Michael Pollan reminds us, we should seek balance as best we can, avoid foods that are heavily processed, and, like humans have for countless millennia, enjoy our time eating and make it social when possible.

Following these suggestions not only helps us but also helps our microbiome. Over the past few hundred thousand years, as our ancestors began to hunt effectively, and then again over the past 10,000 years, as we entered into domesticating relationships with plants and animals, our microbiome shifted and expanded accordingly. It is us and we are it—we are inseparable.

When we consume very imbalanced diets, there are microbial repercussions. We get sick, we get lethargic, and we have trouble digesting. Listening to our gut (and all the critters within it) and responding accordingly have deep roots in our species. We should continue that tradition.

Tradition, however, cannot be our only guide. There are more than 7 billion humans now, and we eat an awful lot. This creates a problem: Our present foodways are not sustainable. Over the last 10,000 years we've been ratcheting up the intensity and density of food production. Today we're overfishing many areas of the oceans to the point of causing massive extinctions of hundreds of species. We've developed mass factory-farming systems such that the cows, chickens, and pigs that many humans eat have nutrients so downgraded that they're potentially unsafe. The modes of mass meat production have also produced a system of suffering for the animals (and many of the human workers) that many find revolting, not to mention immoral. In the developed world, people eat more meat than is necessary, and government regulation means it costs less than it otherwise should. A better systematic, ecological, and creative approach is crucial to making sure humans, and all the species we rely on, continue to do well.

The very first cave art is not of humans; it is of the animals they ate. Our ancestors saw the importance and significance of the animals on which they relied. We can take a lesson from them and get a bit more creative and humane in how we manage the lives of those that we eat.

Aside from being necessary for our growth, health, and development, food is also core to our sense of selves and our communities. Cooking and eating together, sharing food, are key factors in our successful evolutionary history. Managing food and eating is no place to skimp. Here are some food bullets for our creative lives:

- Forage wisely. Seek a balance of affordability, accessibility, nutrition, taste, and enjoyment.
- Eat fresh. Avoid packaged foods with long lists of ingredients. Your microbiome will thank you.
- Eat socially. Do as our ancestors did and get the whole group involved in the collection, preparation, and enjoyment of food; make it an event.

- Create equitable access to food and water in our local communities, the nation, and globally however you can. Small acts of cooperative creativity centered on food can go a long way.

Sex

Sex and relationships are seldom, if ever, simple. Growing up human means growing up in a world of diverse gender expectations, body types, reproductive options, family structures, and sexual orientations. Biology matters. But it's by no means the end of the story. Human sex and sexuality are not static. Being biologically male or female makes a difference in how one experiences the world. Patterns in pregnancy, lactation, birth, menopause, and differences in size and upper-body strength create a set of processes that make women's and men's lives different. But the differences are not as extreme as many think. It's likely that both males and females made stone tools, participated in power scavenging and hunting, cared for young, foraged, innovated, and created as humans expanded, successfully, across the planet over the last 2 million years. There are patterned biological differences, but there is also considerable overlap in what we can do. Most things most humans do every day are not constrained by the extremes of size and upper-body strength or by pregnancy. How sex differences are experienced, shaped, augmented, or reduced depends on the society and the community in which one lives and the choices one makes.

Gender is not the same as sex. But they are so connected in our minds that we often fail to acknowledge the difference. Most people assume the gender differences we experience today are ancient, like sex differences. They are not, at least not in evolutionary time.

Human gender has roots from hundreds of thousands of years ago. In the deeper past it was less extreme and less obvious, at least as measured in the bones and materials left behind by our ancestors. Evidence for the specific gender roles we see today shows up in the last five to six millennia or even just the last few centuries, depending on which aspects we seek. This pattern of recent gender development does not mean gender did not exist in the deep past, just that it was neither as pronounced nor the same as it is today. Gender is not static.

As communities and societies became more complex, so did gender. Gender is, after all, the product of human creativity. Regardless of how one feels about gender, past and present, there is no going backward. Gender differences are here to stay and they are substantial. But we need to remember that the patterns of these differences are not fixed.

For example, contrary to popular belief, the majority of gender differences are not linked to specific biological differences between males and females (which have not changed much in a long time). For example, today in the United States there is gender inequality in economic and political realities. Males, on average, are paid more money for the same jobs than females. Females, who make up just over 50 percent of the population, make up only 20 percent of the US Senate, a key national governing body. Looking at human biology, our fossil and archeological record and human behavior today reveal that both of these patterns are not based on some evolved capacity or on measurable aspects of our biology. There is no evidence that males and females differ in capacities when hired with the same qualifications for the same jobs or that males govern more effectively.

Contemporary overviews across cultures and across our entire species reveal a lot of variation in patterns of sexual desire and behavior. Unfortunately, the fossil and older archeological records give us little guidance on this one. Sexual activity does not fossilize. In the more recent past, especially with the advent of figurative art on pottery, the proliferation of figurines, statues, carvings, and painting, and art on architecture in the last 3,000 to 5,000 years or so provides some evidence. There are numerous depictions of sexual activity in this period. Of all sorts. And graphic. Many objects in the recent archeological record would be classified as pornographic if shown in public in the United States. But all that tells us is what we already knew: Some humans have lots of sex.

Evidence suggests our ancestors were anything but prudes. They likely had some versions of the various patterns of sexuality and attraction we see today. The range of sexual activity and preferences was likely constrained by relationships in communities as well as between them. Given what we know, it is also likely that those who harmed others via coercive sex probably did not fare well. Today sex in humans is regulated and facilitated by histories, laws, traditions, economics, media, literary and theatrical influences, social networks, and individual experiences. How, why, and where we have sex today are also affected by material items (cars, contraceptives, sex toys, lubricants, etc.), exposure to specific practices, revolts against or conformity to social norms, ideals and expectations, fetishes, and so on.

The contemporary landscape of human sexual activity may very well have freaked out our ancestors. Or not. Maybe there was a lot more going on than we can see in the fossil record. We'll never know. The best advice for navigating the complexities is to thine own self be true, as much as possible, and to be open to others following suit. Go back to that first principle in the human two-step: Welcome diversity. Dealing with issues of sexuality is difficult, but taking this implicit advice from our ancestors can help: Don't go it alone. Discussing sexual relationships with partners and with communities, letting them be a part of the social fabric, can help make the complexity of human sexuality more navigable for all.

Sex, gender, and sexuality are frequently tied to marriage and parenting. Two key points derived from our evolutionary history are salient here: (1) Marriage and pair-bonds are not the same thing, and (2) parenting is not a solo (or female-only) activity.

Frank Sinatra sang about love and marriage being like a horse and carriage—inextricably bound—and we listened passionately. Many still identify marriage as a natural goal for humans, with something we call "love" as a necessary component. However, the archeological and historical evidence is pretty clear on this: Marriage is a recent human creation, not something from our deep past. While the goal of seeking marriage and a specific romantic relationship is recent, our drive to form tight pair-bonds is very deep.

We covered the biology in chapter 8: In a biological sense there are two types of pair-bonds, the social pair-bond and the sexual pair-bond. Both types are part of complex social networks that emerged as central patterns in human evolution, as part of our early creative and cooperative ventures. Pair-bonds can involve sexual relationships and what we'd call today romantic attachments. Humans also have extensive social pair-bonding across genders and age categories, probably more than any other species. We can have social pair-bonds with our relatives and our closest friends. They can be with same-sex individuals or different-sex individuals, same age or different ages. Humans also have sexual pair-bonds both heterosexually and homosexually. We tend to expect pair-bonds to be associated with marriage or some other form of culturally sanctioned relationship. However, it is far from clear if all (or even most) married couples are sexually and/or socially pair-bonded.

Importantly, our sexual pair-bonding, like our sexual activity, is not limited to reproduction. In many societies social and political histories have created contexts where heterosexual pair-bonds are sanctioned and homosexual pair-bonds are not. However, this trend is rapidly changing in the early part of the twenty-first century as many societies alter their perspectives on sexuality and marriages: social creativity in action.

Reproduction, it need hardly be said, is one possible outcome from sexual activity. Looking to our past clearly demonstrates that human infants are extremely costly and require massive caretaking. All the evidence we have suggests that humans are communal breeders and that males and females, young and old, had a hand in raising children for much of our history. But in much of the contemporary world, that successful pattern is breaking down.

Along with ideas about marriage, much of the developed world has created a residence pattern that favors single nuclear families (one dad, one mom, and their offspring) living in relative isolation. This recent invention makes parenting more difficult. Combining this residence pattern with the contemporary ideas of gender, infant caretaking becomes largely associated with females, and in many cases with the mothers alone. This combination of residence patterns and assumptions about caretaking is highly problematic for two reasons: (1) Humans evolved infants that are really, really needy, and a single caretaker (or even two caretakers) would be very stressed raising one. (2) Gendering the caretaking responsibilities in such an extreme manner has the potential to both limit the behavioral and social options of females, increasing gender inequality, and limit the exposure of the infant to a diversity of individuals and experiences, thus reducing the stimuli on its developing brain and mind and potentially inhibiting its imagination.

Day care, Head Start programs, and social crèches, even just lots of public spaces for socialization, can ameliorate these challenges. We should take a cue from human evolutionary processes and do all we can to create social and diverse exposure for developing minds and support and equity for females who are reproducing.

Humans have a distinctively complicated, messy, and elaborately cognitive way of having sex, of gendering ourselves, of bonding, and of parenting. These patterns are part of what makes us one of the most adept, complex, and interesting animals on the planet.

Here are some sex and gender bullets:

- We can recognize biological differences between females and males, but also that females and males are not as different as most think. This is a great start.
- Gender is a spectrum, not an either-or human trait. Take comfort that no matter where one falls on the gender spectrum, it's smack dab in the normal range for humans.
- Humans have an expansive range of sexual behavior, and as long as one's own version of it does not involve harm or coercion, it's part of the range of regular human experience. No matter how one seeks to experience sexuality, it is highly likely that one is not alone.
- Humans can develop pair-bonds (even multiple pair-bonds) across the life span. But these are not the same as marriage. Marriage is a recent creative development. Focusing on developing strong social connections first can make the other social goals (marriage, family, partners, or whatever one seeks) easier to achieve.
- Parenting is hard. It's best not to go it alone. If one does find herself with children and no partner(s), depend on family and friends. It is what we humans have done for 2 million years.

Violence

Every time we watch news reports, read updates, or tune in to any media sources, the lead stories are almost always about horrific things. It would surprise no one to see a headline in *The New York Times* that read "Four

Killed in New York City Today." But a much more common occurrence, the more important news story for that day, would be a headline we never see: "7,999,996 People Got Along Today in New York City." We mustn't let a media system based on selling us information drive what we think of as normal for humans.

Our ancestors did not run hand in hand through the daisies for 2 million years. They had conflicts, they fought, and sometimes they killed one another. But most of the time they worked together, innovated and made things, created societies and collaborated to solve the problems the world threw at them. Conflict can drive us to do better. Knowing that we are neither predetermined nor restricted to using violence led Martin Luther King Jr., Nelson Mandela, Rigoberta Menchú, Mahatma Gandhi, Malala Yousafzai, Cesar Chavez, Aung San Suu Kyi, Bob Marley, Betty Williams, Arundhati Roy, and many others to tap into the human power of compassion and community, imagination and hope, and thereby unite broad swaths of people to create peaceful prosperity in the face of violence and cruelty. This process happens every day in small ways as well.

Collaboration, cooperation, and coordination are not the opposites of, or antidotes to, violence and cruelty. In fact, they underlie the most horrific events: the German Holocaust, the mass atrocities in Rwanda, Congo, and Cambodia, and wars across the continents. All of these events could not have happened without intensive collaboration and coordination among the perpetrators. In warfare it is not the most violent army that wins, but rather it's the most cooperative, coordinated, and caring to their comrades that does. That should give us hope for options and alternatives.

Here are some violence bullets:

- No one is violent simply because of her or his genes or sex. Anyone who says these facets of our evolutionary history made her or him a rapist or murderer is lying.
- Conflict is not necessarily a bad thing. It can oftentimes be good. Conflict and competition are not synonymous with violence, aggression, or cruelty.

- Beware of the blaring media. They are trying to sell us something, using horror and fear to do it. Most of the time humans are getting along creatively.
- Violence is an option for humans, not an obligation, fate, or necessity. Cruelty happens, but compassion happens more. Our challenge is to figure out how to use this fact in our daily lives.
- Inequality is tied to violence, and it's here to stay. But it's neither static nor uniform. We can, and should, get creative about how we as individuals, as communities, and as a species develop and manage inequality.

Faith

The human capacity for imagination has led to unbelievable complexity in our world. But no aspect of the contemporary world is more rooted in our imaginative and hopeful capacities than faith. Some form of faith, often a specific belief system, is part of nearly every human's life. Believing in some form of religious creed, and the practice of dogma, is common across the planet. But that does not mean what many think it means. Not everyone is religious. Religions show up in the human record only recently. For most of our history as a species we did not have any particular formalized belief system or institutionalized religious structures.

Nevertheless, it's likely that all human communities had their own set of practices and patterns that bordered on recognizing the supernatural. That leaves humans with a quandary: How do we explain those meanings? Why do things happen? Is there more to the world than what we experience physically? How can we carry on thoughts and conversations in our heads? Is there a mind or a soul and do we all have one?

Our lineage started seriously examining these questions sometime in the last few hundred thousand years. The answers we developed changed the way we see the world and thus changed our lives. Moving from foragers to farmers, from nomads to settled, from stone to iron, from hunters to ranchers, from villages to cities, reshaped how humans think about, and experience, meaning.

If one looks closely at the core tenets and basic processes in most global religions, there is a lot of overlap, even agreement. Surprisingly, this does not keep them from often, and sometimes violently, being in conflict with one another. There is a reason why so many basic tenets of religions overlap: They are part of the same human capacity. There is also a reason why there is much contention and disagreement among global religions: They are institutions. Their power is in part connected to the number and status of their adherents, and they compete for adherents. Thinking about a religious human, someone who believes in a certain creed and practices in regard to meaning and faith, is not the same as thinking about a religion.

The study of our deep past tells us little about today's religions, but it tells us a great deal about human capacities for meaning-making and how they might relate to religious beliefs and practices. The very recent past gives us more insight into religions themselves. Combining these two and thinking about what we've covered in this book provides some bullet points for enhancing our creative lives in regard to the issues around religion:

- If one is not religious, one shouldn't knock religious individuals because they have a particular faith. We should recognize and respect that most humans on the planet belong to a particular religion. We all share the same capacities for making and engaging with meaning. We just do so in different ways.
- If one is religious, one shouldn't think that there is only one way to be good and to understand the world and that it belongs to a particular religious tradition. There are copious data that prove this view wrong.
- We should beware of people using the institutions or particular assertions of religions to destroy or reduce creativity and human potential. Denying our capacities and tendencies as creative species (e.g., complex sexuality, community, science, and art) is profoundly destructive. Religious fundamentalism typically results in repression and abuse and should be opposed.

- No single human tradition or institution, religious or otherwise, has all the answers or owns the right answers. There are many ways to be human. Be generous even as you hold tight to your own beliefs.

Art

Human art is much more than a product, an activity, or an outcome. Art is a way of interacting with, reimagining, and explaining the world as we shape it and it shapes us. It enables us to tell stories and experience meaning.

All of the preceding categories—food, sex, violence, and faith—find some of their most powerful expression in art: the colors, shapes, and presentation style of different cuisines; the graphic representations of sexuality both explicit and implicit along with the real-time drama of sexual intimacy; depictions and evocations of violence from stories of martial valor to horror movies; the power of religious iconography, ritual, and music. All regularly define us as human.

Yet it seems we often struggle to keep art in our lives. This is a problem. From the time our ancestors began doodling on clamshells (about 300,000 years ago), blocks of ochre, and ostrich eggshells, we became locked into a desire to create imagery and meaning. All humans immerse themselves in artistic endeavors as children. But then, unfortunately, many of us stop.

Why? There is, in many societies, an association between art and frivolity. Art is seen as not productive to societal needs. This is an ignorant stance. The capacity to tell a story, to depict a feeling, to sing and dance a sensation, is as important as our ability to make stone tools, to build a fire, to avoid being eaten, to figure out how to raise a crop. These processes remain entangled and intertwined even as these abilities manifest today as writing computer code, constructing a legal argument, or devising a high-energy physics experiment. Art has helped humans do all of these things precisely because it taps into our imaginative capacities and enables our creativity to flourish in ways that are unavailable to other animals. Art gives us a leg up on the world and opens new horizons and vistas, new possibilities. And yet we deride it as frivolous.

Here are some art bullets:

- Everyone is an artist as a child. Why stop? Foster art in children, but continue to foster it in adults. Do something related to art every now and then, and collaborate with friends and family.
- Don't confine what one considers art to "high" and "low" categories. Ballet and street dancing, graffiti and oil paintings, limericks and sonnets, doodles and marble sculptures—one doesn't have to like it all, but it is all art. It maintains humanity.
- Respect your plumber, mechanic, and bus driver in addition to painters, sculptors, musicians, authors, and actors. Those ancestors who made particularly aesthetic stone tools, who were flamboyant and stylized in their defleshing of an elephant, or who created new ways of assembling food before presenting it to the group were all infusing their craft with a sense of art. Craft in everyday life can be artistic.
- Doing something artistic quietly on your own fosters a creativity and imaginative exploration that you can bring to the resounding social life of day-to-day existence.

Science

It is appropriate that our list ends with science. It is, after all, what inspired this book.

Science in the most general sense is old, a process that emerged early in the history of the genus *Homo*. We have long been melding curiosity with imagination, innovation with creativity, and determination with complex teaching, learning, and sharing. The current scientific quests to investigate human evolution and other physical processes, from sight and thought to star formation and the beginning of the universe itself, however, are on a new level.

Asking questions about who we are, where we come from, and where we are going is not new. But the application of scientific approaches to such questions is. For much of human history these questions were answered by stories and myths, community traditions, and incipient religious beliefs. In the last 10,000 to 20,000 years, these probably became more solidified with the development of particular social identities, concepts of property, formalized clans, tribes, linguistic groups, trading networks, and other large clusters of communities. The advent of large-scale and institutional religions added to that mix and created doctrine to answer the questions. The beginning of writing was followed by the formalization of philosophy, a whole area of human specialization focused on those questions. For the past thirty or forty centuries, philosophical inquiries, religious doctrine, and traditional stories dominated the who, where, and why explanations of humanity. But the last four centuries or so, and especially the last two, saw the emergence of the scientific method.

The capacity to deploy a particular mode of inquiry into ourselves and the world around us that is both falsifiable and material-data based sets us up to interpret things in innovative and distinctive ways. Biology and physics bring a new kind of knowledge into the world. But, regardless of the quality and veracity of the data and analyses produced, it is humans interpreting the results. This means that creativity and imagination, plus a lot of societally mediated explanation, will complicate the scientific results, prompting doubt and new hypotheses to be tested. Humans are never completely objective. Anyone, scientist or otherwise, who does not acknowledge that is deluded. So any science we hear of is going to have some creative flourishes. The difference is that in science, no matter what a scientist says, one should be able to look into the data used and make one's own judgment. Everything asserted in this book is drawn from some scientific study, interpreted from a body of available data, or extrapolated from a comparative assessment of different approaches. The trick to thinking about and understanding science is that it is much more accessible than most think. If the roots of science lie deep in our past, then every human today has the basic capacities to understand and participate at some level in scientific inquiry.

Humans need not passively accept what we are told. For example, we accept as common sense that there is an association between hunting, men, and warfare. It just sounds right. Yet, in this book I've laid out a series of arguments demonstrating why this connection is not only not there, but also misguiding and obscuring a bunch of much more interesting relationships. If you disagree, do some science. In every place that I make a point in this regard, check the endnotes to see the publications I've cited to support the points. Read them, have your friends read them, and see if you agree. Do a little research in libraries or on the web, ask people, see where this path of inquiry takes you. We may yet agree to disagree.

There are now many high-quality free online courses and websites that contain a lot of information. And of course you are reading this book right now, so you know that there are books out there that translate evolutionary science into more or less accessible language. Reading is one of humanity's greatest and most distinctive skills. As Isaac Asimov said, science is "a system for testing your thoughts against the universe and seeing whether they match." Science is within your reach.

Here are some science bullets:

- Most science is not rocket science. Humans have the skills to understand a lot more than we think we do. Our particular blend of curiosity, cognitive capacity, collaborative teaching and learning, and creativity enables us to think about and digest information in particularly effective, and imaginative, ways. Using this talent can benefit us all.

- Evolutionary approaches and all of the physical, biological, and social sciences are critical in understanding health, environmental issues, race and racism, aging, gender and sex, violence, and many, many more core issues facing humans on a daily basis. Basic science is as important as arithmetic, reading, writing, and history. We should teach it to children.

- Science is supposed to have a built-in BS detector. If there is no way to assess what scientists are saying, then remain wary. Don't let scientists off the hook; demand clearer and better translations of research into accessible information. Notice the boundary between the methodology and those performing it.

- Live it. Science is about trying to figure out how the world works and seeking the answers in material explanations. Do it every day . . . Enjoy!

Go Forth and Be Creative

Being human is a creative process. But today, with all of our obligations, with all the complexity of the modern world pulling us in a million directions, taking the time and effort to embrace that creativity seems far removed from our daily routine. We have limited time, energy, and effort. But even if it might be more difficult than it was in the past, we, and our families, friends, communities, even our species, need creativity more than ever.

Our ancestors set the stage for us by living creative and cooperative lives, as individuals and in groups. We can't let that go to waste. Two million years ago our small, naked, fangless, hornless, and clawless ancestors with a few sticks and stones surmounted near impossible odds. All because they had one another and a spark of creativity. And so do we.

That spark has grown and burns brightly across the planet. We've developed better tools, clothes, longer and healthier lives, airplanes, ideas of transcendent beauty, spacecraft to interstellar space, and a lot more children. But the challenges have grown in scale as well, and they show no sign of slowing down.

Let's meet those challenges head-on and shoot for another 2 million years of creativity.

NOTES

OVERTURE

1 **"to combine them in extraordinary new ways"** Popova, M., "About," *Brain Pickings,* accessed October 17, 2015, http://www.brainpickings.org/about/.

1 **it is a thoroughly social process** Hodder, I., "Creative Thought: A Long-Term Perspective," in *Creativity in Human Evolution and Prehistory,* ed. S. Mithen, 61–77 (London: Routledge, 1998).

2 **onto the world and transform them into materially resounding reality** Mithen, S., ed., *Creativity in Human Evolution and Prehistory* (London: Routledge, 1998); Montagu, A., *The Human Revolution* (New York: Bantam, 1965).

2 **"people in a good collaboration accomplish more than the group's most talented members could achieve on their own"** Tharp, T., *The Collaborative Habit: Life Lessons for Working Together* (New York: Simon & Schuster, 2009).

2 **move back and forth between the realms of "what is" and "what could be"** Gabora, L., and Kaufman, S.B., "Evolutionary approaches to creativity," in *The Cambridge Handbook of Creativity,* ed. J. Kaufman and R. Sternberg, 270–300 (New York: Cambridge University Press, 2010).

2 **shared intentionality coupled with our imagination** Tomasello, M., and Carpenter, M., "Shared Intentionality," *Developmental Science* 10 (2007): 121–125, DOI: 10.1111/j.1467-7687.2007.00573.x; Tomasello, M., *A Natural History of Human Thinking* (Cambridge, MA: Harvard University Press, 2014).

2 **the species singularly distinguished and shaped by creativity** Fogarty, L., Creanza, N., and Feldman, M.W., "Cultural Evolutionary Perspectives on Creativity and Human Innovation," *Trends in Ecology and Evolution* 12 (2015): 736–754.

5 **since Charles Darwin and Alfred Russel Wallace** Although Charles Darwin rightfully gets the lion's share of the credit for fully developing the first solid theory of evolution, it is important to note that the original idea was presented as a collaboration between Darwin and Wallace (who did spell his middle name with only one *l*). In fact, the whole history of evolutionary thought, which is often attributed to a single creative act by Darwin and then a bit of elaboration by a few other folks, is a perfect example of creative collaboration by thousands of thinkers over the past few centuries.

5   **called the extended evolutionary synthesis (EES)** Jablonka, E., and Lamb, M., *Evolution in Four Dimensions: Genetic, Epigenetic, Behavioral, and Symbolic Variation in the History of Life* (Cambridge, MA: MIT Press, 2005); Laland, K.N., et al., "The extended evolutionary synthesis: its structure, assumptions and predictions," *Proceedings of the Royal Society of London B* 282 (2015): 20151019, http://dx.doi.org/10.1098 /rspb.2015.1019; Pigliucci, M., "An extended synthesis for evolutionary biology: the year in evolutionary biology," *Annals of the New York Academy of Sciences* 1168 (2009): 218–228.

6   **passing of genes, encoded in DNA** Genes play an important role in our development and functioning, not as directors, but rather as parts of a complex system. Terms such as *blueprints, building blocks,* and *code of life* are really poor ways to describe our DNA. It is misleading to talk about genes as doing things by themselves; they exist as part of a larger, integrated system. Epigenetics is the study of all the systems of interactions in development above the level of the gene. It reflects the reality that multiple factors influence the development of an organism and that there are very, very few instances of direct gene-to-trait scenarios. Traits such as body size and shape, face form, and so on emerge from the interaction of many genes and a range of developmental and environmental influences, and behavior is even more complicated.

8   **including dogs, cats, eagles, tyrannosaurs, and humans** Weiss, K., and Buchanan, A., *The Mermaid's Tale: Four Billion Years of Cooperation in the Making of Living Things* (Cambridge, MA: Harvard University Press, 2009).

9   **This sophisticated mathematical modeling** Nowak, M.A., and Highfield, R., *Super Cooperators: Altruism, Evolution, and Why We Need Each Other to Succeed* (New York: Free Press, 2011); Sober, E., and Wilson, D.S., *Unto Others: The Evolution and Psychology of Unselfish Behavior* (Cambridge, MA: Harvard University Press, 1998); ibid.

9   **the distinctive ability to think about times and places** This is our distinctive ability to think about problems, times, and places that occurred in the past and those that could occur in the future. It allows us to mull over challenges that are not in the present moment or the immediate past or future, to percolate ideas and mull over options outside of the contexts of the actual problems. See Bikerton, D., *Language and Human Behavior* (London: UCL Press, 1996); Donald, M., *The Origins of the Modern Mind* (Cambridge, MA: Harvard University Press, 1991); Deacon, T., *The Symbolic Species: The Co-Evolution of Language and the Brain* (London: Penguin, 1997).

10   **niche construction** See "Niche Construction: The neglected process in evolution," School of Biology, St. Andrews University, accessed January 20, 2016, http://synergy .st-andrews.ac.uk/niche/, for an excellent overview.

11   **more than 96 percent with our closest cousin, the chimpanzee** See the science writer Carl Zimmer's excellent and interactive description of this in "Genes Are Us. And Them," *National Geographic,* accessed October 17, 2015, http://ngm.nationalgeo graphic.com/2013/07/125-explore/shared-genes.

CHAPTER 1

15   **cast a sideways glance at me, and walked away** This vignette is drawn from a larger essay on much of my work with macaques: Fuentes, A., "There's a Monkey in My Kitchen (and I Like It): Fieldwork with Macaques in Bali and Beyond," in *Primate Ethnographies,* ed. Karen Strier, 151–162 (Boston: Pearson, 2014).

16   **sidle up next to humans and lean into them** Obviously, as an observer one is not supposed to interact in such a manner with the monkeys, but Teardrop had a way of

sneaking up and settling next to you, such that getting up would have drawn attention from the other group members and caused more of a problem than sitting there.

19 **Primates check their violence** For a concise overview, see Bernstein, I., "Social Mechanisms in the Control of Primate Aggression," in *Primates in Perspective,* 2nd ed., ed. C. Campbell et al., 599–607 (New York: Oxford University Press, 2011).

20 **primates a buffer most other species don't have** There are other highly social mammal species such as whales and wolves that have similar types of social niches.

20 **carve out more space in their lives to innovate** Good overviews of these concepts are in Campbell, C., et al., eds., *Primates in Perspective,* 2nd ed. (New York: Oxford University Press, 2011). See chapters 27, 32, and 38–44 for a terrific set of summaries of primate social complexity and creativity.

21 **they even use a rock as a tool, to pound a piece of food or to scratch an itch** These data are discussed at length in Fuentes, A., "Object rubbing in Balinese macaques (Macaca fascicularis)," *Laboratory Primate Newsletter* 31 (1992): 14–15; Fuentes, A., et al., "Macaque Behavior at the Human-Monkey Interface: The Activity and Demography of Semi-Free Ranging Macaca fascicularis at Padangtegal, Bali, Indonesia," in *Monkeys on the Edge: Ecology and Management of Long-tailed Macaques and Their Interface with Humans,* ed. M.D. Gumert, A. Fuentes, and L. Jones-Engel, 159–179 (New York: Cambridge University Press, 2011). There is also great information on this site and these behaviors in Bruce Wheatley's 1999 book, *The Sacred Monkeys of Bali* (Long Grove, IL: Waveland Press); and Nahallage, C.A.D., and Huffman, M.A., "Comparison of stone handling behavior in two macaque species: implications for the role of phylogeny and environment in primate cultural variation," *American Journal of Primatology* 70 (2008): 1124–1132.

21 **The researcher Michael Gumert** See Gumert, M.D., and Malaivijitnond, S., "Marine prey processed with stone tools by Burmese long-tailed macaques (Macaca fascicularis aurea) in intertidal habitats," *American Journal of Physical Anthropology* 149, 3 (2012): 447–457.

22 **open the mounds and fish for the tasty termites inside** Sanz, C., Call, J., and Boesch, C., *Tool Use in Animals: Cognition and Ecology* (New York: Cambridge University Press, 2014).

22 **A social tradition is a shared bit of creativity** Fragazy, D., and Perry, S., *The Biology of Traditions: Models and Evidence* (Cambridge: Cambridge University Press, 2005). See also Whiten, A., "The Scope of Culture in Chimpanzees, Humans and Ancestral Apes," in *Culture Evolves,* ed. A. Whiten et al. (Oxford: Oxford University Press, 2012): 105–122.

22 **sometimes it spreads into the new group and other times it does not** For overviews of these patterns and many fascinating others, read the book edited by Bill McGrew, Linda Marchant, and Toshisada Nishida, *Great Ape Societies* (Cambridge: Cambridge University Press, 1998).

23 **followed the trend toward social complexity and began making social niches, tools, and social traditions** Malone, N.M., Fuentes, A., and White, F.J., "Variation in the social systems of extant hominoids: comparative insight into the social behaviour of early hominins," *International Journal of Primatology* 33 (2012): 1251–1277; MacKinnon, K.C., and Fuentes, A., "Primate Social Cognition, Human Evolution, and Niche Construction: A Core Context for Neuroanthropology," in *The Encultured Brain,* ed. D. Lende and G. Downey, 67–102 (Cambridge, MA: MIT Press, 2012).

CHAPTER 2

26 **a small creative edge** We can construct such a picture of the LCA via what we know of the living apes and humans and the inferences we make from the fossil record. See

Malone, N.M., Fuentes, A., and White, F.J., "Variation in the social systems of extant hominoids: comparative insight into the social behavior of early hominins," *International Journal of Primatology* 33, 6 (2012): 1251–1277, DOI: 10.10007/s10764-012-9617-0.

28   **both sexes' canine teeth were about the same size** White, T. D., et al, "Ardipithecus ramidus and the paleobiology of early hominids," *Science* 326 (2009): 75–86.

29   **stronger social and bonding relationships with males—a hint of things to come** Ibid.; Lovejoy, O., "Reexamining human origins in light of Ardipithecus ramidus," *Science* 326 (2009), DOI: 10.1126/science.1175834.

29   **Once, in the Afar region of Ethiopia, seventeen hominins** Johanson, D., "Lucy, thirty years later: an expanded view of Australopithecus afarensis," *Journal of Anthropological Research* 60, 4 (2004): 466–468.

30   **marks on animal bones that are about 3.4 to 3.6 million years old** McPherron, S.P., et al., "Evidence for stone-tool-assisted consumption of animal tissues before 3.39 million years ago at Dikika, Ethiopia," *Nature* 466 (2010): 857–860.

31   **or one of the other two closely related hominin species around at the time** Haile-Selassie, Y., Melillo, S.M., and Su, D.F., "The Pliocene hominin diversity conundrum: do more fossils mean less clarity?" *Proceedings of the National Academy of Sciences* 113 (2016), www.pnas.org/cgi/doi/10.1073/pnas.1521266113.

31   **a site called Lomekwi 3** Hovers, E., "Tools go back in time," *Nature* 521 (2015): 294–295; Harmand, S., et al., "3.3-million-year-old stone tools from Lomekwi 3, West Turkana, Kenya," *Nature* 521 (2015): 310–316.

31   **working together in groups and in the manipulation of stones** Heinzelin, J., et al., "Environment and behavior of 2.5-million-year-old Bouri hominids," *Science* 284 (1999): 625–629; Semaw, S., "The world's oldest stone artefacts from Gona, Ethiopia: their implications for understanding stone technology and patterns of human evolution between 2.6–1.5 million years ago," *Journal of Archaeological Science* 27 (2000): 1197–1214.

32   **and they fall into a few different types or species** Spoor, F., "The middle Pliocene gets crowded," *Nature* 521 (2015): 432–433.

34   ***Paranthropus*'s mouths were their main tools** Wood, B., and Strait, D., "Patterns of resource use in early Homo and Paranthropus," *Journal of Human Evolution* 46 (2004): 119–162.

35   ***Australopithecus sediba*** Berger, L.R., "The mosaic nature of Australopithecus sediba," *Science* 340 (2013): 163.

36   **mandible found in Ethiopia at the site of Ledi-Geraru** Villmoare, B., et al., "Early Homo at 2.8 Ma from Ledi-Geraru, Afar, Ethiopia," *Science* 347 (2015): 1352–1354.

37   ***Homo naledi*** Berger, L.R., et al., "Homo naledi, a new species of the genus Homo from the Dinaledi chamber, South Africa," *eLife* 4 (2015): e09560.

37   **that brains are getting somewhat bigger** Antón, S.C., Potts, R., and Aiello, L.C., "Evolution of early Homo: an integrated biological perspective," *Science* 345 (2014): 45–58.

41   **Working together, communicating through gesture and by example, our ancestors learned to cooperate in ways no one else could** While the *Homo-Paranthropus* story I present here is not as straightforward as a time machine, this approach, the using of actual data and academic accounts to construct a narrative and paint a picture of how our ancestors lived, can translate what we know about human evolution from hard-core science into accessible information. The specific details in the story I present are speculative (that is, we can't know for sure that this is how they occurred) but are based on what we know about our ancestors and the ecologies they lived in. The scenario described here is derived from published research in the primary research

literature and books, including the following: Blumenschine, R.J., et al., "Environments and hominin activities across the FLK Peninsula during Zinjanthropus times (1.84 Ma), Olduvai Gorge, Tanzania," *Journal of Human Evolution* 63 (2012): 364–383; Fuentes, A., Wyczalkowski, M., and MacKinnon, K.C., "Niche construction through cooperation: a nonlinear dynamics contribution to modeling facets of the evolutionary history in the genus Homo," *Current Anthropology* 51, 3 (2010): 435–444; Hart, D., and Sussman, R.W., *Man the Hunted: Primates, Predators, and Human Evolution* (New York: Basic Books, 2005); Lee-Thorp, J.A., and Sponheimer, M., "Contributions of biogeochemistry to understanding early hominin ecology," *Yearbook of Physical Anthropology* 49 (2006): 131–148; Pante, M.C., et al., "Validation of bone surface modification models for inferring fossil hominin and carnivore feeding interactions, with reapplication to FLK 22, Olduvai Gorge, Tanzania," *Journal of Human Evolution* 63 (2012): 395–407; Potts, R., "Environmental and behavioral evidence pertaining to the evolution of early Homo," *Current Anthropology* 53, 6 (2012): S299–S317.

43   **eleven different species or subspecies** Wood, B., "Reconstructing human evolution: achievements, challenges, and opportunities," *Proceedings of the National Academy of Sciences* 107 (2010): 8902–8909; Wood, B., and Leakey, M., "The Omo-Turkana Basin fossil hominins and their contribution to our understanding of human evolution in Africa," *Evolutionary Anthropology* 20, 6 (2012): 264–292; Antón, S.C., Potts, R., and Aiello, L.C., "Evolution of early Homo: an integrated biological perspective," *Science* 345 (2014): 45–58.

43   *Homo* **from about 1.6 million years ago until around 400,000 years ago** Sometimes the earliest ones are called *Homo ergaster,* and some of the later ones in Europe are called *Homo antecessor.*

44   **Denisovans are known only from a few bones found in Siberia** See Krause, J., et al., "The complete mitochondrial DNA genome of an unknown hominin from southern Siberia," *Nature* 464 (2010): 894–897.

44   *heidelbergensis*-**Neanderthal-Denisovan line are also found in East Asia** Cooper, A., and Stringer, C.B., "Did the Denisovans cross Wallace's line?" *Science* 342 (2013): 321–323; Hawks, J., "Significance of Neanderthal and Denisovan genomes in human evolution," *Annual Reviews of Anthropology* 42 (2013): 433–449.

45   **They also made small bits of art and body-adornment jewelry and, at least on occasion, buried their dead** It has become very clear that the Neanderthals were "human" in almost every way. They were not human exactly like us today, but they were indeed part of the human niche. See Roebroeks, W., and Soressi, M., "Neandertals revised," *Proceedings of the National Academy of Sciences* (2016), www.pnas.org /cgi/doi/10.1073/pnas.1521269113.

45   **we even carry small bits of their DNA with us today** Villa, P., and Roebroeks, W., "Neandertal demise: an archaeological analysis of the modern human superiority complex," *PLOS ONE* 9, 4 (2014): e96424, DOI: 10.1371/journal.pone.0096424; Cooper, A., and Stringer, C.B., "Did the Denisovans cross Wallace's line?" *Science* 342 (2013): 321–323.

45   **just under 200,000 years ago** White, T.D., et al., "Pleistocene Homo sapiens from Middle Awash, Ethiopia," *Nature* 423 (2003): 742–747, Bibcode:2003Natur.423..742W, DOI: 10.1038/nature01669, PMID 12802332.

46   **by about 25,000 years ago, there were no more "others"** Some have suggested that little pockets of other *Homo* remained isolated (like on Flores and maybe in southern Spain), but these were all certainly gone by 15,000 to 20,000 years ago.

47   **you always get only one race** See Fuentes, A., *Race, Monogamy, and Other Lies They Told You: Busting Myths About Human Nature* (Berkeley: University of California Press, 2012), for a good summary of the science of race; see Templeton, A.R., "Biological races in humans," *Studies in History and Philosophy of Science Part C: Studies in History and Philosophy of Biological and Biomedical Sciences* 44, 3 (2013): 262–271.

47   **nor any other biological measure divides modern humans into subspecies** See the special issue of the journal *Human Biology* 2014 (the official publication of the American Association of Anthropological Genetics) devoted to this topic, http://www.wsupress.wayne.edu/news-events/news/detail/human-biology-reviews-troublesome-inheritance. See also Hunley, K.L., Cabana, G.S., and Long, J.C., "The apportionment of human diversity revisited," *The American Journal of Physical Anthropology* 160 (2016):561–569.

48   **but they are not the focus of this book** See Gravlee, C.C., "How race becomes biology: embodiment of social inequality," *American Journal of Physical Anthropology* 139 (2009): 47–57; Marks, J., "Ten Facts About Human Variation," in *Human Evolutionary Biology*, ed. M. Muehlenbein, 265–276 (New York: Cambridge University Press, 2010); Sussman, R., *The Myth of Race* (Cambridge, MA: Harvard University Press, 2014); Fuentes, A., "A troublesome inheritance: Nicholas Wade's botched interpretation of human genetics, history, and evolution," *Journal of Human Biology* 86, 3 (2015); Fuentes, A., *Race, Monogamy, and Other Lies They Told You: Busting Myths About Human Nature* (Berkeley: University of California Press, 2012).

CHAPTER 3

51   **entitled "Man the Hunter"** Devore, I., and Lee, R.B., *Man the Hunter* (Piscataway, NJ: Transaction Publishers, 1969).

51   **Being the hunted rather than the hunters is the reality at the start of our lineage** Hart, D.L., and Sussman, R.W., *Man the Hunted: Primates, Predators, and Human Evolution* (New York: Basic Books, 2005).

51   **gender differences associated with food that we see today are not evident in our deep past** Dyble, M., et al., "Sex equality can explain the unique social structure of hunter-gatherer bands," *Science* 348 (2015): 796–798.

53   **they branched out** Ungar, P.S., Grine, F.E., and Teaford, M., "Diet in early Homo: a review of the evidence and a new model of adaptive versatility," *Annual Review of Anthropology* 35 (2006): 209–228.

53   **FwJj20 site at Koobi Fora in Kenya** Archer, W., et al., "Early Pleistocene aquatic resource use in the Turkana Basin," *Journal of Human Evolution* 77 (2014): 74–87. For even more evidence that lake-edge ecologies were important for our early relatives, see Roach, N.T., et al., "Pleistocene footprints show intensive use of lake margin habitats by Homo erectus groups," *Scientific Reports* 6 (2016): 26374, DOI: 10.1038/srep26374.

56   **chimpanzees think through using multiple tools for a single task** See, for example, Sanz, C., and Morgan, D., "The Social Context of Chimpanzee Tool Use," in *Tool Use in Animals: Cognition and Ecology*, ed. C.M. Sanz, J.Call, and C.Boesch, 161–175 (Cambridge: Cambridge University Press, 2013); Sanz, C., Call, J., and Morgan, D., "Design complexity in termite-fishing tools of chimpanzees (Pan troglodytes)," *Biology Letters* 5 (2009): 293–296; Sanz, C., and Morgan, D., "Flexible and persistent tool-using strategies in honey-gathering by wild chimpanzees," *International Journal of Primatology* 30 (2009): 411–427.

57   **lots of trial and error, acquire the tool-using skills** Lonsdorf, E.V., "What is the role of mothers in the acquisition of termite-fishing behaviors in wild chimpanzees (Pan troglodytes schweinfurthii)?" *Animal Cognition* 9 (2006): 36–46.

58   **simplest and earliest stone tools** Hovers, E., "Tools go back in time," *Nature* 521 (2015): 294–295; Semaw, S., "The world's oldest stone artefacts from Gona, Ethiopia: their implications for understanding stone technology and patterns of human evolution between 2.6–1.5 million years ago," *Journal of Archaeological Science* 27 (2000): 1197–1214; and Harmand, S., et al., "3.3-million-year-old stone tools from Lomekwi 3, West Turkana, Kenya," *Nature* 521 (2015): 310–313.

58   **do a number of things in sequence** See Dietrich Stout's great overview entitled "Stone Toolmaking and the Evolution of Human Culture and Cognition," in *Culture Evolves*, ed. A. Whiten et al., 197–214 (Oxford: Oxford University Press, 2012).

59   **learn to reliably make good Oldowan tools** Stout, D., and Chaminade, T., "Stone tools, language and the brain in human evolution," *Philosophical Transactions of the Royal Society B* 367 (2012): 75–87.

59   **using 20 to 30 percent of the body's energy during peak growth, between two and seven years of age** Kuzawaa, C., et al., "Metabolic costs and evolutionary implications of human brain development," *Proceedings of the National Academy of Sciences* 111 (2015): 13010–13015.

59   **massive increase in brain size we see in the fossils** Antón, S.C., Potts, R., and Aiello, L.C., "Evolution of early Homo: an integrated biological perspective," *Science* 345 (2014), DOI: 10.1126/science.1236828; Aiello, L.C., and Key, C., "Energetic consequences of being a Homo erectus female," *American Journal of Human Biology* 14 (2002): 551–565; Aiello, L.C., and Wells, J.C.K., "Energetics and the evolution of the genus Homo," *Annual Review of Anthropology* 31 (2002): 323–338.

60   **nearly modern-size brains (more than 1,000 cubic centimeters) appeared by 400,000 to 500,000 years ago** Contemporary humans have brains larger than 1,000 cubic centimeters, averaging about 1,350 cubic centimeters. However, brain size no longer matters, as healthy human brains today range between 1,000 and 2,000 cubic centimeters (human body sizes range quite a lot) and there is absolutely no measurable cognitive difference associated with any of the size differences in this range (for example, Einstein's brain was smaller than average).

60   **tools made the necessary increase in consumed calories possible** Tattersall, I., "If I had a hammer," *Scientific American* 311 (2014): 54–59; Tattersall, I., "Diet as driver and constraint in human evolution," *Journal of Human Evolution* 77 (2014): 141–142.

60   **These tools also had an interesting by-product** Iriki, A., and Taoka, M., "Triadic (ecological, neural, cognitive) niche construction: a scenario of human brain evolution extrapolating tool use and language from the control of reaching actions," *Philosophical Transactions of the Royal Society B* 367 (2012): 10–23, DOI: 10.1098/rstb.2011/.0190; Stout, D., and Chaminade, T., "Stone tools, language and the brain in human evolution," *Philosophical Transactions of the Royal Society B* 367 (2012): 75–87; Coward, F., and Gamble, C., "Big brains, small worlds: material culture and the evolution of the mind," *Philosophical Transactions of the Royal Society B* 363 (2008): 1969–1979.

60   **training hours and actual performance of making the tools** Hecht, E.E., et al., "Acquisition of Paleolithic tool making abilities involves structural remodeling to inferior frontoparietal regions," *Brain Structure and Function* 220 (2015): 2315–2331;

Morgan, T.J.H., et al., "Experimental evidence for the co-evolution of hominin tool-making teaching and language," *Nature Communications* 6 (2015): 6029, DOI: 10.1038/ncomms7029; Stout, D., "Tales of a Stone Age Neuroscientist," *Scientific American* 314 (2016): 28–35.

61 **envisioning multiple stages to the process, before it is even begun** Stout, D., "Stone toolmaking and the evolution of human culture and cognition," *Philosophical Transactions of the Royal Society B* 366 (2011): 1050–1059; Stout, D., "Stone Toolmaking and the Evolution of Human Culture and Cognition," in *Culture Evolves,* ed. Andrew Whiten et al., 197–214 (Oxford: Oxford University Press, 2012); Nonaka, T., Bril, B., and Rein, R., "How do stone knappers predict and control the outcome of flaking? Implications for understanding early stone tool technology," *Journal of Human Evolution* 59 (2010): 155–167.

62 **Rick Potts of the Smithsonian estimates** Potts, R., "Environmental and behavioral evidence pertaining to the evolution of early Homo," *Current Anthropology* 53 (2012): S299–S317.

63 **left piles of tools across the areas over which they roamed** Ibid.; Potts, R., "Evolution and environmental change in early human prehistory," *Annual Review of Anthropology* 41 (2012): 151–167.

66 **attacking and consuming humans** Hart, D., and Sussman, R.W., *Man the Hunted: Primates, Predators, and Human Evolution* (New York: Basic Books, 2005).

CHAPTER 4

70 **Power scavenging** Domínguez-Rodrigo, M., and Pickering, T.R., "Early hominid hunting and scavenging: a zooarcheological review," *Evolutionary Anthropology* 12 (2003): 275–282.

70 **some of the earliest tool-use sites** Semaw, S., "The world's oldest stone artefacts from Gona, Ethiopia: their implications for understanding stone technology and patterns of human evolution between 2.6–1.5 million years ago," *Journal of Archaeological Science* 27 (2000): 1197–1214.

71 **kind of predator it was and how big it was** Domínguez-Rodrigo, M., et al., "Unraveling hominin behavior at another anthropogenic site from Olduvai Gorge (Tanzania): new archaeological and taphonomic research at BK, bed II," *Journal of Human Evolution* 57 (2009): 260–283.

71 **bite of a predator or the gnawing of a rodent** Domínguez-Rodrigo, M., "Meat-eating by early hominids at the FLK 22 Zinjanthropus site Olduvai Gorge (Tanzania): an experimental approach using cut-mark data," *Journal of Human Evolution* 33 (1997): 669–690; Domínguez-Rodrigo, M., et al., "Unraveling hominin behavior at another anthropogenic site from Olduvai Gorge (Tanzania): new archaeological and taphonomic research at BK, bed II," *Journal of Human Evolution* 57 (2009): 260–283.

71 **Gran Dolina site, at Atapuerca in Spain** Saladie, P., et al., "Carcass transport decisions in Homo antecessor subsistence strategies," *Journal of Human Evolution* 61 (2011): 425–446.

72 **not reliant on one type of food over another** Unger, P., Grine, F., and Teaford, M., "Diet in early Homo: a review of the evidence and a new model of adaptive versatility," *Annual Review of Anthropology* 35 (2006): 209–228; Schoeninger, M.J., "Stable isotope analyses and the evolution of human diets," *Annual Review of Anthropology* 43 (2014): 413–430.

72 **Meat was not the only item on the menu** Schoeninger, M.J., "Stable isotope

analyses and the evolution of human diets," *Annual Review of Anthropology* 43 (2014): 413–430.

73 **characteristic of successful human foragers** Dyble, M., et al., "Sex equality can explain the unique social structure of hunter-gatherer bands," *Science* 348 (2015): 796–798; Fry, D.P., and Söderberg, P., "Lethal aggression in mobile forager bands and implications for the origins of war," *Science* 341 (2013): 270–273; Lee, R., *The !Kung San* (Cambridge: Cambridge University Press, 1979).

73 **critical part of the diet for *Homo* early on** Dominy, N.J., et al., "Mechanical properties of plant underground storage organs and implications for dietary models of early hominins," *Journal of Evolutionary Biology* (2008), DOI: 10.1007/s11692-008-9026-7; Laden, G., and Wrangham, R.W., "The rise of the hominids as an adaptive shift in fallback foods: plant underground storage organs (USOs) and australopith origins," *Journal of Human Evolution* 49 (2005): 482–498, DOI: 10.1016/j.jhevol.2005.05.007; O'Connell, J.F., Hawkes, K., and Blurton Jones, N.G., "Grandmothering and the evolution of Homo erectus," *Journal of Human Evolution* 36 (1999): 461–485, DOI: 10.1006/jhev.1998.0285; O'Connell, J., Hawkes, K., and Jones, N.B., "Meat-Eating, Grandmothering, and the Evolution of Early Human Diets," in *Human Diet: Its Origin and Evolution,* ed. P.S. Ungar and M.F. Teaford, 49–60 (London: Bergin and Garvey, 2002).

73 **Alyssa Crittenden and colleagues** Crittenden, A.N., "The importance of honey consumption in human evolution," *Food and Foodways* 19 (2011): 257–273.

75 **chimpanzees' favorite prey is a kind of monkey called red colobus** Watts, D., and Mitani, J., "Hunting behavior of chimpanzees at Ngogo, Kibale National Park, Uganda," *International Journal of Primatology* 23 (2002): 1–28; Wrangham, R.W., and Bergmann-Riss, E.L., "Rates of predation on mammals by Gombe chimpanzees, 1972–1975," *Primates* 38 (1990): 157–170.

75 **spear-like sticks, to be exact** Pruetz, J.D., et al., "New evidence on the tool-assisted hunting exhibited by chimpanzees (Pan troglodytes verus) in a savannah habitat at Fongoli, Sénégal," *Royal Society Open Science* 2 (2015), DOI: 10.1098/rsos.140507.

76 **orangutans hunting** Hardus, M.E., et al., "Behavioral, ecological, and evolutionary aspects of meat-eating by Sumatran orangutans (Pongo abelii)," *International Journal of Primatology* 33 (2012): 287–304.

79 ***Homo* used sturdy spears** Sahle, Y., et al., "Earliest stone-tipped projectiles from the Ethiopian rift date to 279,000 years ago," *PLOS ONE* 8 (2013): 1–9.

80 **the site of Qesem Cave** Hardy, K., et al., "Dental calculus reveals potential respiratory irritants and ingestion of essential plant-based nutrients at Lower Palaeolithic Qesem Cave Israel," *Quaternary International* 398 (2015): 1–7.

81 **raw foods are seldom sufficiently nourished** Koebnick, C., et al., "Consequences of a long-term raw food diet on body weight and menstruation: results of a questionnaire survey," *Annals of Nutrition and Metabolism* 43 (1999): 69–79.

81 **Cooking increases digestibility** Wrangham, R., and Carmody, R., "Human adaptation to the control of fire," *Evolutionary Anthropology* 19 (2010): 187–199.

81 **dangerous bacteria that can grow rapidly on exposed meat** Smith, A.R., et al., "The significance of cooking for early hominin scavenging," *Journal of Human Evolution* 84 (2015): 62–70.

81 **hearths or evidence of smoke on bones and teeth** Roebroeks, W., and Villa, P., "On the earliest evidence for habitual use of fire in Europe," *Proceedings of the National Academy of Sciences* 108 (2011): 5209–5214.

82 **fire and light became catalysts for colossal increases in our creativity and productivity** Wrangham, R., *Catching Fire: How Cooking Made Us Human* (New York: Basic Books, 2009).

82 **evidence of the creation and maintenance of fire** Roebroeks, W., and Villa, P., "On the earliest evidence for habitual use of fire in Europe," *Proceedings of the National Academy of Sciences* 108 (2011): 5209–5214.

CHAPTER 5

86 **in solidarity with the people who suffered the worst of its effects** Solnit, R., "In New Orleans, Kindness Trumped Chaos," *Yes! Magazine,* August 27, 2010, http://www .yesmagazine.org/issues/a-resilient-community/in-new-orleans-kindness -trumped-chaos.

86 **but humans do, again and again and again** Nowak, M., and Highfield, R., *SuperCooperators: Altruism, Evolution, and Why We Need Each Other to Succeed* (New York: Free Press, 2011); Fuentes, A., "It's not all sex and violence: integrated anthropology and the role of cooperation and social complexity in human evolution," *American Anthropologist* 106 (2004): 710–718.

87 **risking themselves for other members of their species that they do not know** There are always rare actions by individual animals that seem to be amazingly compassionate, but they are very infrequent (despite the Internet memes) and not typical of any species. I have seen both male and female monkeys adopt orphaned young in their own group, and there are one-off incidences like a dog saving a baby bunny and raising it or a cat nursing a few orphaned rat pups, but they are rare and not characteristic of either dogs or cats (but this kind of behavior is more common in domestic animals). Interestingly, when we do see events of intensive compassion like this happening with a slightly higher frequency, it tends to occur in species that have big brains and complex and very long social lives and where there are major roles played by older females as anchors for the social structures (such as in orcas and elephants). There are a few occasions of this kind of behavior in other primates, but it is not particularly common.

87 **more than just groups** We also refer to the groups of some very complex social mammals as communities. Chimpanzees, orcas, and elephants all live in types of communities as well. In each of these cases, humans included, the community denotes a higher level of coordination and complexity than just a group.

87 **across an individual's life span** Rodseth, L., et al., "The human community as a primate society," *Current Anthropology* 32 (1991): 221–254; Fuentes, A., "Integrative anthropology and the human niche: toward a contemporary approach to human evolution," *American Anthropologist* 117 (2015): 302–315; Fuentes, A., "Human evolution, niche complexity, and the emergence of a distinctively human imagination," *Time and Mind* 7 (2014): 241–257; Gamble, C., Gowlett, J., and Dunbar, R., "The social brain and the shape of the Palaeolithic," *Cambridge Archaeological Journal* 21 (2011): 115–136.

87 **many challenges to any animals trying to live together in a social group** This is not the same as a herd or a flock. There are large groupings of animals that assemble in more or less the same place and move in a generally coordinated fashion (think of herds of deer or flocks of birds), but they are not the same as a cluster of individuals who all know one another and have social relationships with one another. Herds and flocks are less social and more about being together in numbers for safety and for basic interactions.

88 **The psychologist and anthropologist Robin Dunbar** Dunbar, R.I.M., "The social

brain: mind, language, and society in evolutionary perspective," *Annual Reviews of Anthropology* 32 (2003): 163–181; Dunbar, R.I.M., Gamble, C., and Gowlett, J., *Social Brain, Distributed Mind* (Oxford: Oxford University Press, 2010).

89 **Mammals, however, come out from Mom in varying** And many birds as well. Anything with a reasonably large brain seems to take a bit longer to get going as an infant.

90 **having multiple allomothers** McKenna, J.J., "The evolution of allomothering behavior among colobine monkeys: function and opportunism in evolution," *American Anthropologist* 84 (1979): 804–840; McKenna, J.J., "Aspects of infant socialization, attachment, and maternal caregiving patterns among primates: a cross-disciplinary review," *Yearbook of Physical Anthropology* 22 (1979): 250–286; Burkart, J.M., Hrdy, S.B., and van Schaik, C., "Cooperative breeding and human cognitive evolution," *Evolutionary Anthropology* 18 (2009): 175–186.

90 **extra caretakers aren't always other females** Gettler, L.T., "Direct male care and hominin evolution: why male-child interaction is more than a nice social idea," *American Anthropologist* 112 (2010): 7–21; Gettler, L.T., "Applying socioendocrinology to evolutionary models: fatherhood and physiology," *Evolutionary Anthropology* 23 (2014): 146–160.

90 **more nutritional demands than earlier *Homo* females** Aiello, L.C., and Key, C., "Energetic consequences of being a Homo erectus female," *American Journal of Human Biology* 14 (2002): 551–565; Aiello, L.C., and Wells, J.C.K., "Energetics and the evolution of the genus Homo," *Annual Review of Anthropology* 31 (2002): 323–338.

91 **The anthropologist Sarah Hrdy and other groups of researchers** Hrdy, S.B., *Mothers and Others: The Evolutionary Origins of Mutual Understanding* (Cambridge, MA: Harvard University Press, 2009); Burkart, J.M., Hrdy, S.B., and van Schaik, C., "Cooperative breeding and human cognitive evolution," *Evolutionary Anthropology* 18 (2009): 175–186.

91 **grandmothers** Hawkes, K., "Grandmothers and the evolution of human longevity," *American Journal of Human Biology* 15 (2003): 380–400; Hawkes, K., O'Connell, J.F., and Blurton-Jones, N.G., "Human Life Histories: Primate Trade-offs, Grandmothering Socioecology, and the Fossil Record," in *Primate Life Histories and Socioecology,* ed. P.M. Kappeler and M.E. Pereira, 204–227 (Chicago: University of Chicago Press, 2003); Hrdy, S.B., *Mothers and Others: The Evolutionary Origins of Mutual Understanding* (Cambridge, MA: Harvard University Press, 2009).

92 **undergo menopause** Hawkes, K., "Grandmothers and the evolution of human longevity," *American Journal of Human Biology* 15 (2003): 380–400; Hawkes, K., O'Connell, J.F., and Blurton-Jones, N.G., "Human Life Histories: Primate Trade-offs, Grandmothering Socioecology, and the Fossil Record," in *Primate Life Histories and Socioecology,* ed. P.M. Kappeler and M.E. Pereira, 204–227 (Chicago: University of Chicago Press, 2003).

92 ***Homo erectus* were moving from a group to a community** And there is ample research to support that this indeed was how it happened with our ancestors. See Flinn, M.V., et al., "Evolution of the Human Family: Cooperative Males, Long Social Childhoods, Smart Mothers, and Extended Kin Networks," in *Family Relations: An Evolutionary Perspective,* ed. C.A. Salmon and T.K. Shackleford, 16–38 (New York: Oxford University Press, 2004); Gettler, L.T., "Direct male care and hominin evolution: why male-child interaction is more than a nice social idea," *American Anthropologist* 112 (2010): 7–21; Hrdy, S.B., *Mothers and Others: The Evolutionary Origins of Mutual Understanding* (Cambridge, MA: Harvard University Press, 2009); Gamble, C., Gowlett, J., and

Dunbar, R.I.M., "The social brain and the shape of the paleolithic," *Cambridge Archaeological Journal* 21 (2011): 115–136; Fuentes, A., *Evolution of Human Behavior* (New York: Oxford University Press, 2009).

92   **characterize the process of niche construction** Remember, from the "Overture," that this is the process of evolution where the organisms and their environment react to one another, affecting how each is shaped and shaping the pattern of interactions for generations into the future.

94   **reassemble the entire toolmaking process, flake by flake** Delganes, A., and Roche, H., "Late Pliocene hominid knapping skills: the case of Lokalalei 2C, West Turkana, Kenya," *Journal of Human Evolution* 48 (2005): 435–472; Nonaka, T., Bril, B., and Rein, R., "How do stone knappers predict and control the outcome of flaking? Implications for understanding early stone tool technology," *Journal of Human Evolution* 59 (2010): 155–167.

95   **"the apprentice model"** Sterelny, K., *The Evolved Apprentice: How Evolution Made Humans Unique* (Cambridge, MA: MIT Press, 2012).

96   **which is not with early humans** Adovasio, J.M., Soffer, O., and Page, J., *The Invisible Sex: Uncovering the True Roles of Women in Prehistory* (Walnut Creek, CA: Left Coast Press, 2009).

97   **key for our ancestors and is still key for us today** Fuentes, A., "Integrative anthropology and the human niche: toward a contemporary approach to human evolution," *American Anthropologist* 117 (2015): 302–315; Hiscock, P., "Learning in lithic landscapes: a reconsideration of the hominid 'toolmaking' niche," *Biological Theory* 9 (2014): 27–41; Morgan, T.J.H., et al., "Experimental evidence for the co-evolution of hominin tool-making teaching and language," *Nature Communications* 6 (2015): 6029, DOI: 10.1038/ncomms7029; Stout, D., and Chaminade, T., "Stone tools, language and the brain in human evolution," *Philosophical Transactions of the Royal Society B* 367 (2012): 75–87.

97   **"enskillment"** Ingold, T., *The Perception of the Environment: Essays on Livelihood, Dwelling and Skill* (New York: Routledge, 2000); Ingold, T., "Toward an ecology of materials," *Annual Review of Anthropology* 41 (2012): 427–442.

98   **Work by the archeologist Penny Spikins** Spikins, P., *How Compassion Made Us Human* (Barnsley, UK: Pen and Sword Press, 2015); Spikins, P., Rutherford, H., and Needham, A., "From homininity to humanity: compassion from the earliest archaics to modern humans," *Time and Mind* 3 (2010): 303–326.

98   **the 1.8-million-year-old site of Dmanisi in Georgia** Lordkipanidze, D., et al., "A complete skull from Dmanisi, Georgia, and the evolutionary biology of early Homo," *Science* 342 (2013): 326–331.

98   **she was likely suffering from hypervitaminosis A** Spikins, P., *How Compassion Made Us Human* (Barnsley, UK: Pen and Sword Press, 2015); Spikins, P., Rutherford, H., and Needham, A., "From homininity to humanity: compassion from the earliest archaics to modern humans," *Time and Mind* 3 (2010): 303–326; Walker, A., Zimmerman, M.R., and Leakey, R.E., "A possible case of hypervitaminosis A in Homo erectus," *Nature* 296 (1982): 248–250.

98   **child lived at least five years or more with this syndrome** Gracia, A., et al., "Craniosynostosis in the Middle Pleistocene human cranium 14 from the Sima de los Huesos, Atapuerca, Spain," *Proceedings of the National Academy of Sciences* 106 (2009): 6573–6578.

100   **Homo sapiens sapiens** The last *sapiens* here denotes a subspecies (remember from chapter 1).

CHAPTER 6

103   **people we call the Natufians** Bar-Yosef, O., "The Natufian culture in the Levant: threshold to the origins of agriculture," *Evolutionary Anthropology* 31 (1998): 159–177.

103   **village-living domesticators** Ibid.

105   **added a few tools and some red pigment, then covered the bodies** Maher, L.A., et al., "A unique human-fox burial from a pre-Natufian cemetery in the Levant (Jordan)," *PLOS ONE* 6 (2011): e15815. DOI: 10.1371/journal.pone.0015815.

106   **laid her hand on the puppy before covering them both and sealing the grave** Davis, S.J.M., and Valla, F., "Evidence for domestication of the dog 12,000 years ago in the Natufian of Israel," *Nature* 276 (1978): 608–610.

106   **three main ways in which animal domestication happened** Larson, G., and Fuller, D., "The evolution of animal domestication," *Annual Review of Ecology, Evolution, and Systematics* 45 (2014): 115–136.

106   **commensal pathway begins when another species is attracted to the human niche** Ibid.

106   **are called synanthropic** Zeder, M.A., "The domestication of animals," *Journal of Anthropological Research* 68 (2012): 161–190.

107   **avoided the sharp spears and arrows and fire that the humans wielded** Shipman, P., *The Animal Connection: A New Perspective on What Makes Us Human* (New York: W. W. Norton, 2011).

107   **as hunting partners, and as friends** Olmert, M.D., *Made for Each Other: The Biology of the Human-Animal Bond* (Philadelphia: Da Capo Press, 2009); Shipman, P., *The Invaders: How Humans and Their Dogs Drove Neanderthals to Extinction* (Cambridge, MA: Belknap Press, 2015).

108   **By about 15,000 to 20,000 years ago, we find bones** Larson, G., and Fuller, D., "The evolution of animal domestication," *Annual Review of Ecology, Evolution, and Systematics* 45 (2014): 115–136; Zeder, M.A., "The domestication of animals," *Journal of Anthropological Research* 68 (2012): 161–190; Shipman, P., *The Animal Connection: A New Perspective on What Makes Us Human* (New York: W. W. Norton, 2011).

108   **dogs and wolves began to separate as breeding clusters** While we call dogs and wolves different species today, they remain fully capable of interbreeding and living together; 30,000 years is not quite long enough to get a true speciation in this case.

108   **lives of canids** Canids are the group of mammals that includes dogs, wolves, foxes, coyotes, etc.

109   **Russian researcher Lyudmila Trut** Trut, L., Oskina, I., and Kharlamova, A., "Animal evolution during domestication: the domesticated fox as a model," *BioEssays: News and Reviews in Molecular, Cellular and Developmental Biology* 31 (2009): 349–360.

109   **Neanderthals never befriended dogs** Shipman, P., *The Invaders: How Humans and Their Dogs Drove Neanderthals to Extinction* (Cambridge, MA: Belknap Press, 2015).

110   **serious nutritional stress** Marom, N., and Bar-Oz, G., "The prey pathway: a regional history of cattle (Bos taurus) and pig (Sus scrofa) domestication in the northern Jordan Valley, Israel," *PLOS ONE* (2013), http://dx.doi.org/10.1371/journal.pone.0055958.

110   **taking of young males and the avoiding of females** Zeder, M.A., "The domestication of animals," *Journal of Anthropological Research* 68 (2012): 161–190.

110   **populations stayed stable or even grew** This works only when the overall density of humans is not too high; once we get to large towns and cities, hunting of wild game is no longer really a viable option for feeding the communities.

112 **started to shape the way the forests look and work** Hunt, C.O., and Rabat, R.J., "Holocene landscape intervention and plant food production strategies in island and mainland Southeast Asia," *Journal of Archaeological Science* 51 (2014): 22–33.

114 **correlation between the large seeds and the plant growth** Smith, B.D., "The initial domestication of Cucurbita pepo in the Americas 10,000 years ago," *Science* 276 (1997): 932–934.

114 **Possibly as early as 10,000 years ago** Piperno, D.R., et al., "Starch grain and phytolith evidence for early ninth millennium B.P. maize from the central Balsas river valley, Mexico," *Proceedings of the National Academy of Sciences* 106 (2009): 5019–5024.

114 **need a lot of teosinte** Beadle, G.W., "Teosinte and the Origin of Maize," in *Maize Breeding and Genetics,* ed. D.B. Walden, 113–128 (New York: John Wiley & Sons, 1978); Benz, B.F., "Archaeological evidence of teosinte domestication from Guilá Naquitz, Oaxaca," *Proceedings of the National Academy of Sciences* 98 (2001): 2104–2106; Flannery, K.V., "The origins of agriculture," *Annual Review of Anthropology* 2 (1973): 271–310.

115 **dried corn cob discovered in archeological remains dates to about 6,000 years ago** Piperno, D.R., and Flannery, K.V., "The earliest archaeological maize (Zea mays L.) from highland Mexico: new accelerator mass spectrometry dates and their implications," *Proceedings of the National Academy of Sciences* 98 (2001): 2101–2103; Piperno, D.R., et al., "Starch grain and phytolith evidence for early ninth millennium B.P. maize from the central Balsas river valley, Mexico," *Proceedings of the National Academy of Sciences* 106 (2009): 5019–5024.

115 **Domesticated a number of times over the last 9,000 years** Callaway, E., "The birth of rice," *Nature* 514 (2014): S58–S59; Fuller, D.Q., et al., "The domestication process and domestication rate in rice: spikelet bases from the Lower Yangtze," *Science* 323 (2009): 1607–1610.

115 **in the Pearl and Yangtze River areas** Ibid.

118 **their health deteriorated** Larsen, C.S., "Biological changes in human populations with agriculture," *Annual Review of Anthropology* 24 (1995): 185–213.

118 **being locked in to the land** Bar-Yosef, O., "The Natufian culture in the Levant: threshold to the origins of agriculture," *Evolutionary Anthropology* 6 (1998): 159–177; Ullah, I.I.T., Kuijt, I., and Freeman, J., "Toward a theory of punctuated subsistence change," *Proceedings of the National Academy of Sciences* (2015), www.pnas.org/cgi/doi/10.1073/pnas.1503628112; Kuijt, I., "What do we really know about food storage, surplus, and feasting in preagricultural communities?" *Current Anthropology* 50 (1009): 641–644.

119 **moms wean earlier** The longer a woman nurses her infant, the longer amount of time there is between births. When human moms nurse, there is often something called lactational amenorrhea: The body shuts down fertility while the nursing is going on. This enables the female's body to focus on developing and producing the milk to assist in the growth of the infant. However, if the mom stops nursing, the fertility cycle kicks back in. This is what happened in early farming communities, and the birth spacing went from an infant every three to five years to one every other year or so (more than double the birthrate!).

119 **women have more babies more often** Bentley, G.R., Goldberg, T., and Jasienska, G., "The fertility of agricultural and non-agricultural traditional societies," *Population Studies* 47 (1993): 269–281.

119 **and the population goes up, fast** Larsen, C.S., "Biological changes in human populations with agriculture," *Annual Review of Anthropology* 24 (1995): 185–213.

119 **four times more cavities than hunter-gatherers** There is large variation depending on what kinds of food the people are growing; corn, for example, is much more cavity inducing than wheat. Also, the rest of the diet has an impact as well. See ibid.; Powell, M.A., "The Analysis of Dental Wear and Caries for Dietary Reconstruction," in *The Analysis of Prehistoric Diets,* ed. R.I. Gilbert and J.H. Mielke, 307–338 (Orlando, FL: Academic Press, 1985); Turner, C.G., "Dental anthropological indications of agriculture among the Jomon people of central Japan," *American Journal of Physical Anthropology* 51 (1979): 619–636.

120 **weakening the roots of teeth and the gums surrounding them** Beckett, S., and Lovell, N.C., "Dental disease evidence for agricultural intensification in the Nubian C-group," *International Journal of Osteoarchaeology* 4 (1994): 223–239.

120 **having higher-carbohydrate and lower-protein diets than men in these societies** See summaries in Larsen, C.S., "Biological changes in human populations with agriculture," *Annual Review of Anthropology* 24 (1994): 185–213.

120 **declines in stature with the transition to agriculture** See Cohen, M.N., and Armelagos, G.J., eds., *Paleopathology at the Origins of Agriculture* (Orlando, FL: Academic Press, 1984).

121 **mycobacterium and treponematosis . . . with the advent of animal domestication** Harper, K.N., et al., "On the origin of the treponematoses: a phylogenetic approach," *PLOS Neglected Tropical Diseases* 2 (2008): e148, DOI: 10.1371/journal.pntd.0000148; Larsen, C.S., "Biological changes in human populations with agriculture," *Annual Review of Anthropology* 24 (1995): 185–213.

121 **100 trillion bacteria and other microbial critters** See the NIH Human Microbiome Project site (http://hmpdacc.org) for a fascinating overview of the human microbiome, what it does, and what it is made of. There are a number of good scientific articles and data summaries available on the site.

122 **so did the action of our microbiome** Turnbaugh, P.J., et al., "The effect of diet on the human gut microbiome: a metagenomic analysis in humanized gnotobiotic mice," *Science Translational Medicine* 1 (2009): 6ra14; Takahashi, K., "Influence of bacteria on epigenetic gene control," *Cellular and Molecular Life Sciences* 71, 6 (2014): 1045–1054; Paul, Bidisha, et al., "Influences of diet and the gut microbiome on epigenetic modulation in cancer and other diseases," *Clinical Epigenetics* 7 (2015), DOI: 10.1186/s13148-015-0144-7.

CHAPTER 7

127 **three hundred mass shootings in the United States** The Gun Violence Archive, accessed July 19, 2016, http://www.gunviolencearchive.org/reports/mass-shootings/2015. Here the definition of a "mass shooting" is four or more individuals shot in a single event.

127 **United States dies via homicide annually** "Assault or Homicide," National Center for Health Statistics, Centers for Disease Control and Prevention, last updated July 6, 2016, http://www.cdc.gov/nchs/fastats/homicide.htm.

127 **philosopher Thomas Hobbes** Hobbes, T., *Leviathan* (1651; repr., New York: Penguin, 1982).

128 **competition between males is a core feature of human evolution** Wrangham, R., and Peterson, D., *Demonic Males: Apes and the Origin of Human Violence* (New York: Mariner Books, 1996).

128 **"evolutionary history of violent male-male competition"** Pinker, S., *The Blank Slate: The Modern Denial of Human Nature* (New York: Viking Press, 2002), 316.

128 **many political scientists, such as** Gat, A., "Proving communal warfare among hunter-gatherers: the quasi-Rousseauan error," *Evolutionary Anthropology* 24 (2015): 111–126.

129 **violence and warfare are not core to our deep nature** Wilson, E.O., *The Social Conquest of Earth* (New York: Liveright, 2015).

129 **empathy and altruism have deep roots in our apelike past** De Waal, F., *The Age of Empathy* (New York: Broadway Books, 2010).

129 **rather than becoming less violent as we became more civilized** Fry, D., *Beyond War: The Human Potential for Peace* (Oxford: Oxford University Press, 2007); Ferguson, B., "Pinker's List: Exaggerating Prehistoric War Mortality," in *War, Peace, and Human Nature,* ed. D.P. Fry, 112–131 (Oxford: Oxford University Press, 2013).

130 **Gran Dolina cave site in the Sierra de Atapuerca** Carbonell, E., et al., "Cultural cannibalism as a paleoeconomic system in the European Lower Pleistocene," *Current Anthropology* 51 (2010): 539–549.

131 **a form of psychological intimidation** Otterbein, K., "The earliest evidence for warfare?: a comment on Carbonell et al.," *Current Anthropology* 52 (2011): 439.

132 **fear, and distrust of members of other groups is pretty much how we arrived at modern humanity** Bowles, S., "Conflict: altruism's midwife," *Nature* 456 (2008): 326–327.

134 **primates spend the vast majority of their time resting, feeding, or in positive social interactions** Sussman, R.W., and Garber, P.A., "Cooperation, Collective Action, and Competition in Primate Social Interactions," in *Primates in Perspective,* 2nd ed., ed. C. Campbell et al., 587–598 (Oxford: Oxford University Press, 2011).

134 **competition is checked by networks of relationships** Flack, J.C., et al., "Policing stabilizes construction of social niches in primates," *Nature* 439 (2006): 426–429; Barrett, L., Henzi, S.P., and Lusseau, D., "Taking sociality seriously: the structure of multi-dimensional social networks as a source of information for individuals," *Philosophical Transactions of the Royal Society B* 367 (2012): 2108–2118; Strum, S.C., "Darwin's monkey: why baboons can't become human," *Yearbook of Physical Anthropology* 149 (2012): 3–23.

136 **"demonic aggression in ourselves and our closest kin bespeaks its antiquity"** Wrangham, R., and Peterson, D., *Demonic Males: Apes and the Origin of Human Violence* (New York: Mariner Books, 1996), 108–109.

136 **chimpanzees can be really aggressive** Wilson, M.L., "Chimpanzees, Warfare and the Invention of Peace," in *War, Peace, and Human Nature,* ed. D.P. Fry, 361–388 (Oxford: Oxford University Press, 2013).

137 **use sharp sticks to jab small sleeping primates** Pruetz, J., et al., "New evidence on the tool-assisted hunting exhibited by chimpanzees (Pan troglodytes verus) in a savannah habitat at Fongoli, Sénégal," *Royal Society Open Science* (2015): 140507, DOI: 10.1098/rsos.140507.

138 **evolutionary origins of war** Wilson, M.L., "Chimpanzees, Warfare and the Invention of Peace," in *War, Peace, and Human Nature,* ed. D.P. Fry, 361–388 (Oxford: Oxford University Press, 2013); Wrangham, R., and Peterson, D., *Demonic Males: Apes and the Origin of Human Violence* (New York: Mariner Books, 1996), 108–109.

138 **justification in taking the comparison to that conclusion** See Ferguson, B., "Pinker's List: Exaggerating Prehistoric War Mortality," in *War, Peace, and Human Nature,* ed. D.P. Fry, 112–131 (Oxford: Oxford University Press, 2013); Fuentes, A., *Race, Monogamy, and Other Lies They Told You: Busting Myths About Human Nature* (Berkeley: University of California Press, 2012); Hart, D.L., and Sussman,

R.W., *Man the Hunted: Primates, Predators, and Human Evolution* (New York: Basic Books, 2005); Marks, J., *What It Means to Be 98 Percent Chimpanzee* (Berkeley: University of California Press, 2002), for extensive discussion on the problems with using chimpanzees as analogies for human ancestors, especially when it comes to violence and war.

140 **given extra testosterone, adults' aggression does not tend to increase** Archer, J., "Testosterone and human aggression: an evaluation of the challenge hypothesis," *Neuroscience and Biobehavioral Reviews* 30 (2006): 319–345. See also, Fine, C., *Testosterone Rex: Myths of Sex, Science, and Society* (New York: W. W. Norton, 2017).

142 **more peaceful lot in the last few centuries** The psychologist Stephen Pinker and the political scientist Azar Gat make this argument.

142 **violence in modern mobile forager societies** Fry, D., and Söderberg, P., "Lethal aggression in mobile forager bands and implications for the origins of war," *Science* 341 (2013): 370–373.

143 **fifty intensively studied forager societies** Boehm, C., "Purposive social selection and the evolution of human altruism," *Cross-Cultural Research* 42 (2008): 319–352.

143 **"man's capacity to use violence effectively"** Wilson, M., and Daly, R., "Coercive Violence by Human Males Against Their Female Partners," in *Sexual Coercion in Primates and Humans: An Evolutionary Perspective on Male Aggression Against Females,* ed. M.N. Muller and R.W. Wrangham, 319–339 (Cambridge, MA: Harvard University Press, 2009).

144 **male aggression is an evolved strategy** Chagnon, N., "Life histories, blood revenge, and warfare in a tribal population," *Science* 239 (1998): 985–992.

144 **reanalysis of the original Yanomamö** Fry, D., *Beyond War: The Human Potential for Peace* (Oxford: Oxford University Press, 2007).

144 **genealogies of 121 Waorani elders** Beckerman, S., et al, "Life histories, blood revenge, and reproductive success among the Waorani of Ecuador," *Proceedings of the National Academy of Sciences* 106 (2009): 8134–8139.

146 **lethal violence includes dented or shattered skulls and faces** Debra, M., and Harrod, R., "Bioarchaeological contributions to the study of violence," *Yearbook of Physical Anthropology* 156 (2015): 116–145.

147 **required multiple participants in coordinated action** See Ferguson, B., "War Before History," in *The Ancient World at War,* ed. P. D'Souza, 15–27 (London: Thames and Hudson, 2008); Ferguson, B., "Pinker's List: Exaggerating Prehistoric War Mortality," in *War, Peace, and Human Nature,* ed. D.P. Fry, 112–131 (Oxford: Oxford University Press, 2013); Kim, N., and Kissel, M., *Emergent Warfare and Peacemaking in Our Evolutionary Past* (London: Routledge, 2017). Many of these sites are also those heralded by Steven Pinker in his book *Better Angels of Our Nature* (New York: Viking, 2011).

149 **database of 447 fossil sites from around the globe** Kissel, M., and Piscitelli, M. (in prep), "Violence in Pleistocene Populations: Introducing a New Skeletal Database of Modern Humans to Test Theories on the Origins of Warfare." See also Haas, J., and Piscitelli, M., "The Prehistory of Warfare: Misled by Ethnography," in *War, Peace, and Human Nature,* ed. D.P. Fry, 168–190 (Oxford: Oxford University Press, 2013).

150 **produced them, which likely resulted in the individual's death** Sala, N., et al., "Lethal interpersonal violence in the Middle Pleistocene," *PLOS ONE* 10 (2015): e0126589, DOI: 10.1371/journal.pone.0126589.

150 **hundreds of thousands of years and thousands of fossils** Ibid.

152   **At Nataruk, a site west of Lake Turkana** Mirazón Lahr, M., et al., "Inter-group vio-
       lence among early Holocene hunter-gatherers of West Turkana, Kenya," *Nature* 529
       (2016): 394–398.

153   **sites of Voloshkoe and Vasilyevka** Pinhasi, R., and Stock, J., eds., *Human Bioarche-
       ology of the Transition to Agriculture* (New York: John Wiley & Sons, 2011).

153   **or were missing body parts** Ibid.

153   **Vasilyevka, five of forty-four skeletons** Lillie, M.C., "Fighting for your life? Vio-
       lence at the Late-glacial to Holocene transition in Ukraine," in *Violent Interactions in
       the Mesolithic: Evidence and Meaning,* ed. M. Roksandic, *British Archaeological Re-
       ports International Series* 1237 (2004): 89–96.

154   **rare by comparison to the total number of sites** Ferguson, B., "War Before His-
       tory," in *The Ancient World at War,* ed. P. D'Souza, 15–27 (London: Thames and
       Hudson, 2008); Keeley, L., *War Before Civilization: The Myth of the Peaceful Savage*
       (Oxford: Oxford University Press, 1996).

154   **Talheim and Herxheim . . . and Schletz** Wild, E.M., et al., "Neolithic massacres:
       Local skirmishes or general warfare in Europe?" *Radiocarbon* 46 (2004): 377–385.

156   **is violent from its very origins** Pinker, S., *The Better Angels of Our Nature* (New York:
       Viking, 2011); Gat, A., "Proving communal warfare among hunter-gatherers: the
       quasi-Rousseauan error," *Evolutionary Anthropology* 24 (2015): 111–126.

156   **previously published reviews** Keeley, L., *War Before Civilization* (Oxford: Oxford
       University Press, 1996); Bowles, S., "Did warfare among ancestral hunter-gatherers
       affect the evolution of human social behaviors?" *Science* 324 (2009): 1293–1298.

156   **But these assertions are highly contested** Ferguson, B., "Pinker's List: Exaggerating
       Prehistoric War Mortality," in *War, Peace, and Human Nature,* ed. D.P. Fry, 112–131
       (Oxford: Oxford University Press, 2013).

156   **"grossly distorting war's antiquity and lethality"** Ibid.

159   **ownership of items and property is a key aspect of everyday life** Fry, D., and Söder-
       berg, P., "Lethal aggression in mobile forager bands and the implications for the ori-
       gins of war," *Science* 341 (2013): 270–273; Fry, D., *Beyond War: The Human Potential
       for Peace* (New York: Oxford University Press, 2009).

159   **a new shift in seeing the world** Bowles, S., and Choi, J., "Coevolution of farming and
       private property during the early Holocene," *Proceedings of the National Academy of
       Sciences* 110 (2013): 8830–8835.

CHAPTER 8

163   **species' ability to successfully leave descendants** Sexually reproducing species, that
       is. There are many forms of life that do not sexually reproduce (lots of plants and
       single-celled and simpler animals). But all mammals and the majority of complex
       animals do need sex to reproduce.

164   **STI champions of the animal world** Nunn, C., and Alitzer, S., *Infectious Diseases
       in Primates: Behavior, Ecology and Evolution* (Oxford: Oxford University Press,
       2006).

164   **"Human sexuality is . . . bizarrely unusual by the standards of other animal spe-
       cies"** Diamond, J., *Why Is Sex Fun? The Evolution of Human Sexuality* (New York:
       Basic Books, 1997). See the quote here: http://www.jareddiamond.org/Jared
       _Diamond/Why_Is_Sex_Fun.html.

164   **Humans also have sex in many different ways** Have a look at the Kinsey Institute's
       webpages for a great overview: "Exploring Love, Sexuality, and Well-being," Kinsey In-
       stitute, Indiana University, accessed July 20, 2016, https://www.kinseyinstitute.org/.

164   **For men and women ages twenty-five to forty-four** Centers for Disease Control and Prevention, National Center for Health Statistics, "Sexual Behavior, Sexual Attraction, and Sexual Identity in the United States," data from the 2006–2008 National Survey of Family Growth; and "Teenagers in the United States: Sexual Activity, Contraceptive Use, and Childbearing," National Survey of Family Growth 2006–2008, series 23, number 30; see also "FAQs & Statistics," Kinsey Institute, Indiana University, http://www.iub.edu/~kinsey/resources/FAQ.html.

164   **19 million new sexually transmitted infections occur each year** "Sexual Health, Disease & Sexually Transmitted Infections," Kinsey Confidential, accessed July 20, 2016, http://kinseyconfidential.org/resources/sexual-health-disease/; and "Sexually Transmitted Dieases (STDs)," Centers for Disease Control and Prevention, accessed July 20, 2016, https://www.cdc.gov/std/.

164   **more . . . sex than any other animal** Fine, C., *Testosterone Rex: Myths of Sex, Science, and Society* (New York: W. W. Norton, 2017); Sanders, S.A, et al., "Misclassification bias: diversity in conceptualisations about having 'had sex,'" *Sexual Health* 7 (2010): 31–34; Clarkin, P., "Humans Are (Blank)-ogamous," accessed July, 28, 2016, https://kevishere.com/2011/07/05/part-1-humans-are-blank-ogamous/.

164   **"Gender" is a catchall term** Fine, C., *Delusions of Gender: The Real Science Behind Sex Differences* (London: Icon Books, 2010).

166   **keep sexual reproduction in a system** Becks, L., and Agrawal, A.F., "The evolution of sex is favoured during adaptation to new environments," *PLOS Biology* 10 (2010): e1001317, DOI: 10.1371/journal.pbio.1001317.

166   **go back to their regular, nonsexual lives, or they die** Okay, there is a lot more complication than this for many organisms, but this is the basic pattern.

166   **Females have mammary glands and nipples** Except the mammals called monotremes (like the duckbilled platypus). They have no nipples; they just exude the milk out of sweat gland–like openings in their skin and it coats their hair and the babies lap it up. All other mammals, males and females, have nipples, but usually only females have mammary glands associated with them.

166   **external testicles and often an external penis** In some mammals, such as whales, dolphins, and seals, males carry their genitals internally due to specific environmental constraints.

167   **serve in both sexual and birthing roles** See Dunsworth, H., "Why Is the Human Vagina So Big?" Social Evolution Forum, Evolution Institute, December 3, 2015, https://evolution-institute.org/blog/why-is-the-human-vagina-so-big/.

167   **Both males and females can have orgasms** It is very clear that this is the case in primates, but not as clear in some other mammals. See Campbell, C., "Primate Sexuality and Reproduction," in *Primates in Perspective,* 2nd ed., ed. C. Campbell et al., 464–475 (Oxford: Oxford University Press, 2011).

169   **sexual behavior as part of their social networking, not just for reproduction** Ibid.; Thierry, B., "The Macaques: A Doubly Layered Social Organization," in *Primates in Perspective,* 2nd ed., ed. C. Campbell et al., 229–241 (Oxford: Oxford University Press, 2011).

169   **Chimpanzees have even more complicated sexual lives** Campbell, C., "Primate Sexuality and Reproduction," 464–475, and Stumpf, R., "Chimpanzees and Bonobos: Inter- and Intraspecific Diversity," 353–361, in *Primates in Perspective,* 2nd ed., ed. C. Campbell et al. (Oxford: Oxford University Press, 2011).

169   **apes that have lots of sex** Campbell, C., "Primate Sexuality and Reproduction," 464–475, and Stumpf, R., "Chimpanzees and Bonobos: Inter- and Intraspecific

Diversity," 353–361, in *Primates in Perspective*, 2nd ed., ed. C. Campbell et al. (Oxford: Oxford University Press, 2011).

170   **created a whole new way to have, think about, represent, regulate, and embody sex** Fausto-Sterling, A., *Sexing the Body: Gender Politics and the Construction of Sexuality* (New York: Basic Books, 2000); Donnan, H., and MacGowan, F., *The Anthropology of Sex* (London: Bloomsbury, 2010).

171   **primates, having allomothers** McKenna, J.J., "The evolution of allomothering behavior among colobine monkeys: function and opportunism in evolution," *American Anthropologist* 84 (1979): 804–840; McKenna, J.J., "Aspects of infant socialization, attachment, and maternal caregiving patterns among primates: a cross-disciplinary review," *Yearbook of Physical Anthropology* 22 (1979): 250–286; Burkart, J.M., Hrdy, S.B., and van Schaik, C., "Cooperative breeding and human cognitive evolution," *Evolutionary Anthropology* 18 (2009): 175–186.

171   **extra caretakers aren't always just other females** Gettler, L.T., "Applying socioendocrinology to evolutionary models: fatherhood and physiology," *Evolutionary Anthropology* 23 (2014): 146–160.

171   **a group caretaking endeavor** Hrdy, S.B., *Mothers and Others: The Evolutionary Origins of Mutual Understanding* (Cambridge, MA: Harvard University Press, 2009); Burkart, J.M., Hrdy, S.B., and van Schaik, C., "Cooperative breeding and human cognitive evolution," *Evolutionary Anthropology* 18 (2009): 175–186; Gettler, L.T., "Direct male care and hominin evolution: why male-child interaction is more than a nice social idea," *American Anthropologist* 112 (2010): 7–21.

171   **took on substantial aspects of the care and development of children** Hawkes, K., "Grandmothers and the evolution of human longevity," *American Journal of Human Biology* 15 (2003): 380–400; Hawkes, K., O'Connell, J.F., and Blurton-Jones, N.G., "Human Life Histories: Primate Trade-offs, Grandmothering Socioecology, and the Fossil record," in *Primate Life Histories and Socioecology,* ed. P.M. Kappeler and M.E. Pereira, 204–227 (Chicago: University of Chicago Press, 2003); Hrdy, S.B., *Mothers and Others: The Evolutionary Origins of Mutual Understanding* (Cambridge, MA: Harvard University Press, 2009).

172   **females live long after their reproductive cycling shuts down** Ibid.

172   **contribute to the survival of the infants as they built that particular niche that we call the human community** And there is ample research to support that this indeed was how it happened for our ancestors. See Flinn, M.V., et al., "Evolution of the Human Family: Cooperative Males, Long Social Childhoods, Smart Mothers, and Extended Kin Networks," in *Family Relations: An Evolutionary Perspective,* ed. C.A. Salmon and T.K. Shackleford, 16–38 (New York: Oxford University Press, 2007); Gettler, L.T., "Direct male care and hominin evolution: why male-child interaction is more than a nice social idea," *American Anthropologist* 112 (2010): 7–21; Hrdy, S.B., *Mothers and Others: The Evolutionary Origins of Mutual Understanding* (Cambridge, MA: Harvard University Press, 2009); Gamble, C., Gowlett, J., and Dunbar, R., "The social brain and the shape of the paleolithic," *Cambridge Archaeological Journal* 21 (2011): 115–136.

173   **the standard line for the evolution of human monogamy and marriage** For details of the traditional approach, see Symons, D., *The Evolution of Human Sexuality* (Oxford: Oxford University Press, 1981); Buss, D.M., and Schmitt, D.P., "Sexual Strategies Theory: An Evolutionary Perspective on Human Mating," *Psychological Review* 100 (1993): 204–232; Chapais, B., *Primeval Kinship: How Pair-Bonding Gave Birth to Human Society* (Cambridge, MA: Harvard University Press, 2010); Lovejoy, C.O.,

"Reexamining human origins in light of Ardipithecus ramidus," *Science* 326 (1009): 108–115.

173 **Pair-bonds are not necessarily associated with marriage** Fuentes, A., "Re-evaluating primate monogamy," *American Anthropologist* 100 (1998): 890–907; Fuentes, A., "Patterns and trends in primate pair bonds," *International Journal of Primatology* 23 (2002): 953–978; Curtis, J.T., and Wang, Z., "The neurochemistry of pair bonding," *Current Directions in Psychological Science* 12 (2003): 49–53.

174 **the myth of the nuclear family** See Barash, D.P., and Lipton, J.E., *The Myth of Monogamy: Fidelity and Infidelity in Animals and People* (New York: Holt, 2002); Squire, S., *I Don't: A Contrarian History of Marriage* (New York: Bloomsbury, 2008); Ryan, C., and Jetha, C., *Sex at Dawn: The Prehistoric Origins of Modern Sexuality* (New York: Harper, 2010), for a good set of discussions on this topic.

174 **there are two types of pair-bonds** Fuentes, A., "Patterns and trends in primate pair bonds," *International Journal of Primatology* 23 (2002): 953–978; Curtis, J.T., and Wang, Z., "The neurochemistry of pair bonding," *Current Directions in Psychological Science* 12 (2003): 49–53.

174 **mate with each other over other mating options** Fuentes, A., *Race, Monogamy, and Other Lies They Told You: Busting Myths About Human Nature* (Berkeley: University of California Press, 2012).

174 **are maintained via social behavior combined with the physiology** Ellison, P.T., and Gray, P.B., eds., *The Endocrinology of Social Relationships* (Cambridge, MA: Harvard University Press, 2009); Curtis, J.T., and Wang, Z., "The neurochemistry of pair bonding," *Current Directions in Psychological Science* 12 (2003): 49–53.

174 **emerged as a core pattern in human evolution** Fuentes, A., *Evolution of Human Behavior* (Oxford: Oxford University Press, 2009); Ryan, C., and Jetha, C., *Sex at Dawn: The Prehistoric Origins of Modern Sexuality* (New York: Harper, 2010); Chapais, B., *Primeval Kinship: How Pair-Bonding Gave Birth to Human Society* (Cambridge, MA: Harvard University Press, 2010).

175 **culturally sanctioned outcome of romantic love** See Fuentes, A., *Race, Monogamy, and Other Lies They Told You: Busting Myths About Human Nature* (Berkeley: University of California Press, 2012); Barash, D.P., and Lipton, J.E., *The Myth of Monogamy: Fidelity and Infidelity in Animals and People* (New York: Holt, 2002); Squire, S., *I Don't: A Contrarian History of Marriage* (New York: Bloomsbury, 2008); Ryan, C., and Jetha, C., *Sex at Dawn: The Prehistoric Origins of Modern Sexuality* (New York: Harper, 2010), for further insight on this.

175 **the expected cultural norm in many human societies** And it is important to note that most humans today who are married are in assumedly monogamous marriages. At the same time, humans do socially and sexually pair-bond, but are all married couples sexually pair-bonded? And/or socially pair-bonded? Given the enormous variation in why and how people marry, probably not. But there is very, very little research asking these questions. We currently have no good data on this critical measure.

175 **the nuclear family and husband-wife structure that now typifies much of the world** Squire, S., *I Don't: A Contrarian History of Marriage* (New York: Bloomsbury, 2008).

176 **Sex is biology** Actually, even sex is not this straightforward. There can be a lot of fuzziness even at the level of DNA, and mammals have more of a range of development—at one extreme if totally bio-male and at the other if totally bio-female—but nearly all mammals fall somewhere along a spectrum of mostly male or

mostly female biologically. See Fausto-Sterling, A., *Sexing the Body: Gender Politics and the Construction of Sexuality* (New York: Basic Books, 2000).

176   **gender is the process by which** Nanda, S., *Gender Diversity: Cross-Cultural Variations,* 2nd ed. (Long Grove, IL: Waveland Press, 2014); Wood, W., and Eagly, A.H., "A cross-cultural analysis of the behavior of women and men: implications for the origins of sex differences," *Psychological Bulletin* 128 (2002): 699–727; Fine, C., *Delusions of Gender: The Real Science Behind Sex Differences* (London: Icon Books, 2010); and Fine, C., *Testosterone Rex: Myths of Sex, Science, and Society* (New York: W. W. Norton, 2017).

177   **expectations is a central part of all human cultures** Nanda, S., *Gender Diversity: Cross-Cultural Variations,* 2nd ed. (Long Grove, IL: Waveland Press, 2014).

178   **the gender similarities hypothesis** Hyde, J.S., "The gender similarities hypothesis," *American Psychologist* 60 (2005): 581–592; Hyde, J.S., "Gender similarities and differences," *Annual Review of Psychology* 65 (2014): 373–398.

178   **boys and girls, are more alike than they are different** Zell, E., Krizan, Z., and Teeter, S.R., "Evaluating gender similarities and differences using metasynthesis," *American Psychologist* 70 (2015): 10–20.

178   **recent overviews of gender similarities and differences** Archer, J., "The reality and evolutionary significance of psychological sex differences" (unpublished manuscript, July 2016) Microsoft Word File; see also Fine, C., *Testosterone Rex: Myths of Sex, Science, and Society* (New York: W. W. Norton, 2017).

179   **level of variation among individuals and in populations** Reviewed in Joel, D., and Fausto-Sterling, A., "Beyond sex differences: new approaches for thinking about variation in brain structure and function," *Philosophical Transactions of the Royal Society B* 371 (2016): 20150451, DOI: 10.1098/rstb.2015.0451.

179   **between very specific small areas of the brain** See the overview by McCarthy, M.M., "Multifaceted origins of sex differences in the brain," *Philosophical Transactions of the Royal Society B* 371 (2016): 20150106, DOI:10.1098/rstb.2015.0106.

179   **by which humans acquire gender shapes our neurobiology** Jordan-Young, R.M., *Brain Storm: The Flaws in the Science of Sex Differences* (Cambridge, MA: Harvard University Press, 2011); Eliot, L., *Pink Brain Blue Brain: How Small Differences Grow into Troublesome Gaps—and What We Can Do About It* (New York: Mariner Books, 2010); Joel, D., "Male or female? Brains are intersex," *Frontiers in Integrative Neuroscience* 5 (2011): 1–5; Ingalhalikar, M., et al., "Sex differences in the structural connectome of the human brain," *Proceedings of the National Academy of Sciences* 111 (2013): 823–828; Fine, C., et al., "Plasticity, plasticity, plasticity . . . and the rigid problem of sex," *Trends in Cognitive Sciences* 17 (2013): 550–551; Fine, C., "His brain, her brain?" *Science* 346 (2014): 915–916; ibid.

180   **uptick in energetic costs for female *Homo*** Aiello, L., and Key, C., "Energetic consequences of being a Homo erectus female," *American Journal of Human Biology* 14 (2002): 551–565; Aiello, L.C., and Wells, J.C.K., "Energetics and the evolution of the genus Homo," *Annual Review of Anthropology* 31 (2002): 323–338.

180   **use of handheld spears to stab the prey, is at around 300,000** Conard, N.J., et al., "Excavations at Schöningen and paradigm shifts in human evolution," *Journal of Human Evolution* 89 (2015): 1–17.

180   **both males and females participated in hunts** Estalrrich, A., and Rosas, A., "Division of labor by sex and age in Neandertals: an approach through the study of activity-related dental wear," *Journal of Human Evolution* 80 (2015): 51–63; Kuhn, S.L., and Stiner, M.C., "What's a mother to do? A hypothesis about the division of labor among

Neanderthals and modern humans in Eurasia," *Current Anthropology* 47 (2006): 953–980.

180   **males more on the upper teeth and for females more on the lower teeth** Estalrrich, A., and Rosas, A., "Division of labor by sex and age in Neandertals: an approach through the study of activity-related dental wear," *Journal of Human Evolution* 80 (2015): 51–63.

181   **gender assumptions about men and tools and men and hunting are really, really recent** See Adovasio, J.M., Soffer, O., and Page, J., *The Invisible Sex: Uncovering the True Roles of Women in Prehistory* (Washington, DC: Smithsonian Books, 2007).

182   **these hand images from eight different cave art sites** Snow, D., "Sexual dimorphism in upper Paleolithic European cave art," *American Antiquity* 78 (2013): 746–761.

183   **engaging in sex year-round and across most of their lives** Not that we actually do that. Most humans have a range of ups and downs of sexual activity, and many go much of their lives with little or none.

184   **"sexuality is a somatic fact created by cultural effect"** "Somatic" means "of the body." See Fausto-Sterling, A., *Sexing the Body: Gender Politics and the Construction of Sexuality* (New York: Basic Books, 2000).

184   **equate it with the sexual system of other mammals** Symons, D., *The Evolution of Human Sexuality* (Oxford: Oxford University Press, 1981); Buss, D.M., and Schmitt, D.P., "Sexual Strategies Theory: An Evolutionary Perspective on Human Mating," *Psychological Review* 100 (1993): 204–232; Fisher, H., *Anatomy of Love: The Natural History of Monogamy, Adultery, and Divorce* (New York: Simon & Schuster, 1992).

185   **chemical cascade will lead one toward a pair-bond relationship** Though there are also many who would argue that the female is more drawn to this bonded state and the males resist it. See, for example, the classic Symons, D., *The Evolution of Human Sexuality* (Oxford: Oxford University Press, 1981); Buss, D.M., and Schmitt, D.P., "Sexual Strategies Theory: An Evolutionary Perspective on Human Mating," *Psychological Review* 100 (1993): 204–232.

185   **no robust anthropological, biological, or psychological support for either of these positions** Fuentes, A., *Race, Monogamy, and Other Lies They Told You: Busting Myths About Human Nature* (Berkeley: University of California Press, 2012).

185   **sometime between the last few thousand years and the last few centuries** Ryan, C., and Jetha, C., *Sex at Dawn: The Prehistoric Origins of Modern Sexuality* (New York: Harper, 2010); Fuentes, A., *Race, Monogamy, and Other Lies They Told You: Busting Myths About Human Nature* (Berkeley: University of California Press, 2012).

185   **pair-bond sex reflects the basic evolutionary goal of reproduction is too narrow** Fuentes, A., "Re-evaluating primate monogamy," *American Anthropologist* 100 (1998): 890–907; Fuentes, A., "Patterns and trends in primate pair bonds," *International Journal of Primatology* 23 (2002): 953–978.

186   **what being male or female means biologically** Fausto-Sterling, A., *Sexing the Body: Gender Politics and the Construction of Sexuality* (New York: Basic Books, 2000); Fuentes, A., *Race, Monogamy, and Other Lies They Told You: Busting Myths About Human Nature* (Berkeley: University of California Press, 2012); Fine, C., *Testosterone Rex: Myths of Sex, Science, and Society* (New York: W. W. Norton, 2017).

186   **subcultures of attraction, and politics, are built up around them** Yalom, M., *A History of the Breast* (New York: Alfred A. Knopf, 1997).

187   **on breasts and their size and shape?** See William, F., *Breasts: A Natural and Unnatural History* (New York: W. W. Norton, 2013), for an overview of these debates.

188   **"we are not blank slates, but we are also not pink and blue notepads"** Jordan-Young, R.M., *Brain Storm: The Flaws in the Science of Sex Differences* (Cambridge, MA: Harvard University Press, 2011).

CHAPTER 9

193   **83 percent of the world's population of about 7 billion** "The Future of World Religions," Pew-Templeton Global Religious Futures Project, accessed July 20, 2016, http://www.globalreligiousfutures.org/; "Topics & Questions," Pew-Templeton Global Religious Futures Project, accessed July 20, 2016, http://www.globalreligiousfutures.org/questions.

193   **76 percent of the population self-defines as religious, 3 percent as atheist, 4 percent as agnostic, and 17 percent as nothing in particular** "America's Changing Religious Landscape," Pew Research Center: Religion and Public Life, accessed July 20, 2016, http://www.pewforum.org/2015/05/12/americas-changing-religious-landscape/.

194   **Forty percent stated they would not vote for a Muslim** Saad, L., "Support for Nontraditional Candidates Varies by Religion," Gallup, accessed July 2016, http://www.gallup.com/poll/183791/support-nontraditional-candidates-varies-religion.aspx?utm_source=Politics&utm_medium=newsfeed&utm_campaign=tiles.

194   **Pew-Templeton Global Religious Futures Project** "The Future of World Religions," Pew-Templeton Global Religious Futures Project, accessed July 20, 2016, http://www.globalreligiousfutures.org/.

196   **Where and when did religion show up, and what does it come from** Here we are asking this in an evolutionary sense—when and how did humans start showing evidence of religious behavior? This is not the same as a theological explanation—all religions have internal origin stories and explanations for how they came to be. But it is important to recognize that asking one question (the evolutionary one) is in no way an attempt to deny the religious validity of the other one (the theological one). Both can coexist, as they are working with slightly different types of answers.

197   **Wishing and hope reflect the human ability** Fuentes, A., "Human evolution, niche complexity, and the emergence of a distinctively human imagination," *Time and Mind* 7 (2014): 241–257.

198   **"Why Religion Is Nothing Special but Is Central"** Bloch, M., "Why religion is nothing special but is central," *Philosophical Transactions of the Royal Society B: Biological Sciences* 363 (2008): 2055–2061.

198   **individual and communal imaginations** Imagination does not mean "made up"; imagination is the capacity for perceptual creativity, the hoping and wishing that we have been discussing.

199   **distinct phenomenon that can analytically be labeled "religion"** Bloch, M., "Why religion is nothing special but is central," *Philosophical Transactions of the Royal Society B: Biological Sciences* 363 (2008): 2055–2061; Rappaport, R.A., *Ritual and Religion in the Making of Humanity* (Cambridge: Cambridge University Press, 1999).

199   **four key patterns that appear in most, if not all, practices-and-beliefs** To develop this list Alcorta and Sosis draw heavily on previous anthropological and sociological work on religion, especially that of Mary Douglas, Émile Durkheim, Mircea Eliade, Bronislaw Malinowski, Roy Rappaport, Victor Turner, and Edward Tylor. See Alcorta, C.S., and Sosis, R., "Ritual, emotion, and sacred symbols: the evolution of religion as an adaptive complex," *Human Nature* 16 (2008): 323–359.

200   **a separation of the sacred and the secular** Here most actually use the term *profane*

as an adjective meaning secular or just "not religious or sacred," but most people hear *profane* and think of its use as a verb meaning "to treat (something sacred) with abuse, irreverence, or contempt: DESECRATE" (*Merriam-Webster's Collegiate Dictionary*). So *secular* here simply means not associated with religious ritual or sacred (supernatural) status.

200 **"it creates the sacred"** Rappaport, R.A., *Ritual and Religion in the Making of Humanity* (Cambridge: Cambridge University Press, 1999).

201 **religions label and transform how humans experience emotions and other aspects of life** Tweed, T., "Ancient Crossings and Foraging Religions: from Itinerant Paleoindian Bands to (Mostly) Sedentary Archaic Communities, 9200 BCE–1100 BCE," in *Heavenly Habits: A History of Religion in the Lands That Became the United States* (New Haven, CT: Yale University Press, 2018), which might be considered symbolic.

204 **development of the capacity for symbolic behavior** For example, see Mithen, S., *The Prehistory of the Mind: A Search for the Origins of Art, Religion, and Science* (London: Phoenix, 1998).

205 **set the stage for the emergence of religion** Thomas Tweed outlines this scenario very well in his book in preparation *Heavenly Habits: A History of Religion in the Lands That Became the United States* (New Haven, CT: Yale University Press, 2018).

205 **The two earliest possible burials** Carbonell, E., and Mosquera, M., "The emergence of a symbolic behaviour: the sepulchral pit of Sima de los Huesos, Sierra de Atapuerca, Burgos, Spain," *Comptes rendus palévol* 5 (2006): 155–160; Dirks, P.H., et al., "Geological and taphonomic context for the new hominin species Homo naledi from the Dinaledi chamber, South Africa," *eLife* 4 (2015): e09561.

206 **often in the same spaces where people were living** Pettitt, P., *The Palaeolithic Origins of Human Burial* (London: Routledge, 2011).

206 **evidence of daily and mundane (secular) activities going on in and around them** Hodder, I., and Cessford, C., "Daily practice and social memory at Çatalhöyük," *American Antiquity* 69 (2004): 17–40.

207 **"religious imagination and the human quest for meaning"** Van Huyssteen, J.W., *Alone in the World? Human Uniqueness in Science and Theology* (Grand Rapids, MI: William B. Eerdmans, 2006).

207 **"the religious system . . . is an exquisite, complex adaptation"** Sosis, R., "The adaptationist-byproduct debate on the evolution of religion: five misunderstandings of the adaptationist program," *Journal of Cognition and Culture* 9 (2009): 315–332.

208 **language that enabled the ubiquitous presence of religiosity in humans** King, B., *Evolving God: A Provocative View on the Origins of Religion* (New York: Doubleday, 2007); Jeeves, M., ed., *Rethinking Human Nature: A Multidisciplinary Approach* (Grand Rapids, MI: William B. Eerdmans, 2009); Rappaport, R.A., *Ritual and Religion in the Making of Humanity* (Cambridge: Cambridge University Press, 1999); Van Huyssteen, J.W., *Alone in the World? Human Uniqueness in Science and Theology* (Grand Rapids, MI: William B. Eerdmans, 2006).

208 **precedes, and enables, the emergence of religion** Rappaport, R.A., *Ritual and Religion in the Making of Humanity* (Cambridge: Cambridge University Press, 1999); Rossano, M.J., "Ritual behaviour and the origins of modern cognition," *Cambridge Archaeological Journal* 19 (2009): 243–256.

208 **played (and still plays) a core role in human evolution** Coward, F., and Gamble, C., "Big brains, small worlds: material culture and the evolution of the mind," *Philosophical Transactions of the Royal Society B* 363 (2008): 1969–1979; Sterelny, K., *The*

Evolved Apprentice: How Evolution Made Humans Unique (Cambridge, MA: MIT Press, 2012).

208   **the social lives and ecological landscapes of early humans** Sterelny, K., and Hiscock, P., "Symbols, signals, and the archaeological record," *Biological Theory* 9 (2014): 1–3; Stout, D., "Stone toolmaking and the evolution of human culture and cognition," *Philosophical Transactions of the Royal Society B* 366 (2011): 1050–1059.

208   **possibility that a new skill of making meaning emerged** Fuentes, A., "Human evolution, niche complexity, and the emergence of a distinctively human imagination," *Time and Mind* 7 (2014): 241–257.

209   **the origin of religion and religious belief are adaptations** Johnson, D.D.P., and Bering, J.M., "Hand of God, mind of man: punishment and cognition in the evolution of cooperation," *Evolutionary Psychology* 4 (2006): 219–233; Norenzayan, A., *Big Gods: How Religion Transformed Cooperation and Conflict* (Princeton, NJ: Princeton University Press, 2013); and Johnson, D., *God Is Watching You: How the Fear of God Makes Us Human* (Oxford: Oxford University Press, 2016).

209   **normal functioning of the human cognitive system** These would fall into the areas of "cognitive science of religion" (CSR) or "evolutionary cognitive science of religion" (ECSR), whose practitioners are primarily in cognitive psychology and religious studies, philosophy of mind, neuroscience, and social and cognitive anthropology.

209   **we are self-aware** Called "theory of mind."

209   **supernatural agents at play underlying many observed or perceived phenomena** See the following for this position and some overviews and critiques: Atran, S., *In Gods We Trust: The Evolutionary Landscape of Religion* (Oxford: Oxford University Press, 2002); Bering, J.M., "The Evolutionary History of an Illusion: Religious Causal Beliefs in Children and Adults," in *Origins of the Social Mind: Evolutionary Psychology and Child Development*, ed. B. Ellis and D. Bjorklund, 411–437 (New York: Guilford Press, 2012); Boyer, P., *Religion Explained: The Evolutionary Origins of Religious Thought* (New York: Basic Books, 2001); Watts, F., and Turner, L., *Evolution, Religion, and Cognitive Science: Critical and Constructive Essays* (Oxford: Oxford University Press, 2014).

210   **that the particular "Big God(s)" religions** Norenzayan, A., *Big Gods: How Religion Transformed Cooperation and Conflict* (Princeton, NJ: Princeton University Press, 2013).

210   **the role of supernatural punishment** Johnson, D.D.P., and Bering, J.M., "Hand of God, mind of man: punishment and cognition in the evolution of cooperation," *Evolutionary Psychology* 4 (2006): 219–233; Johnson, D.D.P., *God Is Watching You: How the Fear of God Makes Us Human* (Oxford: Oxford University Press, 2016).

210   **ended up outcompeting other religions and that is why they are dominant** See Fuentes, A., "Hyper-cooperation is deep in our evolutionary history and individual perception of belief matters," *Religion, Brain and Behavior* 5, 4 (2014): 19–25, DOI: 10.1080/2153599X.2014.928350, for a broader discussion of these.

213   **Our models and hypotheses need to keep this in mind** Ibid.; Rappaport, R.A., *Ritual and Religion in the Making of Humanity* (Cambridge: Cambridge University Press, 1999).

213   **semiosis—the use and creation of symbol** Here I am relying on the philosopher Charles Sanders Peirce's system of semiosis (for a good overview see Atkin, A., "Peirce's Theory of Signs," in *Stanford Encyclopedia of Philosophy*, article published October 13, 2006, substantive revision November 15, 2010, acccessed July 20, 2016, http://plato .stanford.edu/entries/peirce-semiotics/). Peircian semiotics are used by anthropologists to explore human evolution and the development of symbols in the human past (e.g.,

Deacon, T., *The Symbolic Species: The Co-evolution of Language and the Brain* [New York: W. W. Norton, 1997]; Kissel, M., and Fuentes, A., "From Hominid to Human: The Role of Human Wisdom and Distinctiveness in the Evolution of Modern Humans," *Philosophy, Theology and the Sciences* 3, 2 [2016]: 217–44).

214   **the human tendency to be religious** Rappaport, R.A., *Ritual and Religion in the Making of Humanity* (Cambridge: Cambridge University Press, 1999); Van Huyssteen, J.W., *Alone in the World? Human Uniqueness in Science and Theology* (Grand Rapids, MI: William B. Eerdmans, 2006).

216   **proposed by theologians and scientists** See, for example, Deane-Drummond, C., *The Wisdom of the Liminal: Evolution and Other Animals in Human Becoming* (Grand Rapids, MI: William B. Eerdmans, 2014); Van Huyssteen, J.W., *Alone in the World? Human Uniqueness in Science and Theology* (Grand Rapids, MI: William B. Eerdmans, 2006); Deane-Drummond, C., and Fuentes, A., "Human being and becoming: situating theological anthropology in interspecies relationships in an evolutionary context," *Philosophy, Theology and the Sciences* 1 (2014): 5.

216   **eventually leading to religious belief** See, for example, Deane-Drummond, C., "Beyond Separation or Synthesis: Christ and Evolution as Theodrama," in *Darwin in the 21st Century: Nature, Humanity and God,* ed. P.R. Sloan, G. McKenny, and K. Eggleson (South Bend, IN: University of Notre Dame Press, 2015); Van Huyssteen, J.W., *Alone in the World? Human Uniqueness in Science and Theology* (Grand Rapids, MI: William B. Eerdmans, 2006).

217   **naturalness to the human religious imagination** Van Huyssteen, J.W., *Alone in the World? Human Uniqueness in Science and Theology* (Grand Rapids, MI: William B. Eerdmans, 2006).

218   **a better moral or altruistic person are wrong** See, for example, Decety, J., et al., "The negative association between religiousness and children's altruism across the world," *Current Biology* 25 (2015): 2951–2955; Galen, L.W., "Does religious belief promote prosociality? A critical examination," *Psychological Bulletin* 138 (2012): 876–906; Sablosky, R., "Does religion foster generosity?" *Social Science Journal* 51 (2014): 545–555.

CHAPTER 10

221   **"the expression or application of human creative skill"** "Art" in OxfordDictionaries .com, accessed July 21, 2016, http://www.oxforddictionaries.com/us/definition /american_english/art.

221   **"expresses important ideas or feelings"** "Art" in *Merriam-Webster's Collegiate Dictionary Online*, accessed July 20, 2016, http://www.merriam-webster.com/dictionary/art.

221   **"Art is not a thing—it is a way"** Popova, M., "What is Art? Favorite Famous Definitions, from Antiquity to Today," *Brain Pickings*, accessed July 20, 2016, https://www .brainpickings.org/2012/06/22/what-is-art/.

222   **intense interpretation of life** Knight, K., and Schwarzman, M., *Beginner's Guide to Community-Based Arts* (Los Angeles: New Village Press, 2005).

222   **"more creative in their behavior than any other living species"** Mithen, S., *Creativity in Human Evolution and Prehistory* (London: Routledge, 1998).

222   **was Washoe** Carey, B., "Washoe, a Chimp of Many Words, Dies at 42," *The New York Times*, November 1, 2007, http://www.nytimes.com/2007/11/01/science/01chimp .html.

223   **and she greatly enjoyed the opportunity to do it** Fouts, R., and Mills, S.T., *Next of Kin: My Conversations with Chimpanzees* (New York: William Morrow, 1998).

223 **elephants and other apes, all in captivity** For a good overview, see Boxer, S., "It Seems Art Is Indeed Monkey Business," *The New York Times*, November 8, 1997, http://www.nytimes.com/1997/11/08/arts/it-seems-art-is-indeed-monkey-business .html.

223 **for the female viewer to enhance their displays** Kelley, L.A., and Endler, J.A., "Male great bowerbirds create forced perspective illusions with consistently different individual quality," *Proceedings of the National Academy of Sciences* 109 (2012): 20980–20985.

224 **sensually attractive or pleasing** For a range of the philosophical, literary, and other academic takes on this topic, see Umberto Eco's books *The History of Beauty* (Rome: Rizzoli, 2004) and *On Ugliness* (Rome: Rizzoli, 2007); Scrunton, R., *Beauty: A Very Short Introduction* (Oxford: Oxford University Press, 2011); Cahn, S.M., and Meskin, A., *Aesthetics: A Comprehensive Anthology* (New York: Blackwell, 2007).

227 **"and jewelry of behavioral modernity"** Ochre is a kind of pigment. Hiscock, P., "Learning in lithic landscapes: a reconsideration of the hominid 'toolmaking' niche," *Biological Theory* 9 (2014): 27–41; Sterelny, K., and Hiscock, P., "Symbols, signals, and the archaeological record," *Biological Theory* 9 (2014): 1–3.

227 **collaboration we don't see in other animals** Vaesen, K., "The cognitive bases of human tool use," *Behavioral and Brain Sciences* 35 (2012): 203–218.

227 **creating shapes and forms from stone** McPherron, S.P., "Handaxes as a measure of the mental capabilities of early hominids," *Journal of Archaeological Science* 27 (2000): 655–663, Mithen, S., "Social Learning and Industrial Variability," in *The Archaeology of Human Ancestry,* ed. J. Steele and S. Shennan, 207–229 (London: Routledge, 1996).

228 **"golden ratio"** See, for example, Pope, M., Russel, K., and Watson, K., "Biface form and structured behaviour in the Acheulean," *Lithics: The Journal of the Lithic Studies Society* 27 (2006): 44–57.

228 **fit in the range of the golden ratio** Ibid.

228 **tool styles emerge clearly by this time** Lycett, S.J., and Gowlett, J.A.J., "On questions surrounding the Acheulean 'tradition,'" *World Archaeology* 40 (2008): 295–315; Ashton, N., and White, M.J., "Bifaces and Raw Materials: Flexible Flaking in the British Earlier Palaeolithic," in *From Prehistoric Bifaces to Human Behaviour: Multiple Approaches to the Study of Bifacial Technology,* ed. M. Soressi and H. Dibble, 109–123 (Philadelphia: University of Pennsylvania Museum of Archaeology and Anthropology, 2003); Wenban-Smith, F.F., "Handaxe typology and Lower Palaeolithic cultural development: ficrons, cleavers and two giant handaxes from Cuxton," in "Papers in Honour of R.J. MacRae," ed. M.I. Pope and K.D. Cramp, special issue, *Lithics: The Journal of the Lithic Studies Society* 25 (2006): 11–22; Wynn, T., and Tierson, F., "Regional comparisons of the shapes of later Acheulean handaxes," *American Anthropologist* 92 (1990): 73–84.

228 **site called Boxgrove in England** Pope, M.I., "Behavioural Implications of Biface Discard: Assemblage Variability and Land-Use at the Middle Pleistocene Site of Boxgrove," in *Lithics in Action: Lithic Studies Society Occasional Paper No. 8,* ed. E. Walker, F.F. Wenban-Smith, and F. Healy, 38–47 (Oxford: Oxbow Books, 2004); Pope, M.I., and Roberts, M.B., "Observations on the Relationship Between Individuals and Artefact Scatters at the Middle Palaeolithic Site of Boxgrove, West Sussex," in *The Hominid Individual in Context: Archaeological Investigations of Lower and Middle Palaeolithic Landscapes,* ed. C. Gamble and M. Porr, 81–97 (London: Routledge, 2005).

229 **This making of "place" is wonderfully demonstrated deep in the Bruniquel Cave in southwestern France** Jaubert, J., et al., "Early Neanderthal constructions deep in Bruniquel Cave in southwestern France," *Nature* 534 (2016), http://www.nature .com/doifinder/10.1038/nature18291.

229 **used as a cutting or chopping implement** Carbonell, E., and Mosquera, M., "The emergence of a symbolic behaviour: the sepulchral pit of Sima de los Huesos, Sierra de Atapuerca, Burgos, Spain," *Comptes rendus palévol* 5 (2006): 155–160.

229 **There is evidence of some groups of *Homo* using ochre by at least 280,000 years ago** Watts, I., Chazan, M., and Wilkins, J., "Early evidence for brilliant ritualized display: specularite use in the Northern Cape (South Africa) between ~500 and ~300 Ka," *Current Anthropology* 57 (2016): 287–310.

230 **small dried spots of red pigment** Roebroeks, W., et al., "Use of red ochre by early Neandertals," *Proceedings of the National Academy of Sciences* 109 (2012): 1889–1894.

230 **including black pigments** Bonjean, D., et al., "A new Cambrian black pigment used during the late Middle Palaeolithic discovered at Scladina cave (Andenne, Belgium)," *Journal of Archaeological Science* 55 (2015): 253–265.

230 **study of beaded headbands** Wiessner, P., "Style and social information in Kalahari San projectile points," *American Antiquity* 48 (1983): 253–276; Wiessner, P., "Reconsidering the behavioral basis for style: a case study among the Kalahari San," *Journal of Anthropological Archaeology* 3 (1984): 190–234.

231 **we start to see beads more regularly** Kissel, M., and Fuentes, A., "From Hominid to Human: The Role of Human Wisdom and Distinctiveness in the Evolution of Modern Humans," *Philosophy, Theology and the Sciences* 3, 2 (2016): 217–44.

231 **just two species in the genus *Nassarius*** Bar-Yosef Mayer, D.E., "Nassarius shells: preferred beads of the Palaeolithic," *Quaternary International* 390 (2015): 79–84.

232 **messages there were are locked in the past** Stiner, M.C., "Finding a common bandwidth: causes of convergence and diversity in Paleolithic beads," *Biological Theory* 9 (2014): 51–64.

232 **talons in the vast collection** Radovčić, D., et al., "Evidence for Neandertal jewelry: modified white-tailed eagle claws at Krapina," *PLOS ONE* 10 (2015), DOI: 10.1371 /journal.pone.0119802.

232 **from birds and wore them in some fashion** Finlayson, C., et al., "Correction: birds of a feather: Neanderthal exploitation of raptors and corvids," *PLOS ONE* 7 (2012), DOI: 10.1371/annotation/5160ffc6-ec2d-49e6-a05b-25b41391c3d1.

233 **pattern on the inside of the shell** Joordens, J.C.A., et al., "Homo erectus at Trinil on Java used shells for tool production and engraving," *Nature* 581 (2014): 228–231.

233 **done to occupy the imagination** This process could have started much earlier, with doodling in the dirt or with ashes, but there is no way we could recover such evidence without a time machine.

233 **in multiple locations around the world** Hodgson, D., "Decoding the Blombos engravings, shell beads and Diepkloof ostrich eggshell patterns," *Cambridge Archaeological Journal* 24 (2014): 57–69.

233 **they lead us to think and imagine** Ingold, T., *Lines: A Brief History* (London: Routledge, 2007).

234 **both of these claims are fiercely debated** Bednarik, R.G., "A figurine from the African Acheulian," *Current Anthropology* 44 (2003): 405–413; Kissel, M., and Fuentes, A., "From Hominid to Human: The Role of Human Wisdom and Distinctiveness in the Evolution of Modern Humans," *Philosophy, Theology and the Sciences* 3, 2 (2016): 217–44.

235   **humans' relationships with other animals** Porr, M., and de Kara, M., "Perceiving Animals, Perceiving Humans. Animism and the Aurignacian Mobiliary Art of Southwest Germany," in *Forgotten Times and Spaces: New Perspectives in Paleoanthropological, Paleoetnological and Archeological Studies,* 1st ed., ed. S. Sázelová, M. Novák, and A. Mizerová, 93–302 (Brno: Institute of Archeology of the Czech Academy of Sciences; Masaryk University, 2015).

235   **and some covered with red ochre** Adovasio, J.M., Soffer, O., and Page, J., *The Invisible Sex: Uncovering the True Roles of Women in Prehistory* (Washington, DC: Smithsonian Press, 2007).

235   **perspective one gets when looking at one's own body** McDermott, L., "Self-representation in Upper Paleolithic female figurines," *Current Anthropology* 37 (1996): 227–275.

236   **South Africa dating to about 100,000 years ago** Henshilwood, C.S., et al., "A 100,000-year-old ochre-processing workshop at Blombos Cave, South Africa," *Science* 334 (2011): 219–222.

236   **milk from a wild bovid** Villa, P., et al., "A milk and ochre paint mixture used 49,000 years ago at Sibudu, South Africa," *PLOS ONE* 10 (2015): e0131273, DOI: 10.1371/journal.pone.0131273.

237   **site called called Leang Timpuseng** Aubert, M., et al., "Pleistocene cave art from Sulawesi, Indonesia," *Nature* 514 (2014): 223–227.

237   **El Castillo in Spain** Pike, A.W.G., et al., "U-series dating of Paleolithic art in 11 caves in Spain," *Science* 336 (2102): 1409–1413.

237   **recent ones were finished about 13,000 years ago** Visit "The Cave of Altamira," Museo de Altamira, accessed July 20, 2016, http://en.museodealtamira.mcu.es/Prehistoria_y_Arte/la_cueva.html; or, better yet, visit Altamira in person.

238   **human face in art starts to take shape** Ibáñez, J.J., González-Urquijo, J.E., and Braemer, F., "The human face and the origins of the Neolithic: the carved bone wand from Tell Qarassa North, Syria," *Antiquity* 88 (2014): 81–94; Kuijt, I., "The regeneration of life: Neolithic structures of symbolic remembering and forgetting," *Current Anthropology* 49 (2008): 171–197; Kuijt, I., "Constructing the Face, Creating the Collective: Neolithic Mediation of Personhood," in *Verbs, Bones, and Brains: Interdisciplinary Perspectives on Human Nature,* ed. A. Fuentes and A. Visala (South Bend, IN: University of Notre Dame Press, 2017); see also Hodder, I., "An Archeology of the Self: The Prehistory of Personhood," in *In Search of Self: Interdisciplinary Perspectives on Personhood,* ed. J.W. van Huyssteen and E.P. Wiebe (Grand Rapids, MI: William B. Eerdmans, 2011), 50-69.

239   **musicality is a fundamental part of being human** Mithen, S., *The Singing Neanderthals: The Origins of Music, Language, Mind and Body* (Cambridge, MA: Harvard University Press, 2007).

239   **"melody to communicate information"** Mithen, S., "Overview," *Cambridge Archaeological Journal* 16 (2006): 1, 97–100.

240   **Not everyone agrees with this scenario** See commentaries by Clive Gamble, Ian Morley, Allison Wray, and Maggie Tallerman in "Review Feature: The Singing Neanderthals," *Cambridge Archaeological Journal* 16 (2006): 97–112.

240   **dance and movement are central** Sheets-Johnstone, M., *The Primacy of Movement* (Amsterdam: John Benjamins, 1998).

241   **argues for mimesis** Donald, M., *A Mind So Rare: The Evolution of Human Consciousness* (New York: W. W. Norton, 2001).

241   **a few sites in the area of what is today Germany** Higham, T., et al., "Testing models for

the beginnings of the Aurignacian and the advent of figurative art and music: the radiocarbon chronology of Geißenklösterle," *Journal of Human Evolution* 62 (2012): 664–676.

241 **flute was made and played** You can hear a clay replica of the early flutes played here: Jones, J., "Hear the World's Oldest Instrument, the 'Neanderthal Flute,' Dating Back Over 43,000 Years," Open Culture, February 10, 2015, accessed July 20, 2016, http://www.openculture.com/2015/02/hear-the-worlds-oldest-instrument-the-neanderthal-flute.html.

CHAPTER 11

245 **in their households** "Toothbrush Beats Out Car and Computer as the Invention Americans Can't Live Without, According to Lemelson-MIT Survey," MIT News, January 21, 2003, http://news.mit.edu/2003/lemelson.

246 **Thales of Miletus** See the peer-reviewed *Internet Encyclopedia of Philosophy* for details on Thales and many other aspects of philosophical history and theory: O'Grady, P., "Thales of Miletus (c. 620 B.C.E.–c. 546 B.C.E.)," *Internet Encyclopedia of Philosophy,* accessed December 18, 2015, http://www.iep.utm.edu/thales/.

247 **uniform field of gravity around our planet** Check out the European Space Agency's gravity pages: "Science," European Space Agency Earth Online, accessed July 20, 2016, https://earth.esa.int/web/guest/missions/esa-operational-eo-missions/goce/science.

248 **enabled their discovery** Kaplan, S., "Einstein Predicted Gravitational Waves 100 Years Ago. Here's What It Took to Prove Him Right," *The Washington Post*, February 12, 2016, https://www.washingtonpost.com/news/morning-mix/wp/2016/02/12/einstein-predicted-gravitational-waves-100-years-ago-heres-what-it-took-to-prove-him-right/.

249 **13.77 billion years old** See "How Old Is the Universe?," National Aeronautics and Space Administration (NASA), accessed December 18, 2015, http://map.gsfc.nasa.gov/universe/uni_age.html.

249 **science is merely a methodology** "Science," in *Merriam-Webster's Collegiate Dictionary Online*, accessed July 20, 2016, http://www.merriam-webster.com/dictionary/science.

249 **The Science Council** "Our Definition of Science," The UK Science Council, accessed July 20, 2016, http://www.sciencecouncil.org/definition.

249 **"person who gives the right answers, he's one who asks the right questions"** Both the Asimov and Lévi-Strauss quotes come from a great compilation of definitions and thoughts about science put together by the author and blogger Maria Popova in her blog *Brain Pickings*: Popova, M., "What Is Science? From Feynman to Sagan to Asimov to Curie, an Omnibus of Definitions," *Brian Pickings*, accessed July 20, 2016, https://www.brainpickings.org/2012/04/06/what-is-science/.

250 **select, modify, and use to get food** Hunt, G.R., and Gray, R.D., "Diversification and cumulative evolution in New Caledonian crow tool manufacture," *Proceedings of the Royal Society of London B* 270 (2003): 867–874.

252 **chimpanzee groups with access to nuts and stones** Boesch, C., et al., "Is nut cracking in wild chimpanzees a cultural behaviour?" *Journal of Human Evolution* 26 (1994): 325–338.

255 **styles of the subsequent tools** Braun, David R., et al., "Oldowan behavior and raw material transport: perspectives from the Kanjera Formation," *Journal of Archaeological Science* 35 (2008): 2329–2345.

255   **they communicated with one another** Morgan, T.J.H., et al., "Experimental evi-
      dence for the co-evolution of hominin tool-making teaching and language," *Nature
      Communications* 6 (2015): 6029, DOI: 10.1038/ncomms7029; Stout, D., "Stone tool-
      making and the evolution of human culture and cognition," *Philosophical Transac-
      tions of the Royal Society B* 366 (2011): 1050–1059; Sterelny, K., and Hiscock, P.,
      "Symbols, signals, and the archaeological record," *Biological Theory* 9 (2014): 1–3.

256   **site of Schöningen** Conard, N.J., et al., "Excavations at Schöningen and paradigm
      shifts in human evolution," *Journal of Human Evolution* 89 (2015): 1–17.

257   **fall (are pulled by gravity) at approximately the same rate** See "The Monkey and the
      Hunter," American Physical Society: Physics Central, June 20, 2013, accessed July 20,
      2016, http://www.physicscentral.com/explore/action/monkey-hunter.cfm; and Wolfe,
      J., "The Monkey and the Hunter," Physclips, accessed July 20, 2016, http://www
      .animations.physics.unsw.edu.au/jw/monkey_hunter.html, for examples and the math.

258   **whole array of other thrown items** Other animals are able to figure out the basics of
      this equation (archer fish, for example, are good at spitting water at an angle to knock
      insects into their ponds and capture them; see http://www.wired.com/2013
      /11/archerfish-physics/). But no other animals apply this to a range of objects, modify
      the objects for the purposes of throwing, and develop a whole repertoire derived from
      this basic equation. That is something only our ancestors, and we, have done.

258   **added variables and complexities** See Ehryk, "How to calculate the velocity needed for
      a rocket to get to a L1 point (escape a body without orbiting)?" Physics, Stack Overflow,
      March 19, 2014, accessed July 20, 2016, http://physics.stackexchange.com/questions
      /104337/how-to-calculate-the-velocity-needed-for-a-rocket-to-get-to-a-l1-point-escape-a;
      and Pettit, D., "The Tyranny of the Rocket Equation," for NASA, May 1, 2012, accessed
      July 20, 2016, http://www.nasa.gov/mission_pages/station/expeditions/expedition30
      /tryanny.html.

259   **complex investigative mind** Wadley, L., Hodgskiss, T., and Grant, M., "Implications
      for complex cognition from the hafting of tools with compound adhesives in the
      Middle Stone Age, South Africa," *Proceedings of the National Academy of Sciences* 106
      (2009): 9590–9594.

259   **by 70,000 to 80,000 years ago** Wynn, T., "Hafted spears and the archaeology of
      mind," *Proceedings of the National Academy of Sciences* 106 (2009): 9544–9545.

259   **the development of adhesives** Wadley, L., Hodgskiss, T., and Grant, M., "Implica-
      tions for complex cognition from the hafting of tools with compound adhesives in the
      Middle Stone Age, South Africa," *Proceedings of the National Academy of Sciences* 106
      (2009): 9590–9594.

268   **horrific policies, oppression, and atrocities** Sussman, R., *The Myth of Race* (Cam-
      bridge, MA: Harvard University Press, 2015); Marks, J., *Why I Am Not a Scientist*
      (Berkeley: University of California Press, 2009).

268   **still some who do the same** Like Nicholas Wade's repugnant book: *A Troublesome
      Inheritance: Genes, Race and Human History* (New York: Penguin, 2014).

268   **"of true art and true science"** From Maria Popova in her blog *Brain Pickings*: Popova, M.,
      "What Is Science? From Feynman to Sagan to Asimov to Curie, an Omnibus of Defini-
      tions," *Brain Pickings*, accessed July 20, 2016, https://www.brainpickings.org/2012/04
      /06/what-is-science/.

268   **"artists and scientists are not so different from one another"** Senior Adviser for
      Program Innovation for the U.S. National Endowment for the Arts, O'Brien, B.,
      "The Imagine Engine at the Intersection of Science and Art," Live Science, January 3,

2014, accessed July 20, 2016, http://www.livescience.com/42320-intersection
-science-art.html.

CODA

271 **"and there transform them into reality"** Montagu, A., *The Human Revolution* (New York: John Wiley & Sons, 1965): 2–3.

271 **shared his dream** King, Martin Luther, Jr., "I Have a Dream" (speech, March on Washington for Jobs and Freedom, Washington, DC, August 28, 1963).

274 **The big-box store and strip-mallification of the United States** David Giffels, *The Hard Way on Purpose: Essays and Dispatches from the Rust Belt* (New York: Scribner, 2014).

275 **the swimmer Diana Nyad** Myre, G., "On Fifth Try, Diana Nyad Completes Cuba-Florida Swim," NPR.org, September 2, 2013, http://www.npr.org/sections/thetwo -way/2013/09/02/218207861/diana-nyad-in-homestretch-of-cuba-florida-swim.

275 **"without the sting of failure to spur us to"** Bloch, H., "Failure Is an Option," *National Geographic*, September 2013, http://ngm.nationalgeographic.com/2013/09 /famous-failures/bloch-text.

277 **"food deserts"** The USDA defines food deserts as "parts of the country vapid of fresh fruit, vegetables, and other healthful whole foods, usually found in impoverished areas. This is largely due to a lack of grocery stores, farmers' markets, and healthy food providers." ("USDA Defines Food Deserts," *Nutrition Digest*, American Nutrition Association, 38 (1), accessed July 20, 2016, http://americannutritionassociation.org /newsletter/usda-defines-food-deserts.)

277 **many poor urban areas** Noble, Kimberly G., et al., "Family income, parental education and brain structure in children and adolescents," *Nature Neuroscience* 18 (2015), http:// www.nature.com/doifinder/10.1038/nn.3983.

277 **via mother's milk** Ballard, O., and Morrow, A.L., "Human milk composition: nutrients and bioactive factors," *Pediatric Clinics of North America* 60 (2013): 49–74, DOI: 10.1016/j.pcl.2012.10.002.

277 **better when lightly cooked** Wanjek, C., "Reality Check: 5 Risks of a Raw Vegan Diet," *Scientific American*, January 16, 2013, http://www.scientificamerican .com/article/reality-check-5-risks-of/.

278 **death for children under five** "Diarrhoeal Disease," Fact Sheet n. 330, World Health Organization, April 2013, http://www.who.int/mediacentre/factsheets/fs330/en/.

278 **should seek balance as best we can** DeNoon, Daniel J., "7 Rules for Eating," WebMD, March 23, 2009, http://www.webmd.com/food-recipes/20090323/7-rules -for-eating.

278 **are heavily processed** If a food item has more than five to seven ingredients, it is likely processed; if it has more than two that are human-manufactured chemicals, it is heavily processed.

279 **massive extinctions of hundreds of species** See this overview from the World Wildlife Fund: "Overfishing," World Wildlife Fund, accessed July 20, 2016, http://www .worldwildlife.org/threats/overfishing.

282 **not something from our deep past** Remember from chapter 8.

291 **contain a lot of information** The BioAnthropology News Facebook group page is a terrific place to start (https://www.facebook.com/groups/BioAnthNews/).

ACKNOWLEDGMENTS

I owe the greatest thanks to my partner, Devi Snively. Without her support, feedback, critiques, edits, challenges, insights, and companionship this book, and my career, would not exist. I also owe a lifetime of gratitude to my parents, siblings, and extended family, who show me again and again the meaning of community and caring, and who exemplify the values of teaching and learning. I also want to acknowledge the contributions of my canine kin who've, since my childhood, shown me the importance of other species.

The content of this book is particularly influenced by the last decade of interactions with colleagues, students, and friends who've asked me insightful questions and challenged me to think, and explain, more effectively. There is no way I can name them all. Here I offer an abbreviated list of those who've directly influenced some aspect of my thinking, research, or writing specifically related to this book. I am sure I am inadvertently overlooking a few, and for that I apologize. I am also sure there are some errors now and again in the text and for those I take full and exclusive credit.

I thank (in no special order): Jim McKenna, Joanne Mack, Marc Kissel, Celia Deane-Drummond, Susan Blum, Christopher Ball, Lee Gettler, Greg Downey, Daniel Lende, Katherine C. MacKinnon, Christina Campbell, Rebecca Stumpf, Julienne Rutherford, Michelle Bezanson, Libby Cowgill,

Jon Marks, Sue Sheridan, Maurizio Albahari, John Hawkes, Milford Wolpoff, Rachel Caspari, Karen Rosenberger, Karen Strier, Robert Sussman, Paul Garber, Tim Ingold, Adam van Arsdale, Matthew Piscatelli, John Terrel, Mark Golitko, Harry Greene, Rahul Oka, Vania Smith-Oka, Ian Kuijt, Meredith Chesson, Deborah Rotman, Natalie Porter, Catherine Bolton, Carolyn Nordstrom, Alex Chavez, Patrick Gaffney, Donna Glowacki, Hope Hollocher, Mark Hauser (the archeologist), Douglas Fry, Eben Kirksey, Carolyn Rouse, Susan Anton, Leslie Aiello, Laurie Obbink, Polly Wiessner, James Calcagno, Ian Tattersall, Philip Sloan, Thomas Tweed, Richard Sosis, Aku Visala, Erin Riley, Lisa Jones-Engel, Michael Gumert, Michael Alan Park, Jan Beatty, Oliver Davies, Kevin Laland, Jeremy Kendall, Cordelia Fine, Peter Richerson, Mary Shenk, Luis Vivanco, Robert Welsh, Walter Rushton, Barbara Harvey, Eugene Halton, Cliff Shoults, Ken Dusek, Rita and Walt Haake, Sarah Coakley, James Loudon, Michaela Howels, Nicholas Malone, Anne Kwiatt, Amy Klegarth, Kelly Lane, Jeffrey Peterson, Amanda Cortez, Rieti Gengo, Angela Lederach, Julia Feder, Adam Willow, Becky Artinian-Kaiser, Marcus Baynes-Rock, Felipe Fernandez-Armesto, Wentzel van Huyssteen, Patrick Bateson, Kim Sterelny, Dietrich Stout, Jan-Olav Henrickson, Markus Muehling, Eugene Rogers, William Storrer, Robin Lovin, Conner Cunningham, Ripan Malhi, Neil Arner, Grant Ramsey, Dominic Johnson, and Andrew Whiten.

I owe an amazing debt of gratitude to Melissa Flashman at the Trident agency for seeing the possibilities, working with, and having faith in me from the beginning of this project. I thank Emily Loose for pushing me on words, concepts, and details in shaping the book proposal. I am forever indebted to Stephen Morrow at Dutton for helping define, craft, and develop this project from a good idea into the book you are holding in your hand. I also want to extend a heartfelt thanks to the others at Dutton who helped make this book happen, especially Eileen Chetti (copy editor), Alice Dalrymple, and Madeline Newquist.

INDEX

ABOUT THE AUTHOR

AGUSTÍN FUENTES has published more than 135 academic articles, essays, and book chapters, and authored or edited fifteen academic books. In addition to chasing monkeys, apes, and humans in jungles and cities across the planet, he explores the lives of our evolutionary ancestors and what people actually do day in and day out across the globe. He is a professor and chair of anthropology at the University of Notre Dame.